In the Kacch

D0613432

IN THE KACCH

A Memoir of Love and Place

Kevin McGrath

McFarland & Company, Inc., Publishers

Jefferson, North Carolina

An earlier version of the final chapter, "Kacch," appeared in *Temenos Academy Review*, 13, 2010.

LIBRARY OF CONGRESS CATALOGUING-IN-PUBLICATION DATA

McGrath, Kevin, 1951–
    In the Kacch : a memoir of love and place / Kevin McGrath.
        p.   cm.
    Includes bibliographical references and index.

    ISBN 978-0-7864-9653-2 (softcover : acid free paper) ∞
    ISBN 978-1-4766-1760-2 (ebook)

    1. Kachchh (India)—Description and travel.   2. McGrath, Kevin,
    1951—Travel—India—Kachchh.   3. Kachchh (India)—History,
    Local.   4. Kachchh (India)—Social life and customs.   5. Love—
    India—Kachchh.   6. Kachchh (India)—Social conditions.   7. Social
    change—India—Kachchh.   I. Title.

    DS485.C8M35 2015
    954'.75—dc23   2014045959

BRITISH LIBRARY CATALOGUING DATA ARE AVAILABLE

Front cover photograph by Leanna McGrath

Printed in the United States of America

McFarland & Company, Inc., Publishers
  Box 611, Jefferson, North Carolina 28640
  www.mcfarlandpub.com

To Pragmulji III
Sawai Bahadur of All Kacch
vibhrājamānāṃ vapuṣā tapasā ca damena ca...
(She, with a beautiful form of shining radiance,
with heat, and with command...)
MBh. I,65,10

Contents

Acknowledgments

My gratitude is due to many individuals who have shared their time, conversation, and hospitality with me over the years during the production of this book, as well as to the many Kacchis who have offered such kindness to my family and to myself for so long.

To Mr. L.D. Shah and his son Suman, I am profoundly indebted for their great generosity, friendship, and good company. Also, to His Highness, the Maharao of all Kacch, and to the Maharani, I am deeply grateful for their benevolence on many extended occasions. To Zainul Abuddin Pir, to Mr. Vinod Bhatt and family, to the Bhujwala family, to Judy Frater, to Krutarthsinh & Yashodara Jadeja, to Mr. Pramod Jethi, to Maharajkumar Siddhrajsinhji and Kanchende Jhala, to Dr. Pankaj Joshi, to Jagdish Kharve, to Ivan and Nana Koschmider, to Dr. Punit Khatri and his wife, Nita, to Dr. Vijay Kumar, to Abdul Morana, to Mr. Kantisen Schroff, to Kamlesh & Jaydeep Shah, to Col. Manmohan Sodha, to Jugal Tiwari, to Drs. Pulin and Prashant Vasa and Jayu, and to Dilip Vaidya, I am sincerely grateful for all their munificent goodwill and amity.

I am also grateful to Leila Ahmed, to Ali Asani, to Homi Bhabha, to Amarananda Bhairavan, to Sugata Bose, to Thomas Burke, to John Carey, to Diana Eck, to Rena Fonseca, to Gurcharan Das, to Richard DeLacy, to Lilian Handlin, to MK Jayasinhji Jhala, to Gregory Kallimanopoulos, to Leonard van der Kuijp, to Daniel and Sara Mason, to Bijoy Misra, to Parimal Patil, to Dr. Maurice Pechet, to Amartya Sen, to Shashi Tharoor, to Alex Watson, to William Weitzel, and to Nur Yalman for their great intellectual generosity and many personal kindnesses while I was working on this book.

Preface

The District of the Kacch is an area—essentially a large island during the monsoon months—in the west of India, bordering on the Sindh of Pakistan and the Arabian Sea. It is a desert region where mariners, nomads, warriors, and traders have migrated and settled over the centuries, and where a Maharao, the king, continues to hold office even today. This story is specifically about the Kacch, but more generally about how India came to me. It is about my attraction to the place and how that attraction was mediated by love for certain people there: not only for the woman who was with me and for our children, but also for our friends in that region, those who profoundly colored our time with amity and kindness. This book is about love of place and love of person, about how those two passions converged, and about the weather. It is about a love for the spiritual and unworldly beauty of a particular terrain and about human affection in the light of irresistible temporal transience: a memoir of life and situation, both of which are disappearing. It is not a personal narrative, but more an account and testimony of life in place and the love which both of these forces inspired and elicited. It has been written in an attempt to lengthen or sustain those emotions for just a little longer in time. Sometimes in life we are fortunate enough to discover the beautiful, which then, by nature, vanishes from our presence; these lines are an attempt to rediscover that perfect experience—something which is actually and primarily visual, but ultimately only audial in form.

I can say only what I have seen and what I have heard, for what else is there? Yet during most of our lives, we are merely actors performing only what we have received. Repetition is the nature of this process—repetition of desire as well as of action and value—and we are not actually seeing or hearing anything. Now and again, however, for a just few moments, we sometimes pause and become aware of the moral potence that adheres to human life, and in those instants, we perceive with renewed transience the great possibilities of sensitivity and coherence: an opportunity for honest and unoccluded consciousness. Then, it is as if the tissue that enfolds experience and the interstices of time are briefly removed and the just forces of life are unveiled. In those scarce seconds, we perceive our true worth.

Friendship is always accompanied by responsibility and by a necessary reciprocity or obligation; it is not so much the emotions of friendship that establish relations, but the awareness of our profound mutuality—of being *able* to give—that establishes this perennial human condition. The core of this book concerns such a mood, as it exists not only between people, but also between places and people, and it begins, like all great loves, with a profound state of absence. It is friendship that supplies us with our moral station on earth, and I consider love—including its defects—just as I would view the understanding of beauty, as within the rubric of such friendship. From the beginning we are all migrants, going from here to there and from place to place, but we also move from person to person and from community to community, forgetting and overlooking. How these two situations converge and coincide, and then perhaps separate again, informs the impulse that runs throughout this book: the subtle bonds of temperament that bind us to our environments and the aesthetic and emotional bonds of human company that attach our hearts to other hearts. Yes, just like the clouds above, even the indigenous is also perpetually in motion.

What ensues on the following pages are the words that capture some of those images and feelings that were to me most wonderful and enthusiastic in many and various ways. The chapters are composed and arranged so as to give five different perspectives or dimensions to what I have learned of Kacch, followed by a brief *coda*.

Part One

I. Dhrangadhra: On the Mainland

Arriving back in India was at first disorienting; loitering about the ancient greatness of Delhi with all its present hectic ways was confounding, and I recall little of those initial days apart from their exuberance. All that I mentally possessed were vague memories from childhood of youthful visits to India as well as a professional working knowledge of classical Sanskrit literature and Indic society. After a week I flew down to Ahmedabad, crossing the jade landscape of the Doab, and then took a train up—the Kacch Express—which marked my real ingress to the subcontinent; by then all indication of the West had gently evaporated.

In that vast sprawling conurbation of Ahmedabad—a truly Indian and neither an imperial nor colonial city—there had recently been days of communal rioting, and at least a thousand people had perished. As the train moved through the outskirts of the city, the air stank of kerosene fires and of carnage, of bloodshed, riot, and unburied corpses: the odor coming in the window was unmistakable. In the eyes of people on the train, I could sense a visceral fear as the carriage became quiet. What had begun as a local *fracas* soon became tumescent, magnified by the chicanery of gangs and thugs, to be exacerbated by unscrupulous politicians: communal violence that sank into a ravine of class, caste war, and felony, fanned by gangs of young men.

The station platform itself had been in darkness, the electricity having gone off. Groups of shadowy figures moved about pools of candlelight or the sputtering sallow glow of gas lamps. Pilgrims and groups of Moslems were identifiable by their dress as people hurried across the tracks and climbed onto unlit trains. A hint of threat lingered in the air; there was not the usual bustle and hubbub, but rather a somnolent and cloistral quiet. There was sentiment of barbarity, of iron bars and cans of kerosene, and of human bestiality, grains of which all of us carry in our blood like a malaise.

3

Ahmedabad station had a subdued and guilty air about it as if pretending that the brutality had not occurred; even the loquacious tea-sellers were reserved and indolent. There were military everywhere, with tense anxious eyes, walking about in pairs and carrying rifles or automatic weapons.

This was the ferocity upon which every animal society is founded: the nucleus was revealing itself, for ultimately and tragically, war, violence, and animadversion are patterns of human consciousness. For those in love, this is an unbearable thought, for the possibility is too awful, incomprehensible in that it is absolute if not eternal. What is it that is wrong with human beings, I wondered, beginning to feel that I should not be where I was. Yet here I was, sole on the station at Ahmedabad, walking uneasily.

The last time that I had been in the sub-continent was only a year previous, but that had been in the south, aboard a ship as it made its way around the coast; I was alone and on a lecture tour for my university. How rich had been those nights up on the bridge of the vessel, the hot tropical air buffeting and fragrant under an Indian Ocean sky; the Southern Cross had been visible as the ship plowed through sensuous darkness. Deccan India was different from where I was presently, being neither Moslem nor Sanskritic, and the climate was not temperate. In a way, the south was beyond me, was linguistically and culturally too far off. Its temperament was different, and I had felt an outsider there; whereas in Gujarat it was as if I could live and walk forever; it was familiar ground where my ghosts and ancestors abounded. The last time that I had been in this province was about twenty years ago when—as a young scholar—I had been visiting the temples on Mount Abu one spring. Now as I began to renew my relationship with Gujarat, I began to make myself forget the West and to love only India, for now that must be sufficient. Life gives everything and then slowly retrieves everything, so what is the purpose of memory in this case, I wondered, except to prolong our losses?

During the last month in Cambridge before I came East, I had met a woman whose conversation had been concerned with Cervantes, and our dialogues had circled about the infinite inventiveness and inward reality of that hero and the majestic sweetness of his fraternity. Now, I missed the brilliance of Leanna, her brittle intelligence that could follow any track, and it was her image and voice that kept me attached to the West. Never before had I been so captivated by a woman, and that left me suspicious, skeptical of myself. I was not prepared to submit to love, so I had fled; yet nothing had changed.

Arriving at Dhrangadhra—a small town just to the east of the Little

Rann of Kacch and my final destination—I was met by a driver at the station and taken—via the *rajdham*, the main palace—to a nearby villa within its own separate grounds, where I was the guest of my friend Harshraj Jhala. Passing through heavy iron and wooden gates with a yellow lion and solar disc painted upon them, we entered into a tropical woodland, with trees everywhere. A square, whitewashed building stood amid paths and avenues, with an ornamented parapet above and a deep veranda below; the roof was supported by spirally carved pillars and a decorative railing. Instantly, I was seduced by the place and its quiescent, lyrical beauty.

That first morning I awoke early—it was before three—to a great clattering of wings in one of the trees outside of the room. A snake must be hunting among roosting parakeets, for the plaintive voice of a throttled bird continued for almost a minute, slowly subsiding; dogs were barking in the town, and music was being played somewhere. For a while I lay soaked in perspiration, then moved to a drier and cooler part of the bed. The outline of the narrow teak four-poster lent a perspective against the high ceiling, where a fan spun and sent down its wash of air. Like a propeller, it drove the room through darkness, sounding like the thrumming engine of a ship. All of the windows were covered with a stout steel mesh to exclude reptiles and small quadrupeds, and I could discern the outline of a gekko feeding on insects, crawling slowly across the metal.

Having looked at the time, I rose and drank some water and went up onto the roof; all was pacific, and beneath a candid moon a warm breeze blew. From the edge of town I could hear the motors of trucks starting up and moving out onto the roads. Here, the night was tuneful with the venal sound of birds—cuckoos and koels—and the long slow mournful *miaou* of peafowl crying across the gardens. Several times during those early nights, I would rise and go up onto the roof, listening, watching, breathing the tepid air, locating myself and resetting my mental and emotional compass beneath skies thinly covered with small cloud. What a relief it was to be there and to feel the rest of life fall away: I could almost hear the clanging as all those previous days of remorse dropped from me.

Each dawn, taking a bottle of water, I would go up onto the roof and be refreshed by the air and watch the birds. Loosening the thick brass chain and pushing open the copper-plated door to avoid its sharp bronze rosettes, up there I was private and unobserved, yet in my heart I was always watching for Leanna, wanting her to appear. Many gray and black vultures were roosting in a salai tree next to the villa, and now and then a small piece of down from their preening would float onto the roof. Occasionally, one would leap into the air and glide low over my head towards another tree. Sometimes small creamy-yellow herons would shoot past, and lime-green parakeets were always in the air, noisy, agile, and swift; with their long narrow tails and curved wings, they were wonderful fliers, lively and brisk, rocketing about like small green missiles. Raucous peafowl sometimes roosted on the parapets during the night, launching themselves as I came up in the pre-dawn, and two dogs on the veranda below, a male and female, were always sleeping or disporting themselves along the paths that radiated from the building.

Here on the edge of the desert, a negligible monsoon hesitated and held back, and during early mornings, the light was gray and there were plentiful clouds passing low and quickly. One or two drops of rain would stain the russet tiles of the roof, but that was all: a few capillary and astringent speckles. One afternoon, sitting on the veranda, I watched a pigeon in the dust, recumbent due to the heat, its wings flat upon the ground, its beak open, panting with satisfaction.

Love of place is as valid as love of person in how it informs consciousness. I did not quite understand why I had returned to Gujarat for I was not Indian, and yet there was something perhaps atavistic in the acoustics of speech during infancy—I had been born and had grown up in Asia—which for me could only find rest or habitation in this land. In our lives we do not seek the reality, for that has always perished, but its closest and most available metaphor. For if we do not try to find what it is that evades us, we shall never really apprehend ourselves. Yet somehow it was only that woman in Cambridge who was evading me; already, after only a few days, I was beginning to feel isolated and solitary, and I wished that she was with me and that we could walk. I missed her fierce and radical intelligence, always so cutting.

The villa had once been what an earlier Jhala monarch—and the present one was the forty-seventh in line—had given to some of his women to use as a retreat. It was a simple structure with a large oblong audience hall at the center, where a few pieces of marble furniture stood, including a low throne. High on the walls, a series of ten large paintings and some portraits of earlier royalty were hanging. The one that I admired most was of a hero standing in a river, removing his armor to give to the deity Indra, who was disguised as a mendicant, and from a flourishing chromatic and organic sky above, the father of the hero, Surya the Sun, was watching. I had once written a book about that hero—Karna—a figure like Achilles who had lived a life out of time, unconcerned by the present except for his preoccupation with fame.

Baddhu Singh, the head of staff, resided with his family in a house across from the main building. Alongside, he kept his cows and goats, and his wife would milk the animals of a morning, muttering to them as she did so. They had two daughters and two sons. The gardens of the villa, which was at some distance from the main palace, were of various levels; they were decrepit, collapsed, disheveled, and intersected by paths and connecting platforms. The lower terrace had once been a pond fed by ornate channels; there, a pavilion was overgrown with vines, and pomegranate trees had rooted in its fabric. Stone heads and torsos were hidden among foliage where cobras and mongeese lived with their families, and statues—copies of Bharhut work—green and yellow with lichen, stood paused as if in soundless dance. A mason's yard stood next to the villa, from whence came a steady sound of hammering and tapping. It was like an English country graveyard, with blocks of sandstone scattered higgledy-piggledy and half-finished discarded statuary upon the ground, and it reminded me of Wiltshire or Hampshire and something in my youth, for my father had been British and I had strong recollections of rural English seasons.

Slowly I began to adjust to the tempo and pattern of life: the strident nights, the myriad mosquitoes chewing at one's ankles and feet, the lack of water that sometimes occurred, and the habits of Baddhu Singh's household. There was a purity and resilience to life here that was both intricate and visually stunning. Yet despite the vigour of it all and the extraordinary complication of living, once or twice I felt a pang of unease and I was reminded of the poet Ovid, sequestered on the Black Sea coast of Pontos, and of how solitude could be an idiom of punishment, slow and cruel, where mastery was abnegated and all companionable speech silenced. They were hot, sunless, shadowless days of waiting for monsoon to arrive, with now and then a single raindrop, and I spent hours up on the roof, pacing back and forth, watching the flight of birds: bats, vultures, peafowl, parakeets, as all simultaneously inhabited just one tree. Once a busybody crow was actually upon the back of a vulture and pecking angrily at its neck; another time, a crow was chasing a large bat through the air, scratching at the latter with its claws. It was remarkable how certain birds, like crows and sparrows, lived in parallel community with human beings.

From the houses that nestled up against the high walls of the grounds came a miscellany of noise: radio music, the amplified chanting from temples, a constant din of motor vehicles and their horns, bicycles, rickshaws, and thousands of pedestrians in the bustling dirty compression of bazaars. There was the call of *muezzin* at certain times of the day, so familiar from other parts of the world that I had known, and the many voices of *animae* that lived about the place: wild dogs, feral pigs, camels and buffalo, bullocks. All fitted together symphonically into an opulent and steady blare. Sometimes the rasping clatter from the colony of bats in the tamarind trees would reach an enormous crescendo before fading. If it was a weekday, there would be the sound of singing and monodic recital of lessons from a nearby school. Before dawn each day there would be a clashing of cymbals and fanfare of bass drums as devotees beat the bounds of their temple quarter.

I would rise and work, sitting at a small *escritoire* that stood in my room. This was soon covered with vulture feathers and fallen pieces of carved masonry that I had picked up: finials and scrolls, a head. The fan would be spinning, creating a vortex in the air to keep off the mosquitoes whose biting left a gnawing prickle and succeeding rawness of nerves. There was a large rat who lived in the kitchen and made a racket each night as it investigated the pots and pans left over from dinner. After dawn had arrived, Baddhu Singh, unshaven and barefoot, would bring in a pot of tea on a tray, sugary, ginger-flavored, milky tea. One of Baddhu Singh's daughters would bring breakfast over an hour or so after the tea had arrived. Following that, having bathed and washed away the odor from the night's perspiration, I would walk the grounds observing the multitude of trees, sketching a little, and examining the fallen sculptures, mostly replicas of Gupta or early Buddhist style. Then I would work at my desk another hour or so before going out to walk, attuning my thought to this new and vastly spacious life. In those times I was just beginning a study of the feminine in the Sanskrit epic *Mahabharata*: that was ostensibly why I had returned to India, to try to match the textual material with new data from field work. Unlike the West, where epic poetry was a phenomenon of the past and a frozen medium, in India the epics remained viable and dynamic and were an important living element of modern culture: in drama, cinema, literature, and advertising, as well as in ritual. Everyone knew of the heroes and their cults, and they retained a moral and spiritual force in society.

As the days settled to an order of repetition and familiarity, I took to walking more each morning out into the country. The town ended abruptly, as if an invisible line demarcated the edge, beyond which was a lake and then desert. Off the steps to the water, women laundered and boys swam; further along the shore was a line of tents where Harijan refugees from the recent earthquake camped. Wild dogs played and growled, and feral pigs trotted aimlessly and unhappily about the far littoral: theirs was a terrible rebirth, living on ordure.

The monsoon had passed without fruition, it seemed, and this year, once again, there was a possibility of drought. There had been a hint of precipitation in the weak citron light that morning, behind the clouds, but that was all. The monochrome humid sky continued unchanged, ungiving and relentless, always discordant with the cry of crows, a clamour that never halted during daylight hours. Rock was everywhere, for Dhrangadhra lay upon a reef of sandstone, and the town and its environs were occupied by masons' yards: the quarrying and rendering of stone was an important livelihood. This was the stone from which the palaces had been built, and the old town walls and gateways, as well as many of the older houses. Always, there was a steely tap-tapping of chisel and hammer; it stretched over the air like an audial skein, and everywhere, there were chips of stone and heaps of mineral dust.

Often I would stroll over to the palace and wander about the grounds where gardeners were omnipresent, planting and hoeing and irrigating young trees, citrus and frangipani. There were several masons' yards in the estate, where men worked to repair and restore the building's several acres of embellished stone structure damaged during the earthquake. Wreckage from the *seismos* was visible everywhere, although it was not catastrophic as it had been farther west. Cracks were apparent in the architecture of the buildings, and there were many bits of fallen ornament. The earth was littered with broken sculpture; several of the towers had been bound up with steel rods or covered with bamboo scaffolding where they were badly fissured. At times I would rest upon one of the terrace walls or beside one of the dry marble pools and, taking out a small monocular from my bag, would study the upper parts of the edifice. It was a long and irregularly constructed palace, built at three periods, and from a distance in the flat arid landscape it appeared vast—like a little town—with its many towers and domes and rooves. The walls were originally a pale yellow but were now stained by years of repeated monsoons. Rows of sapphire-blue glass windows lined the upper registers, except for the *zenana*, the women's quarters, where there were no windows, only *jalis* or stone screens. Parakeets were everywhere, dashing and cutting about, screeching happily. They were joyful birds, beautiful to watch.

Days began to merge, and nights. I still used to rise in the small hours before dawn and go up onto the roof and sit in the cool as the pendulum of things became temporarily neutral; a small fragile moon hung low above the west, with Venus at her side. Just before the light began to tinge the air with cornelian, bats would begin to glide homeward from their forays, silent and large. Their black membranous four-foot wingspan hissed overhead, and sometimes I would duck if they passed too close. They always circled a tree once before turning in to land. The vultures would occasionally flap their enormous wings and resettle themselves noisily at the top of their roosts, and peafowl would be shrieking throughout the night, a loud and plaintive wail. Silhouetted in crepuscular light, the statues of the parapet were fixed and stony, injured torsos worn by rain and heat and broken by the shuddering of earthquakes. Herons began to pass high above as the light ascended, and minute purple sunbirds shot through the air.

On the roof at that hour, mosquitoes attacked, and my whole body was instantly perforated and stung with their delicate poison. With the onset of day, a breeze picked up, coming from off the lake, where brown waters reflected the sky. Figures would be already crouched along the shore, performing ablutions or doing laundry. Pigeons, doves, cuckoos began to land on the tower at one corner of the building, and the water supply would suddenly come on, gushing lustily into a hidden copper tank. High on the air, fly-catchers were like swift dots against the altitude, black marks upon a gray surface; the far-off sound of a train's whistle was audible, and from neighbouring temples came the matutinal reverberation of chanting and drums and choral refrain. About the walls and grounds, small striped mammals, *kiskoli*, began to scurry about chasing each other. The peafowl complained like Edwardian ladies protesting against ravishment: *no-ooh, no-ooh*. They possessed the single loudest cry of all the creatures in the garden.

The roof itself was heaped with piles of loosened tiles and cracked elements of parapet. Soon the vultures began to take off, one by one, passing low; the swish and crackle of their long-boned wings came close as they swept gracefully through the air. Aerodynamically they were designed for mass, with large bulky bodies and rectangular wings and retractable necks, and a curious musty odor would linger momentarily as they passed. So the boisterous day engaged and settled to its diverse and diffuse arrangements. Baddhu Singh breezed in and out checking the plumbing, for one of the tanks would often overflow and cascade.

Being here was like living upon an invisible and elastic surface that was constantly flexing and stretching: reality had a way of accepting yet ignoring one. Wherever I walked about the town or through the landscape, across the low rippling hills, there was always this sense of play and absorption. My own sense of person and of the selves about me was constantly engaged at the periphery, and that slightly removed fixation was always alert, responsive, and unspoken. Not only that, but the axis between the human and the physical world was different in the tropics; Dhrangadhra was on the twenty-third parallel, and for a westerner, the rules of society were not only imperceptible but perhaps not even accessible. For Hindus, the family is to structure as re-incarnation is to time; the two ideas are similar if not conceptually identical. Only their support or substance differs, one being metaphorical, the other being metonymical. These two threads provided the warp and weft of life here.

Now, as the rains at last fell with great force and the earth emitted a gravid odor and in the temple outside of the villa's heavily bound gates a tympanum was being beaten hour after hour, it was as if that subtle plane between human activity and its material substrate was being reaffirmed and reactivated. As wives stood in doorways looking out and men cycled to work holding umbrellas, and as blithe children dashed between courtyards, splashing puddles at each other, everyone was jubilant with the weather. The rain was to be joyously celebrated, and there were no boundaries to this mood of happiness.

The last time that I had been in this part of the world—almost two decades previously—I had moved across time and landscape as I traveled the triangle about Jodhpur, Bikaner, and the lake on Mount Abu, continually honing my ideas about India and its retrievable past. This time as I walked out across the stones and sand or wandered about the dusty lanes of the town, I was troubled by my internal and unheeded passion. The sound of moderate rain upon the leaves and paths of the grounds was soothing, conciliatory, as the life of people and birds, even of the dogs and pigs, slowed down and became softer, more instilled.

Baddhu Singh's young daughter rocked back and forth upon a swing on the veranda outside of my room—a thick carved mahogany board like a door, suspended by steel rods—singing quietly to herself as the bars squeaked smoothly. Her legs were stretched out before her to generate motion, and her hair and scarf fell outward as she descended. She would do that for hours, chanting a song about Sita and Ram, a hero and his consort, in her low, sonorous, and bird-like voice. As rain trickled and dripped outside, the plashing and the repeated syllables fused harmoniously.

"Jaya Sita-Ram, Jaya Sita-Sita Ram," she sang to herself again and again through the hours. "Sita Jaya-Ram, Sita Jaya-Jaya-Ram."

Each morning she would light incense in the main hall before a portrait of the goddess Shakti-Ma, who rode upon a lion displaying weaponry in her many arms. There were several icons of the Devi about the villa, and sometimes they would be festooned in garlands of jasmine or marigold. Often, the girl also made obeisance to the portraits of former princes and princesses, hung high up on the walls, staring down in sad acuity.

With the rain, Baddhu Singh's wife and children spent more time on the veranda, chatting and laughing and using the swings. The peafowl and vultures became quieter, hunched into their wings, and the dogs ran about, chasing and snarling. The earth became more and more sodden, dyed ochre and sienna by the mud, and walking became disagreeable. Everyone was happy, though, for after several years of drought, it was feared that this year a state of emergency might have been declared, as had happened in the eighties. Afternoons became a stupor of heat and rain, and I was confined to the house; much of the time I spent at my desk, barefoot, wearing only a sarong, drinking tea and working, carefully chasing down and cornering metaphors, line by line. Even in the rooms, nothing was dry any more. Clothes were damp and books and paper were limp; ink spread out upon the pages when I wrote. It was cooler, though, which was exhilarating after so much blank, deadening heat.

"Time is a burden and we seek to be weightless," I wrote, trying to build up a system of correspondence among images. "Words are light, and poetry possesses the least mass of all language, as its metaphors are artificial. The poetry of love is the most lucid and transparent and the best lens for a human soul."

Now and then I ventured out, walking up to the main palace, where one evening I had an informal audience with the Maharaja and Maharani, sitting upon a roof terrace in the north wing of the palace, the *mardana*, or men's quarters, drinking lime water as we conversed at dusk. She spoke of the devastation caused by the earthquake, and he talked of current urban crises, the domestic unease, and calls for war. He had been nineteen years of age when he had ascended the throne, and during the fifties and sixties he had sat in *Lok Sabha*, or parliament, as a citizen member. The Maharaja spoke with such quiet erudition and firmness, one had a sense of his complex and large involvement in this new, burgeoning India.

"How awful it was," he said, describing when the Emergency came and democracy was suspended. "What a dreadful woman she was," he added, speaking of Indira Gandhi. He reminisced about Mahatma Gandhi and Nehru, and the lineage of Indira and Rajiv and now Sonia and her children, Rahul and Priyanka. "What does this say about our political constitution?" he exclaimed. "They are just like us in their dynastic way. Rahul will have to deal with civil insurgence. Kashmir, Manipur, Assam, they will be his test. Then there is the problem of governance itself."

It was only after Independence, when the Maharaja entered government as a private individual, that his wife had come out of seclusion or *purdah*. "That was not easy," she said. "My granddaughters ask me about it all the time now. I think they miss it," she laughed.

His Highness was liberal with his memories of that nascent period of Indian democracy, exploring his recollections carefully and with pleasure. He had been educated in England and recalled those days with affection; he was the last living ruler to have signed the Instrument of Accession, admitting the kingdom into the new state in 1948, and was the final living prince of that old and simpler world. As evening gathered about us and the servants moved closer, the stories of this gracious, unassuming couple transported me; a forsaken and decorous society was revealed in their conversation of a reconciled and less degraded world.

I realized that this was a special moment and, like Parzifal, wondered what question I should ask before everything vanished. What interrogative would make the world coherent again in the face of so much political violence and seismic ruin? The era which this pair had lived through was visibly misplaced, and I felt feckless, unable to promise something courteous for them. What could I say? And the interview left me feeling troubled.

Often on my visits to the palace, I stopped to examine some herostones, *stambhas*—twelve of them were in the palace grounds—of postmedieval origin and not fabricated from a local stone. I had begun to sketch and decipher their inscriptions, for there was something somber and intensely evocative about those columns, with images of armed men—some on horseback—their spears and swords and bucklers elevated. Eleven were dedicated to fallen heroes, and one was to a widow, a *sati* who had immolated herself upon a deceased husband's pyre. Her upright arm was carved onto the stone, the palm of the hand outspread in a final signature of the wife's devotion, with the arm and open hand as if in gesture of farewell and token of an equal heroism to her partner's death in combat. Those *stambhas* with their dark lopsided stance fascinated me.

Unfortunately the inscriptions were often indecipherable, being worn or defaced, yet they captured my attention for many an hour and were a small gray keyhole onto another world: images charged with expression, with grief and the disdain of achieved fame, cynical and proud and withdrawn forever into silence as they stared out into the present world. The heroism of these figures presupposed and evoked an absolute; that is what overcame them, for heroes are ones who elicit and establish an absolute, dramatized by their heroic action. Heroes were figures of time, insofar as they were ones who could determine when to go out of time. I posted a few of my drawings to Leanna, who was now in Greece, along with some sketches of the buildings and birds.

"We assume perfection and that the perfectible is possible," I wrote to her, "but that is only an idea. The question really is, what is the genesis of that idea of an absolute, for it is beyond and prior to the idea and repels us as if we were hirsute and uncouth fools, inappropriate in its presence. Art in that sense is only protocol," I added. "There is the city and there are the ways leading to it and one wonders what language is spoken within its walls. For there, grammar and syntax are all, whereas for us who exist in time, it is the figures of speech that bear meaning and pathway, the wonderful and continual metaphors."

The irony—as I knew so well—was that even the human spirit and simple human affection are metaphorical and that the real and only true exploration was to comprehend the nature of such transitions. This was also the problem that faced the migrant: love of place and love of person and the oscillation of mental freedom that breaks necessity's compulsiveness. This was my present quandary.

The long rasping screech of the bats whenever the rains paused became nightmarish and maniacal; they were big creatures with the teeth of large felines, and in the hours before dawn their sound was cacophonous upon the saturated air. I longed for an afternoon of walking again, but that was a messy and tedious activity at present; it was not worth becoming so tainted with mud and mire. Within the sunless gloom of monsoon, as the volts fluctuated, the light bulbs either were extinguished or their luminosity flickered at about a low amber color, and the fans would sometimes cease to turn, unpredictably beginning again later. Once I came home to find candles lit in the main audience hall and the women dancing with clashing brass *thali* plates, practicing for a wedding. The shadows from their flowing *saris* cast long, vivid shapes upon the tall white walls as they moved through arcs and gestures, whirling and laughing.

Monsoon was traditionally a licit time for lovers, and there were many early paintings depicting scenes of tryst beneath tempestuous skies, with clouds stained livid and indigo by the rains, with luminous threads of yellow lightning snaking downward. Egrets would mark that dark air whitely. It was a time to remain indoors for the private and slow slaking of mutual desire. With the rains, cobras were out, driven from their nests by flooding, which meant that the dogs were barking and growling all night. The bitch had come in heat, and several males had broken into the grounds through one of the lower gates. There was a lot of snarling and whimpering between fighting rivals.

One midnight, waking repeatedly—one of Baddhu Singh's cows had been lowing for hours at the rear of the villa—I had dreamed of Leanna and Cambridge, where we had been walking along the river beneath the plane trees. I wished that she was here on the edge of the desert far from an ocean, for she was like a nerve for me, coding experience. She would have loved this part of Gujarat, especially during the cooler winter months when skies were clear and sheer blue and a saffron-colored sunlight cast fluid, lucid shadows. Yet she was someone who would always emotionally outdistance me, and in my thought and perceptions she was always present. I had never been obsessed by a woman before, and I felt perplexed if not embarrassed by the preoccupation that I was unable to jettison. I felt like Swann, forever circling about Odette in his mind.

It was as if she were the superfluity that supposed all other hierarchies of meaning. Her trajectory was resisting mine and I was unsure why that was: why had I separated from her without declaring my love? What was she doing in Athens, I wondered, and with whom? It was as if the deities had sliced a piece of fruit into two halves upon the roof one night—the moon performed the operation—and we were inimitably divided and suddenly another world manifested itself as curtains parted. Time was always precise, if not conclusive, and there was no dialogue with time.

The next day, when Baddhu Singh brought tea at seven and light began to fall into place again, the rainfall had ceased and the racket of animal and bird noises from the grounds diminished with the retreat of darkness. I laughed to myself as I sipped the tea: Leanna would not have liked the tumultuous uproar of the nights here; sleep had always been a problem for her and she complained frequently about the night. She was too restless, overly nimble and busy in her thought, and sleep was always a struggle for her, forever evanescent and evasive. Yet here in the thick moist air, sleep was unlike western sleep, for its richness and depth of fold; it possessed a redolence and immediacy that was translucent, buoyant enough to be mildly affectionate and yet undemanding. Sleep here was of such a density and texture that no firm equivalence between waking and unconscious existed, as if there was a mutual sensitivity between the two states, osmotic and constantly exchanging.

More and more I stayed within the bounds of the garden, perambulating the grounds accompanied by listless dogs; the town drew me less and less as days and weeks settled into sequence. The numberless species of life, birds, insects, trees, the quadrupeds—especially the tortoises—all made for an earthly paradise; there was such happy and prolific vitality within those garden walls. The only time that I ventured out was either to walk into the desert or to visit the main palace. Quiet, speechless, observant, introspective, and yet fully attuned to the visual and audial qualities of life that surrounded me, it was as if an unraveling was at work as a world exhumed its intricacies and forces, and I felt more and more sapient and precise in my ways, conscious of the value in delay. The rains had changed the color of everything; there was more *chiaroscuro* about the earth; everything was moist, steeped in fertile water; and there was no sky as cloud flew past at low altitude. Women worked on the terraces of arable fields, clearing irrigation ducts of their detritus, chatting and discussing husbands and children. Their deeply dyed *saris* threw bright stains of light amongst the viridian foliage and clay paths.

Baddhu Singh's younger son would often come to say hello before he set off towards school each morning. As the youngest, he had received all the gifts of the family: mischievous, a boyish dandy, yet deeply kind and thoughtful as only children can be, he delighted in affection as the cherished sibling, adored by his sisters. He was always curious about my books and whatever happened to be on my desk, and each morning he never failed to ask about how my lady was that day, pointing to the photograph of my desired paramour.

That night I awoke before three, troubled, feeling dissatisfied and incomplete. Sleeping alone could be irksome, and I longed for the affection and familiarity of Leanna resting beside me, for the shape of her figure and her warmth and the perfection of her anatomy. How absurd and ridiculous it was to love someone and remain undeclared: I was puny. Mosquitoes were particularly voracious that night, and taking a bottle of water, I paced the grounds in the dark along the avenues. There was assurance in that contact with the cool redolent earth, and the air was full of small sounds: the twitching of foliage and grasses, the clicks and rasps and jagged chatter of bat vocabulary. The contact with earth when I walked in the grounds was comforting, a sensation of pebbles and stone steps upon the skin of my feet.

Back inside, I wandered about the faultlessly appointed rooms, their dimensions and white walls deeply satisfying, as if volumes composed musically. Upon the roof the cloud had lifted and some stars were visible—the Pleiades especially—old familiars that I had gazed upon from many places on the globe. Through the monocular I could identify each white spot, small suns in themselves. What was it that the Maharaja had said the day previously? That the soul has no skeleton. That was how I felt now: boneless and noetic and detached from life without this woman.

Once dawn came—opalescent and aerial, cinnamon-toned—all the usual voices in the grounds below were raised: calves, goats, humans, birds, canines. I remembered that I had been dreaming of Leanna; we had been swimming together, and I wondered where she was now and with whom, if I would ever see her again or if she would only exist as an idea, senseless and imperceptible, composed of memories and phantasies. In the dream, her nudity had been something marvelous and wonderful, shining perfectly, and I wondered how she thought of me, if she had any intimation of what I was feeling. In the dream we had visited Elephanta island, where the statues—massive, smooth, black, motionless stones in gloomy caves—were poised as if time itself had been reified into the dense polished mineral of a deity gazing out upon dustless space.

Whenever I went up to the palace in those days, I always visited the hero-stones where they stood in their separate railed-off garden next to a stand of bamboo. They fascinated me for their resemblance and for their illegible inscriptions and for their crude archaic antiquity and discoloration. I became strangely attached to those vanished lives and occupied with trying to decipher the carved *devanagari* words that described the achievements. Death was in counterpoint for a hero, for ontologically it was the hero who asserted and confirmed the boundaries of human existence, wilfully and efficaciously. They were the borderers inhabiting the extremes of life, which was what their agency defined and demarcated. Born once into living and a second time to the volition where they defied or elected death, they were twice-born, forever revived by the songs that recalled them. Death—so brief and lacking in particulars and qualities— was made to conform first by the hero and then by the recapitulating poets. Conversely or by implication, that periphery could be demarcated as a point where memory and recollection ceased to exist. It was the same in a landscape, when the magnitude of perspective and dimension were beyond any human capacity for perception, for then the sublime came into being.

On the following day, I walked around the lake, pausing to rest on the far side, from where I could see what looked like storks, with long delicate wings and stiletto beaks, tentatively wading and scrutinizing the water. The palace was enchanting from a distance, with crimson walls and its pinnacles and domes hidden by ashoka trees: it was another world. I imagined the Maharaja and wife telephoning each other from their separate wings, or sitting of an evening within the upper courtyard, tuning into a small wireless in order to learn of political developments. Harshraj, the second son of the family, had recently arrived, and when I reached the palace, he was reading a newspaper and we greeted and spoke about his journey, the region, family affairs, an impending visit from the Chief Minister of the province—the man who had done nothing to stem the rioting in Ahmedabad, thus fostering the mayhem—who was due to arrive at noon. Barely had Harshraj spoken when an aged helicopter made a low fly-over above the grounds, momentarily hovering and swaying as if in salute to the Maharaja, before going off to land in town.

"There goes iniquity," Harshraj commented, looking away, as if the sight of the helicopter was unseemly. "I am not sure what the amoral really is," he sighed, "but I suppose it is a force that is utterly disconnected and without social awareness, in denial of social principle. Unlike solitude and creativity, such ambition can only be unaware; it lacks the equilibrium of memory and can only suffer and transmit its suffering. It is the nightmare of being unique," he added. "One day that man could become Prime Minister, such is the irony of our democratic state." He spoke of his Rajput kin in other states to the north, detailing the abstruse kinship relationships that obtained and the systems of marriage at work, of the obligations that he had towards them as a prince, a *kumar*, and of exactly how his line extended back to the eleventh century.

He spoke about how he had to find spouses for the elder two children of Baddhu Singh, and how he would go about it, just as twenty years ago he had provided Baddhu Singh with a wife.

"The matching of a private soul with social expectation," he smiled. "Language and its gentle vibrations."

We chatted about the planting of trees in the grounds, of the virtues of jujube compared to aloe, and of how different the present natural life was compared to a hundred years ago. Then there had only been agriculture and animal husbandry, and in those days the Maharaja had possessed his own cavalry troop and stable of elephants.

"Independence and Nehru changed all that, but at least we were not shot like in Russia," Harshraj laughed. "The proportions of life in the region were so much more equable in times before the present," he said. "Now, the quantity of human beings living within the same realm of land had so multiplied that everything was unstable: water, fuel, food, sanitation, even the quality of the air. The symbols of life were equally out of order and the landscape overwhelmed by this corrosion of natural measure, and as the present declined, the town became tawdry and commercially tasteless."

After breakfast the next day, I set off into the desert again and soon passed squads of young soldiers performing drills along a road that ran beside the lake. One or two of the men at the rear greeted me with bold smiles. Out in the desert without a compass, it was difficult to maintain any sense of direction, for the sun was obscured behind a low and reluctant sky. A fine green veil overlay the dust and stones, caused by the recent few days of shower. It was a treeless and exposed landscape with occasional gulleys cut into the soil by infrequent deluges. Occasionally, bones littered the earth—jaws, vertebrae, ribs—left by scavengers. There were few birds, laggars and babblers, and I realised what a haven the palace and villa were with their walled grounds and dense plantation, with ponds and shelter. To the west I could see where irrigation from deep-bore wells facilitated cultivation: beryl-colored fields where mango and millet were growing, surrounded by stone walls heaped with thorns.

It was a long walk, and my feet and ankles were cut and abraded. Returning, I found myself passing through an infantry encampment, where files of troops and officers stared belligerently at me. At the entrance the sentry questioned me severely. It was a reminder of how things stood with Pakistan, less than two hundred miles to the west, a timely indication of an uncertain reality, subcutaneous and potentially devastating, a violent stratum beneath what appeared to be pacific life. Arriving back at the palace, extremely thirsty, I again sat for a while with Harshraj beside a pond, discussing the fish and local politics, drinking many glasses of lime water that Baddhu Singh brought. It was evening then and Harshraj wanted to go for a drive out to a local tank that he knew, a dam built for irrigation purposes.

We soon set off, and the ancient car found its way along narrow tracks through scrub and terra-cotta earth. Small brown quail and partridge were about, and once the vehicle startled a hare: it froze and gazed at us, twitching enormous pink transparent ears. Often we passed Rabari herdsmen with flocks of sheep and goats. They were unlike the town-folk, tall and powerful, splendid with their turbans and embroidered jackets. At one spot we halted beside a snake shrine far out in the landscape, heaped with flat stones, where a long yellow banner snapped and flicked in the gusts. Arriving in the gray dusk at an expanse of windswept mere, we left the car and walked along a thin path; to the west the sky glowed like pearl. The water was driven, and there were low beige waves mirroring a luminous sky. To the east a mild blue-green ambience shone. The lake itself was shallow and bordered with reeds, and here and there sandy islets were washed by the waves. A group of flamingoes gently made their way along one of these spits, and in the monsoon air their subtle pink was radiant.

Two tall sarus were making their way along another sandy bank, and in the dusk the wet sand sparkled with light; the carmine marks of the birds' heads were perfectly distinct—the only pure color in the area. We strolled for a long time along an elevated bank, Harshraj limping with the aid of a cane, as he had twisted an ankle. He recounted tales of his youth, of when he and his younger brother used to go off on horseback and travel for days towards Jodhpur, where his uncle was Maharaja. Irrigation—bore-wells and deep submersible pumps—was changing the landscape as a reliable and constant supply of water enabled the cultivation of formerly barren tracts. With terrestrial change came social change, for with these new hydraulic systems, the water table had fallen from twenty feet to two hundred feet, and traditional methods of water harvesting no longer functioned. Further crisis and instability ensued.

Sandpipers flitted about and lapwings called loudly. Curious bright emerald bee-catchers followed us for a while. Ibis and heron and a tall solemn crane patrolled the shallows, and there were several varieties of duck, uncommon for this time of the year, Siberia being their usual home during these months. There was an air of refined solitude about the vista that was almost northern; a tepid monsoon light with a furtive sky and absence of shadow brought serenity to the scene as if the wind emitted lucence. There was a magnitude about the place that was exclusive. Apart from the few streaks of green where a tree grew or some grasses and reeds flourished, the lack of general color made for a great tranquility that pulsed with vivid detail. To behold such an expanse of water with its small driven waves in such a desert was pleasurable.

On the way back we halted in a Rabari village to visit an old friend of Harshraj and to drink a dish of tea with him. Sitting upon string beds in an unlit courtyard surrounded by camels and ruminating buffalo and dozens of silent curious children, Harshraj and the old chief spoke of how their respective years had been. Later, when we arrived back at the palace, bats were flying in and out of the *darbar* hall and green mosquito coils were burning beneath the chairs. Hawks were shooting across the gardens, and peafowl were stalking among the shrubbery.

How to recede or retreat, I wondered, withdraw from this javelin of time so that the beauty of the days and life did not merely arise and flash open like an eye blinking and then close. Slowness was all, for focus and for quantity, as the feeling of transience was becoming too poignant, for days—at the villa and palace and out in the desert—were surcharged and replete. I was more and more aware of how discrete and momentary all this was as I struggled to grasp it closer, and I was forgetting Leanna. Monsoon deepened again, but without precipitation, and dawns were blustery, the wind coming in long pliant promiscuous waves. It was curious to experience a gale without any proximity to the sea; it seemed antithetical. At the villa, different trees made different sounds as leaves rubbed against each other and their limbs moved. Beside the house, the dogs were beguiled by the olfactory qualities of where the cow had recently given birth to a young male calf. Obviously perplexed and exhibiting distaste, they sniffed about the spot, returning again and again.

That day was the first of the four snake-festival days, the *Nagpanchami mela*, and I woke from siesta groggy and stupefied to the clatter of amplified music coming over the walls; full of sleep, I went and sat on the veranda. Half-way down the main avenue that bisected the gardens, I suddenly noticed that one of the peacocks was displaying its fan and strutting back and forth. Suddenly a mongoose appeared jumping up the steps, followed by a long and irate black cobra, erect and fierce. The two dueled together casually, slowly, and dramatically for several minutes; the mongoose occasionally nipping at the back of the snake when it turned. The mammal was both teasing and fearless, and the peacock fluttered nearby, watching. There was nothing deadly about the engagement; rather, it had qualities of play and ritual or protocol as this trio performed.

I and Baddhu Singh's younger son watched for half an hour, and then the cobra, as if bored, vanished. The scene had been graceful and mannered, without anger or violence; it was not as if this had been a duel of life and death. The mongoose then came up the avenue, pausing to look at us almost politely, and went off towards the side of the villa, where a fountain stood. The dogs were still snoozing, oblivious. There had been a theatrical quality about the scene; it had been so without tension or charge as to seem formal and unembittered, without contest or savagery, as if it were a mere demonstration of hierarchy, lacking in all haste or threat of death.

Outside in the early evening, the roads were packed with promenaders. Youths were cruising up and down with arms linked and wearing their best clothes; families were strolling and children towed balloons. There were dozens of stalls and hawkers about, and blankets were spread upon the ground with wares neatly aligned. The *mela* itself consisted of two big-wheels and several kinds of carousels; all were jammed with people. I purchased a small paper icon of Durga, the goddess astride her lion mount, something for my desk. The road along the lake was also busy, with crowds dressed in their best and walking or sitting upon the grass beneath trees. At the palace I noticed that someone had thrown a garland of marigolds about one of the hero *stambhas* and had daubed the stone with sandal paste as an act of devotion.

A debonair Harshraj was wandering about the grounds with a gardener surveying the young banyans, which had recently been planted, and accompanying their stroll, I admired his pragmatism and idealism, his quirky creativity that had no illusions. He was attempting to reconstruct a different role for sovereignty in postmodern conditions. At the time of Independence, over forty percent of India by area had been under the rule of princely states, yet it was a system that vanished overnight, as cities came to overwhelm the countryside in terms of political weight; gone was the moral entity of the village. Nowadays consumerism and the commodity had become the rule. Harshraj worked with ideas and kindred connections, with prospects; it was a bit like the mongoose and the snake, the making of formal and ritual gestures of advancement. For idealism, even if it did not succeed, could actually resist time and establish social zones; family and clan were his life's medium.

"The promise and not the authenticity is everything; the trick is not to become too materially involved or attached. Seven percent of Indians today are nomadic," said Harshraj. "Human migration poses such a curious relationship to place, for there is sorrow for the abandoned and yet a studied integration of the new. Usually songs express all this. Early migrants always proceeded on foot, and the transitions between districts were slow and comprehensible. There is something about walking as a locative activity," he said, "that is always fitting. Human mobility—and even my ancestors came from inner Asia to these parts—sets up an ungiven relationship with a territory. It has nothing to do with the utility or munificence of a land or why would the desert or the arctic be populated, but with some other mysterious affinity. How is it today," he asked, "when people migrate from Africa or Asia to the Americas, how do they compose themselves if the geocentric or spatial—as a force rather than simply a vessel—is cancelled from their lives when they inhabit cities?"

"Here," he added, "how can kingship function now, when that primacy of the earth no longer obtains? We cannot survive merely by being tenacious," he laughed. "We represent a hierarchy generated by land, by landscape, pre-urban and pre-modern. Now with population inflating the cities and capitals dominating politics, all our relationships are yielded and defunct. How shall we survive, where is our earth, the villages? What happens to a society," he asked, "where land is no more a matter of love and where kinship is no more a defining characteristic and where human beings only exist in terms of individuality and contract; how do the male and feminine then unite? Or does that make for a greater range of love, as there exists more potential for illusion and phantasy? Given the lack of initial place and original kinship, what principles then organize consciousness? I cannot even imagine that state," he laughed. "Does art then become purely self-referential, displaying and promoting only its own medium?"

"A creature without awareness of place or kinship has no cosmology: that is a ghost, a detached spirit of consciousness," he said. "Although, perhaps individual love—the male-feminine axis—can redeem a person from such a selfless abyss. What it is that then focuses those two entities so that they become mutually visible and their depths become perceptible and apart from sexuality? Place and also the paradigms of kinship are like the rules of spoken language or visual perspective, the logic that supplies us beings with an elementary meaning. Then kingship is totally bound up with place. As for liberty," he said, "it is more of an apprehension, an awareness that fires us like heat or light with current and mobility, an awareness that flows within a system of signs. Perhaps in the West today, the fact that human segregation is not a given but is to be constantly proven—between the sexes at least—is, *in potentia*, a condition of great possible freedom. I think that it is generally ignored though. Humanity prefers illusion to autonomy. The problem is, who effects those illusions, for all of culture is nothing but a screen."

Inside the palace, the hall was deserted, and I glanced over the day's newspaper and sat beside the pool to watch the fish. Harshraj's wife and one of his aunts came down, and we exchanged greetings and chatted for a while. Both were distinctly beautiful women, mature, strikingly dressed in cerise and mauve *saris*, and delicately jewelled with rubies and diamonds. They gossiped and laughed, talking about their daughters. I soon left them, going homeward that night towards the villa amazed at how dedicated these people were to their kin and society; it was so unlike how we lived in the West, and I felt indecent and naïve.

The next morning, Harshraj and I set off towards the Rann, and we were soon speeding off in the land rover with a boy in the back to look after the tiffin boxes. After an hour or so of skirting the desert, we made a detour in order to visit Halvad, about a kilometer away, where the clan had once resided before moving to Dhrangadhra. We passed along an attractive avenue of mature banyans that lined one side of a lake and then entered the town proper, slowly making our way through crammed bazaars, until we came to the walls of a palace-stronghold. The gates were impregnable structures plated with iron and bronze, bolted and barbed. Within, another world opened up, of grasses and overgrown ruin, of late medieval disorder and dejected collapse. Pillared and bracketed, a pavilion stood inside the entrance, where an aged watchman now lived; his *charpoy*, a string-bed, was covered with a few possessions. This old gentleman revered Harshraj and took the dust from his feet and opened up a postern in another great barred entry—heavily reinforced with thick iron—and we passed through a second high ruddy sandstone wall. Inside, the earthquake had wrecked much of the configuration of rooms. The plan was that of a traditional form, with vast walls surrounding an inner courtyard with quarters built against the sides. Dozens of carved teak pillars had fallen, their serpentine brackets collapsed with them. Plaster and stone littered the ground as walls and floors had tumbled down. Vines had begun to grow amongst the jumble, and wreckage and silence were everywhere. The central courtyard was made up of four large sunken pools with four stone walkways leading to a central point where an octagonal tower was raised up as a tall isolated column, elegant and perfect. Its eight floors were marked by delicately carved oriel windows, the emblem on the family standard. Cracked and fissured, slightly inclined, it stood integral and focal to the whole edifice, decorated and exquisite. The pools were dry and thick with vegetation and refuse; ragged citrus grew here and there.

The guardian opened the studded and bolted tower door, and we entered into the lowest room. Bats flew about our heads, twittering and disturbed by the sudden light. There was nothing but detritus within except for a carved spiral staircase of rosewood. Fractures were everywhere in the fabric of the tower; only strength of design and material held it intact. We climbed up a couple of levels, avoiding the hundreds of bats, before we retreated. Enormous bees' nests were also littered about, sickly-smelling and dirty. The bees were hazardous, Harshraj commented, and we left.

So we wandered, Harshraj recounting tales of various rajas and their deeds. We mounted onto the roof, where a carved throne and stone benches lined the crenellation; all was in desuetude and spoilage, inhabited only by snakes and birds. Beyond was the lake, and the air coming off it was fresh and cool. To one side were long *ghats*, where dozens of women were laundering; further, a thick stain of gray smoke indicated a cremation. Curiously, there were eighteen small islets on the lake, each with a stone structure and iron fittings: these were well-heads. It seemed paradoxical for wells to be sited within a lake, but during severe drought they supplied an emergency source of water. The seventeenth-century economy had been that sage and efficient, for the menace of water scarcity was intrinsic and perpetual to this part of the world. At each corner of the palace, other less tall towers stood, each with countless embellished oriel windows. Some of the rooms were still complete, light and airy, with walls covered in mirrors and ceilings painted with birds and green foliage. An atmosphere of melancholy and dilapidation was about the place.

"It would take too much money to restore it now," said Harshraj unhappily. "It's gone. Dhrangadhra is bigger and more magnificent, but this was the most beautiful." He spoke with sorrow in his voice. "This would make a wonderful academy for the arts, but who has the money?" In fact he was to pass more than a decade carefully restoring this palace and conserving its old beauty.

The roof where we stood was littered with torn feathers and bits of dried bloody flesh of pigeons, caught and eaten by falcons. The central tower gave an appearance of visual integrity, but that was all, for decay had seized the place. What remained was enchantment, a sense of former Rajput warrior life, *kshatriya* culture at its most refined and mature. That architecture so gracious and civilized could fall into such disrepair and dissolution was distressing; all was reverting to debris and not to be redeemed as a lost and complex ceremonial world withdrew from remembrance. Although the building was essentially a fortress, its tone was that of studied pleasure, of detailed and urbane delight, sophisticated and particular. Time's erasure—one minute of the earth's trembling—had toppled such an acme. Only the voices of mynahs and parakeets touched these walls now.

We set off westward again, having taken a dish of tea with the old bespectacled guardian and his wife. Milestone after milestone, the road was like an arrow; where there was water, there were fields—the golden fluid causative of life—otherwise it was waste. In a few more hours we began to cross the salt territory of the Little Rann and entered the Kacch. For me it was suddenly and quite mysteriously one of the loveliest places on earth, and to return after so many years was a renewal of joy and excitement.

Here and there were empty river-beds where small rivulets trickled or stagnated and herds of camel watered. We passed through miles of shallow salt pans, white and dazzling, where occasionally a crane stood. The landscape was perfectly horizontal, only given perspective by a long line of giant electricity pylons. Far to the west was the port of Kandla, India's largest *entrepot*, situated next to the gray city of Gandhidham, which had been built to house some of the hundreds of thousands of refugees from Partition and its violently enforced binary life. As it was a concrete city, it had suffered badly from the tremors, and then water relief had been a major problem. On the road now, increasingly, were hundreds of overheated lorries, filthy, slow, and with open cabins, their motors emitting volumes of black diesel fume. They transported swaggering cargoes of salt or goods shipped through Kandla. Punctured or stripped tires or mechanical failure was common, and many trucks were pulled over to the side of the road undergoing repairs. There was a eerie quality about the place, severely desolate and mildly threatening.

Sometimes a weary file of camels passed going in an eastward direction, thin tired beasts crossing a bitter and treeless land. The animals were loaded with polished metal pots, tent gear, and wooden beds, as women dressed in black walked alongside. This was a bad year for the pastoralists—one of a series—due to the lack of monsoon. There was nothing about but sand and stone and salt and a flat zero sky. There were no kites or crows in the air, and even wild dogs were sparse. The vehicle sped along like a dart, mile after mile, as we sat in silence looking out upon a hot desert whose air plunged in through the open windows; far off towards the north, a low blurred range of hills became visible. Sometimes the driver smoked a thin local cigarette, spitting out the butts.

Signs of seismic spoliation became common, where buildings had folded inwardly like cardboard. One consequence of relief work was the construction of many small and identical prefabricated dwellings, all square and archetypical: thin walls bolted together with tin rooves and small verandas. These new lodgings were the simplest possible design, reproduced immediately and hundredfold. Houses in these parts were not so much for accommodation but for storage, as people lived outside or upon terraces; they provided the material element of kinship and were only used for shelter during monsoon.

The road was well metaled for strategic reasons, as we were now coming up towards the frontier with Pakistan. At this point the desert lacked even acacia scrub, was nothing but stone upon stone, and even the sand was coarse. It was obvious how civilization in its germination had been founded upon hydraulic schemes, water harvesting and irrigation: without that, there was nothing. Even in the West, rivers and seas had always been contingent for settlement. This was a type of landscape that I had not experienced before, not even in Africa; it was unaffected and uninfluenced by humanity, yet it felt more than uninhabited and untouched. When I had first visited the Rann on a previous occasion, twenty years ago, I had been much farther west and the terrain was not as weirdly remote. Oddly, I felt very much at home here, as if it were deeply familiar; there was something both inaccessible about this region and yet intimate.

There was a nil quality about the district, irrefragable and unchangeable; like the absolute zero of temperature, it was as if this land was not to be affected in any way. Even the driver and the usually effervescent Harshraj had become mute, and the boy was asleep in the rear. Outside of the vehicle, the heat became more intense, tangible and solid, blasting through the open windows as we sped over the birdless shrubless land; even leopard or antelope could not exist out there. At the middle of the day in a flare of light and reflected heat, we halted at a low bridge across a brackish tidal bed. The boy prepared a meal and set it out, murmuring *"Bismillah"* as we began to partake, and we ate without speaking, famished by our long travel. Around us the marsh glowed with an intense ungiving whiteness and the edge of the water was crusted with a thick gritty deposit like rock; the wind coming off the Rann was strong, fiery, and ungentle. Everything about the climate was hostile and unsupportive of life but subtle and delicate at the same time. After we had eaten, I strolled along the viaduct to where I could step down and reach some water in order to wash. Dipping my fingers into the waves, the liquid was hot and the salinity slimy. I rinsed my hands and splashed some water onto my face and hair, and immediately there was a stinging sensation about my lips and cheeks caused by the high alkalinity. It took about an hour to cleanse the discomfort.

Soon we passed through the commune of Rapar, its main street crowded with stalls, bullocks, camels, dogs, and tribesmen. This was unlike any of the villages farther east; it was more central Asian and less oriental. The dust and noise from the hubbub filled the land rover as we gradually bumped through the place, and many women wore their *saris* as veils drawn across their faces. It was like a scene from *Kim*, as slowly we crossed eastern Kacch and drove north towards the small outlying island of Khedir. Suddenly the road entered upon a long causeway of several miles–duration, and it was like being in the Antarctic. Everything was absolutely white, both earth and sky, with no distinction between the two zones. The world was lifeless; whiteness was everything—like Yama, Death—and the sea was completely salt-encrusted. It was ominous, as we drove on across the pitted surface for mile after mile without any indication of living creature or movement, only heat and glare. All of us in the vehicle were taciturn, uneasy.

An hour later we were approaching the hamlet of stone-built Dholavira, our destination. The tranquility of the situation was astonishing: it was completely quiet, even the air was unmoving, and the surrounding plain was thoroughly stilled, without bird or lizard or any motion. We came to an army camp where several vehicles—cannon or missiles—were covered with camouflaged netting and the road was partially blocked with sandbags and we were forced to halt. Harshraj asked a captain where the *purana qila* was, the old fort, and the officer, having inspected us carefully, detailed two troopers to accompany us. We were now within forty kilometers of the border, and the salient hills of Pakistan were visible in the distance, an area that had become a volatile locus for enmity and friction.

As we bumped along in low gear, the site became more obvious: a prominent coffee-colored mound where great stone walls marked one edge, and higher, more architecture was discernible. We stopped and left the vehicle near some huts and, taking a couple of bottles of water, walked over to the ruins. The absolute repose and hush of the place was insuperable. This was the site of one of the earliest human cities, dating back to the third millennium, and it marked the beginnings of urbanization in human culture. Substantial gateways with pillars still remained, and grooves for locking-posts indicated access to an upper town. Formal lanes, enormous rock-cut cisterns, an elaborate plumbing system: all signified a highly rational and sophisticated polity. The ground was littered with potsherds.

For several hours we wandered about the streets and foundations, now and then halting to pick up a piece of terra cotta or mineral: the base of a jar, a piece from a woman's stoneware bracelet, a broken chert knife-blade, steatite beads, chalcedony and jasper fragments, and tiny polished weights. It was astounding, being within a city of such magnitude and mature complexity, far out upon this desert plain of silence. There was a balminess to the air that was surprisingly pacific, and the sky above was the color of diamond, where a few blue-gray doves scattered: the alkalinity of the earth must have had an effect upon the sky's refraction. To the west, in a subtle impenetrable haze, was another small island, and further north lay the ranges of Pakistan.

I had visited many ancient sites in my life, especially in Greece, but none partook of such imposing and supramundane beauty; none were of such archaic majesty and mystery. There was such an air of the ceremonial and pre-temporal about those giant walls. It was untroubled by the lives that presently covered most of the earth, as if poised in its own aeon, without context and unqualified by the millennia that had followed the city's demise. The atmosphere was intoxicating, inaccessible to normal perception; it was another Jerusalem, vibrant and unreal. The light lacked currency and disclosed nothing; a metropolis had inexplicably dissolved, leaving only a trace of former magnificence and power, uncomplicated by time and the consequent disorders of humanity. The great age of the settlement and its extraordinary complexity, sophistication, and obvious civic wealth were stunning; it had been an extremely well-planned and affluent port. The walls and hydraulic systems, the great magnitude of the place, all indicated power and worldliness. It was also the only Indus Valley site to exhibit a large stone inscription with twenty tall characters of script found upon the wall at the entrance to the citadel. No one knows why the extensive and rich civilization suddenly decayed and became moribund; there was no trace to indicate cause of collapse, be it drought, flood, pestilence, epidemic, or a change in the course of waterways: none of these fully accounted for the abandonment.

It was not only the architectural perfection and rational intricacy of the position that was overpowering; the primordial landscape about was spectacular and unnerving, too non-human for comprehension. It was a stupefying experience, being there: the candor of the site was disturbing and the emptiness lucent and unbounded. It was utterly without content except for the archaic walls and the myriad ceramic fragments scattered upon the sand and dry stony earth, sherds and raw agates and large chips of rock-crystal. There were small copper beads that had once been worn by women about their necks, fragments of slim lithic blades lay about, and there were even fractured bits of shell that had once been worn as bangles, long before the Indo-Aryans had migrated into the sub-continent. Here time possessed a completely different dimension that neither reason nor imagination could apprehend. It felt as if light had abstracted itself, that time was effaced and no longer bore any simulation of creature habit or routine. The panorama was as a still life, suspended in solution. An eventless world where no memory was at play, it was so without temporal or visual perspective; human weakness had been fully eliminated in this visible reminiscence of unflawed rest: something had transfigured and ascended. The dramatic solitude of the site overwhelmed me with its emollient silence and strong aquamarine light. It was unreal and strangely composed, both vanished from the present and yet vastly unchanged, suspended out of time.

A few hours later, exhausted, numbed, and exhilarated by the experience, we were on the road again, back towards Dhrangadhra. By late afternoon we were among human habitation, the starved and thirsty white cattle and the settlements of circular mud dwellings with conical grass rooves. We spotted a few *nilgai* or blue buck, far off and trotting across the plain. I sat in the back of the vehicle with Harshraj, both of us saying nothing, staring out as the car galloped across the miles through desiccated and windless terrain as evening drew on and fires were kindled. As we drove back across the hot sweet desert and little Rann, I felt that I had witnessed something unearthly and not of this life. Yet there remained the ominous feeling as to why a site of such magnitude and assets could become so nameless and absolutely deserted; what inhuman force had accomplished that dissolution? The driver lit a stick of incense that burned at a small shrine on the dashboard, and he occasionally opened the door to expectorate, for he was chewing *paan*. As we at last turned onto the Kandla road and approached the main causeway out of the Rann, the way became busy with cargo trucks again; the glare from their headlamps shooting through the night, illuminating the faces of the two men and the boy. Thereafter the hours blurred with darkness and fatigue.

In the days that ensued, the landscape of Dholavira—unperturbed by human chronology and with its distant island hovering in lucid kinetic light—returned to me again and again, dominating my hours and nights. In the centuries of its flourishing, the city must have been close to the sea and its wealth derived from mercantile trading; where else could such power have come from? Earthquake must have changed the shoreline and course of the Indus. If only there had been more time to spend there, to camp for some days and assimilate the place more thoroughly. Yet perhaps the transience of our visit had been sufficient and appropriate, for the site had almost been too much. I wondered if I would ever return, yet knew that I never would. Something about the spot made it impossible; emotionally it was not feasible, and the profoundly elusive and yet intrinsically present quality of the landscape haunted me for weeks.

Life at Dhrangadhra continued in an uneventful tempo. One day—as there was no bank in the town—I had to drive for several hours to another municipality. The transaction itself took about two hours, and I returned with a large sealed bundle of small-denomination notes in a paper bag, feeling embarrassed by the physical quantity of my money. Another day, a shaggy gray and black rhesus monkey the size of a young man appeared in the grounds, lone and looking troubled. The crows constantly mobbed it as it swung about the trees. Baddhu Singh's younger son was delighted and tried to approach the animal when it came down to one of the fountains. It snarled with an angry grimace of large canine teeth and made as if to attack, which thrilled the boy. It must have inadvertently been transported by a truck and come into the gardens for refuge.

Harshraj was preparing to leave, and the palace began to resume what must have been its usual closed life. He had filled the hall with activity and people, and now much of the furniture was already shrouded in long white sheets and the place felt derelict and vacant; the fish ponds assumed a life of disregard. Harshraj himself became constrained, preoccupied with meetings and persons who had postponed visiting until the end. His daughter's yoga teacher and family, the local astrologer, the family of the court painter, the colonel of the garrison—all suddenly began to show up, along with creditors. Servants were going about in a desultory manner, and solitary fans whirred in the deserted *darbar* hall. Cushions with the royal insignia upon them and banners suspended on the walls seemed lonely and out of place; the great copper war-drums appeared more lopsided and dusty. Portraits that were covered in a dense yellow-brown dust from off the desert were sheeted, and brass-bound chests—mounted on small wooden wheels—were padlocked, as were all the *armoires* that held books. The billiard table was clothed in a stained shroud of silk. Now that

Harshraj and his vitality were departing, an air of futility came over the palace.

He departed at noon on the subsequent day. The servants lined the main front steps as the car waited; even the Maharaja's staff came down from the *mardana*. Harshraj appeared alone, having made farewells to his wife and daughter in private. Serious and meditative, he said goodbye to each member of the household. The staff were patently saddened and distressed, acutely lugubrious. He was obviously unhappy himself to depart but restrained all demonstration of sentiment. The old white car started up, and that was it, as the gateman in his beret saluted. That night, I walked about the grounds in the warm pink evening, strolling through the gardens, admiring the birds. One peacock descended from a tower in a long straight spectacular glide right across my sight; an almost full moon offered up its cool light. Some roses were already blooming, and the kestrel flew from pediment to pediment, whistling. Abdul, one of the staff, came out, and we walked without speaking for a while.

"What will you do now that Harshraj is gone?" I asked.

"*Shanti*," the other replied. "Peace."

Later, walking home along the lake road, I felt suddenly alone. The town had been busy earlier with another *mela*, but now that it was late, everything was hushed. Dholavira's irreducible presence still preoccupied me with its lucid, irrefragable potence of place. It was as if I had been permitted a glimpse of something rare and unbearable and now had to decipher that, to decode its absence of signal: the lack of continuum between past and present needed to be supplied. As I stood on the roof that night before going down, I thought to myself that the potential for happiness in this place was very high indeed; one could live here with content. Some words of Harshraj—from our last conversation—came back to me. He had said that because it was the duty of a *kshatriya* always to give and to offer, they should never thank anyone for a gift.

"Gratitude was unnecessary," he had said, "for life itself was a matter of bestowal and one's only obligation was always to provide, to be generous above all else, for life was only an ideal. It is important to give more than one receives in life: that is the only true creativity."

After I had bathed and before I retired, a cold shudder came over me; an icy shivering passed through my body as if I was being stabbed, and for a few minutes as I prepared for bed, I was shaking. It was a horrible feeling, come from nowhere. I took a mattress up onto the roof, trying to escape the hundreds of mosquitoes. The warm breeze was fond and comforting, and above, the night sky gently wheeled. Completely exhausted by the recent days and experience, I fell into a weightless sleep.

One of the dogs was howling below on the veranda before dawn, the pining uxorious male. Baddhu Singh must have tied the bitch up elsewhere. Mosquitoes bit my lips during the night, the only part of my body that was exposed, and they became swollen. For a long time I lay there watching the system of heaven and constellations, meteors and satellites, listening to the drum rhythm of the stars. Grus, the crane, was in the meridian, with Cassiopeia below. It was reassuring how much I had grown to love this place.

That day I moved all of my things up to the roof: books, writing equipment, various *bric-à-brac* that I had acquired and had gathered about me: rocks, pieces of carved stone, vulture feathers, potsherds. I spent more and more time up there. The sun and moon were my feet, in a cornelian sky.

II. Mandvi:
The Old Sea Coast

India received us without ado as we touched down at Mumbai airport and cleared customs. We then went across the terminal to wait for our flight up towards Bhuj, the capital of Kacch. There, out in the middle of the Kacchi desert, it was shockingly hot when we arrived, for the monsoon had not yet come. The city was vastly larger than what it had been twenty years before when I had last visited, and now due to the earthquake of four years previous, rubble was piled everywhere and new buildings were being constructed on all sides.

Dazed from flying—we had come from Athens, where we had at last been married, in a small Byzantine chapel on the Hill of the Muses—we settled into a guest-house that nestled against the old palace walls. Much of that building had fallen during the earthquake, and great heaps of rendered sandstone were everywhere. In fact, much of the old parts of the town were like a combat zone—the Balkans—or like Berlin at the end of the last war. We were woken early by sounds of devotion from nearby temples in the pre-dawn and then by the grating and revving noise of commercial vehicles arriving and departing: trucks preparing to set off in the late cool of the night. A slender moon was visible through the grill of the windows as we lay abed during those warm dark hours, the rotors of a fan clicking on the ceiling.

Leanna and I were deliciously happy during those days, and on one of our first evenings we strolled out to the Hamirsar tank, now almost empty of water. At the *ghats*, women were bathing and doing laundry as the jade-colored water rippled with a steady breeze coming off the desert; cranes and herons flew about. During that time clouds had gathered and piled up and the strong flaunting wind increased, but still no monsoon arrived. We waited in Bhuj for several days, retrieving sleep and slowly settling our feet upon this hot stony soil. Each morning we would walk about the city, much of which was either a shambles or newly built concrete structure. The first few minutes of that earthquake—there had been others during the centuries equally as devastating—must have been horrific and terrible, a nightmare of supernatural distress for those who survived. Grief was not possible, our hotelier told us, with so many dead.

It was disorienting to be back in India and in the Kacch once again, and everything felt slightly two-dimensional. On our final afternoon in Bhuj, before we set off towards coastal Mandvi, we walked out to the *chattris*, which had once stood just beyond the lake at the edge of the town. Now these ancient cenotaphs of long deceased Maharaos—often cremated with their many and living mistresses—were surrounded by a suburb of concrete bungalows. Twenty-one years ago when I had been there alone, I used to walk out of the old city gates—now gone—and stroll around the deserted lake to enjoy the solitude of an evening and to sit beside the *chattris* and multitudes of neatly aligned hero-stones, watching the hawks and kestrels as they hunted; small bats and wild dogs were the only other life as a golden dusk rose upon the air and became pink. Fortunately I had sketched those structures in a notebook, for after the earthquake, most of the memorials were heaps of broken rubble and fenced off with barbed wire to prevent pilfering of fallen masonry, many items of which had probably already been removed and sold in Mumbai. Years ago the air and the light of the desert and the dark crimson hills of the distance had faded into ending day and silence; now all was hubbub and ruin and populace, for time and its proliferating disorder had altered everything. The petrol and diesel engine had overcome this still world; noise was prolific and quietness rare. Much of the new architecture was *kitsch* with an overt demonstration of new wealth and novel sense of prerogative.

Mornings began early in Bhuj, with ringings and clangings from numerous temples that clashed upon the heavy air as the sun arose from the surrounding dry hills. A low serum-colored light appeared to rise upward from the ground, casting linear and geometric shadows sideways. Leanna lay supine and asleep beside me, a pillow upon her head, and I softly touched her back and quietly rose and went outside and ordered tea, taking my books and a bottle of water with me out onto the balcony above the narrow street. The collapsed walls and decayed windows of the palace next door still remained in shadow, where huge jagged and diagonal cracks marked the rotten building; the vast gates had been looted from Halvad in the late sixteenth century, when the Kacchis had defeated the Jhalas. Unseen crows were already busy and discordant upon the air, and pariah dogs were barking and pigs were squealing and grunting. The tower with its pink-striped stones, now lopsided, caught the first noose of light coming off the sands. Soon, the noise of motorcycles and rickshaws was filling the day with a buzzing and hooting.

Before we set off towards Mandvi—which was to be our final destination—we drove up towards the Rann, due north of Bhuj, just for a glance, a reminder of that great white saline and deserted world. Leanna had not seen it before, and I wanted to show it to her. The day was potently hot, mercury standing at forty-four degrees in the thermometer, and being out in that light was as if one were drugged, as consciousness soon became extinct. All mental nuance and abstraction vanished, leaving us feckless and without emotion as we sat in the back of an old and creaking vehicle as it sped down a long straight road. The horizon in front of us was flat and void, and soon the black hills about Bhuj were passed. Now and then we would see a boy with a few lonely camels, hobbled and grazing upon *prosopis* thorn. Occasionally we would pass small villages whose households consisted of round mud-walled and thatched buildings low upon the ground, seemingly submerged in a fluctuating haze of opaque heat. I loved the intense vast solitude of the place, but Leanna caviled at its inhumanity, its rocks and stones and lack of any life but for snakes and foxes; besides, the heat was stupefying her. This was perhaps the most ancient landscape that I had ever perceived, far more ancient than the region about Zarax in southern Greece, where my intellectual and emotional home had been—long ago—for two decades. It was a landscape that I knew intimately with an immediacy that was unhesitating; this earth was already within me, was what I understood and where I felt instantly established.

Our destination was Kalo Dungar, a hilltop overlooking the Great Rann, which stretched out in an aerial haze for some miles towards Pakistan. Just beneath the hill was a small shrine, outside of which brahmin pilgrims and a *saddhu* were sitting, drinking tea and conversing. Their *ashram* nestled above a deep ravine, and beyond it lay the great open expanse of a desolate world. They politely gave us *chai* and watched us drink. There was no love song in that place, no indication of man or woman and no sense of child nor of household: it was a situation where the human soul had depleted itself in order to receive back its own emptiness. The enormity of the supra-terrestrial view, its wind and sky, had only barely touched upon human history four or five thousand years previously, before earthquakes had shifted the course of rivers and the area had become desert; then all had become dormant and immersed in parched heat.

Later that night, as the vehicle ran along the curveless unswerving road through dozens of miles of hot sugary-smelling night air, after the lion-colored sun had gently settled away, we sat closely in the back of the car, exhausted by the day's effort.

"Time is slowly diminishing us," said Leanna. "We are constantly being removed and dissolved. Children are the only ones in life ever to be gaining upon the world. If we are to ever retrieve meaning or some insinuation of meaning, consciousness must be a steady pursuit, never to be presumed. Yet this heat eradicates me; nothing is possible."

"Beauty consists in slowness, the inhibition of time," I said. "That is why I like that place."

"No, it was too empty for me, Kevin. I need people. You know, we forget almost all of our life, glimpsing now and then a few inhabitants, a few moments or instants. Sometimes the Homers of this world observe the more translucent forms, the true figures who patrol time, and through their art they are able to describe for us their insight. Such poets dwell in that other world and not this, and they relate to us how we really are in the universe. They are generous and benignant, sad for the eternal distress of humanity and the suffering incurred by greed. Homer would never stay in Kalo Dungar."

"Well, he might do at the end of his life."

"Yes, the end."

The next day we arrived at Mandvi, having driven down from Bhuj at noon. The topography through which we passed, once we were out of the desert, was prosperous and well irrigated. Mandvi—which means customs house—had changed since my previous visit. Much had gone—the town gates and fortified circuit walls—and much had been extended and built up. It was no longer a small sleepy port but a busy and hectic town, affluent and flourishing. Once it was famed for the "most skillful pilots, good seamen, adventurous merchants, and strong boats" of the Indian Ocean, and this continued, although Somali piracy is presently causing much disorder for the Mandvi carrying trade between the Gulf, India, and East Africa.

The coast was still pristine in extent, tides in the shallow river slowly came and went, and always there were small clouds travelling inland. Miles and miles of bare shore extended on both sides, fringed by thorny scrub, and the palace of the Maharao gleamed like a dark embossed jewel far to the west. The inhospitable turmoil of the Arabian Sea during monsoon had not changed, and brown seething waves were breaking ferociously upon the sand. Cremations were still being performed along the water's edge near the breakwater that sheltered the harbor on its western side. Each morning, flashy green parakeets would perch and noisily chatter on the wires that ran outside our balcony, and the unkempt dogs who had been sleeping in a huddle next to the road that ran along the riverside would snarl and snap as they awoke. Leopard-colored smoky dawns rose up onto the day, and upon the road itself there was always traffic: pedestrians, cyclists, tractors, camels, bullock-carts, ponies, donkeys, trucks, motorcycles, and the occasional elephant on its way to a temple or fair. Farther away, on the far side of the Rukhmavati river—the shining, radiant one—Jain temples were silhouetted among trees, with long orange pennons fluttering from their spires. On the other side of the bridge, in the Moslem quarter, minarets stood out against the sea air, their green pennants constantly flapping in the trade wind.

At last I was back after so many years of absence, and now I had a wife. Cambridge and all my grueling academic years quite rightly seemed on the other side of the earth. Although Mandvi was no longer idyllic and possessed a slight urban and modern tone, I loved the hectic audacity of life there. Below the bridge, along the edges of the river, seventy or so gigantic *kotiya* dhows were moored, anchored, beached, or in process of construction. The shipwrights had not changed, and they gently built these giant wooden vessels, hammering and sawing the teak into perfect marine form. Great hulls were propped up on scaffoldings of mangrove, the names of the vessels written rudely on the keel in red paint: *Maskan, Al Sharif, Sanjeeda.* Upon the western shore of the town there were now huge wind turbines, the propellers of which turned with a powerful thrumming as they generated electricity from the steady breeze. These gave the place a surreal air, dispelling anything sublime. Mandvi beach had become a resort for newly married couples and tourists from Ahmedabad, who would romp and cavort fully clothed in the shallows as breakers crashed down around them. The colossal windmills gave the spot an extra *cachet* of the modern.

Our rooms, in a building that had once been a hospital, were large and spacious. The place was close to the bridge and the Bhuj road, however, and a constant whir and grind of traffic filled the immediate air with noise and fumes. A pair of black-painted British cannon were set into the walls of one of the residual bastions of the former perimeter, just next to our balcony. Egrets and ibis stalked the mud-flats of the river and water buffalo wallowed in the ooze. As our veranda faced east, the dawns would heat up the rooms instantly with a pre-monsoon glare of heat. The bright sunlight of the day soon mixed with the saturated and saline humidity to cause a dazzling brilliance that was shocking to the eyes: a reaction occurring between the ultraviolet light and the alkaline aerial moisture effecting a radical luster. The midday light was of a flaring, almost chemical potence that I had never experienced before.

Walking during the day was unpleasant, and we soon became dehydrated and stunned by the imperial sun. Nights were sweet, however, as bright green fluorescent lamps from outside the many mosques shimmered in the warm darkness. We slept naked and uncovered, damp with perspiration and an odor of heat beneath the spinning rotors of the fan, with windows open onto any breeze, and newly married, after so many years of mere association, the night hours were delicate and splendid. In all my life I had never imagined how archetypal to human consciousness the actual form of marriage was, and I was amazed at this paradox.

During one of those early evenings we drove out in a motor-rickshaw to the palace, a few miles along the coast. The tranquility and privacy of the grounds were refreshing, and the place was deserted apart from a few sleepy barefoot staff. A small Moslem shrine was perched high on the dunes between the shore and the palace, and we spent some hours there as the light settled and the sea grew dark, before returning to the teeming and commercial racket of the town with its refuse and marginal impoverishment and the endless fractional struggle of humanity. Survival was not to be taken for granted or assumed, and life there had lost its symmetry with nature, was in part desperate, illiterate, ill-nourished, and poorly accommodated. Modern India was beset with a terrific need for forbearance among its details, yet this new India was soon destined to become—like its neighbor China—one of the great powers of the twenty-first century as the West struggled and declined. Its poor were the ballast to this movement, a dangerously shifting and smoldering cargo.

One night I dreamed of Harshraj, who was one of the few Indians whom I knew to live a life of easy sophistication, having traveled and experienced the West and rejected it. Happy and continuously youthful with his wife and daughters, he lived a reflective life. He had often spoken well of Mandvi and had stayed there as a guest of the Maharao on several occasions, yet I wondered what he would think of the port now. Dhrangadhra too had suffered from the twentieth century and its lack of control or equation and also from seismic wreckage. I recalled him saying—one night as we sat up on the roof of the palace, the town below sunk away into a cool darkness—how form must always adhere to and follow function.

"If function is always for the good of human-kind," he said, "then our lives must always formulate an optimism. That is our one obligation in life," he added, "whatever our station."

As I sat upon the balcony of a morning after the sun had just risen and the world had revived, the heat brushed closely up against my skin as the pages of my notebook became damp and tacky with perspiration, and the ink of my pens guttered and dripped. Leanna still slept inside the shuttered and curtained room, beneath a whirring fan. For once in my life, love of place and love of person had coincided, and I had secured some title to my *nostos* or homecoming, to a preponderant reality where responsibility and gratitude were both stable. When she rose, I closed my books, and we drank tea together on the terrace at the rear of the building, which was still in shadow. I felt a continual and overwhelming gratitude towards the world for giving me a life with this woman.

"Prophecy is different here in India," she said as we sat on the stone bench. "Here, our conscious is founded upon a different basis of ideas and images, and our depths are not as they are in the West. It is not simply that we receive different images during the day," she added, "nor is it that the visible and diurnal world is different here—unlike how we lived in Greece or Cambridge—but that our dark selves, our profoundly immaterial introspective and interior worlds, are also completely different. None of those images bear any relation to or identity with what we now experience in a daily way: the hypostasis is dissimilar. India is a perfect place for Cervantes," she laughed. "I suppose what I mean," she continued, "is I am curious as to why that should be the case. Why is it that our inner world is so different here? Do you see? It is not only that our physical world is unlike, but that our deeply phenomenal world is not the same. Is that not strange, for where does it leave us?" she said.

"Is that not immortality?" I asked.

"No, definitely not, for that is too limited a metaphor. I am speaking of non-being. These introspective views bear no similarity nor identity with the physical world. You are too western, you know, Kevin," she laughed.

"No, I am not. I am deeply and profoundly inspired here. I was born in Asia, remember. This is my homecoming, being here with you."

We sat on the terrace as the traffic rushed and rattled and made its various ways about the town. Just below us a tall and mature date palm was home to a family of parakeets and a crow, who were busily and vociferously contesting with each other. As the pale quartz of the June sky, a thin lazulite blue, grew hotter and hotter, we retreated back to our rooms.

One afternoon soon after that exchange, we were walking along the deserted shore, far past the wind turbines.

"I find those great slow ticking propellers tremendously beautiful," said Leanna, "despite their imposition upon the landscape. There is something fitting, almost divinely archaic about them. They are like minimalist objects of devotion and remind me of Easter Island statuary or of Kykladic sculpture. There is something about the culture here that is not exactly idyllic, and yet the pastoral is its aesthetic, with its flocks and shepherds and plowing oxen. Despite all the modern *furor*, there is something so pacific and benign about this world that does not exist elsewhere in India, regardless of the filth and ordure."

"Yes, I am sure that what Samuel Palmer or Poussin painted was just as unswept."

We walked for an hour or two, the day not being as hot as it had been of recent, and then halted and swam in the extremely saline and powerful surge, not venturing too far out because of an irresistible undertow; it was a kind of swimming that I had not experienced before. We swam up and down in the shallow surf and then lay upon the sand enjoying our unusual solitude. Clouds began to gather in the west above the distant silhouette of the palace, not as individual forms but as a uniform mauve-gray coloration, as if the monsoon were at last about to break. We dressed and set off homeward, as an occasional murmur of thunder was audible upon the wind.

That night as we sat dining on the veranda, it did rain, but it was more of a light pricking rain that did not penetrate beyond any surface, hardly affecting anything but the scent of the air, which changed dramatically into something earthen and organic. About the moon that night, an aura of copper shone, and in the south, hundreds of miles away, the sky was irradiated by slow pulsing flashes of light that intermittently shone for seconds, then instantly faded with an almost sexual intensity. The following day, the dawn was low and powerful and long dark horizontal clouds covered the horizon in all directions. A cool breeze came from the east—different from the wind that had been blowing since we arrived—and we could hear the bells of temples across the river. There was more cirrus in the sky that day, but no one in town was fooled into thinking that monsoon was imminent.

It amazed me how swiftly the sun rose up above the horizon once its first limb had moved into the day, with a velocity of which we were usually not aware, for there existed no reference apart from those initial instants when the speed was obvious and fully displayed. Once that point had passed and the planet was risen there remained no mediate comparison to give the moment distinction. For about two or three seconds the actual mechanical celerity of time was briefly and overtly revealed; at dusk it was not the same, for the symmetry was different. The velocity of our blood within the carnal body was another dynamic of which we also remained generally unaware, and yet it was similarly fundamental to how our lives were organized. Both sun and blood in their swiftness installed every other motion for us, in time. I say this because the days then were streaming past as if both they and we were unaware of the other; Leanna and I were so deeply involved with only ourselves at that period, hazy with the sudden and novel fascination of an unexpected love and its reality of unpremeditated union.

A week or so later, we returned to the palace to enquire if the Maharao had returned from Mumbai.

"No, not yet," they said, shaking their heads sadly. "He was at Bhuj, though," they added, and would be arriving soon.

We went up to the top of the building, onto the roof and sat beneath its topmost *chattri*. Leanna read, and I sat in the shade looking out over the surrounding country and sea. At one point a dark squall came over, and rain pelted down as air and sky became gray. Instantly everything cooled as the water splashed and drenched the sandstone and marble surfaces. Once the rain had ceased, Leanna went below and wandered the grounds. I remained up there relishing the solitude and silence, admiring the empty Indian Ocean and watching peafowl stalk the gardens. I loved to observe my wife when she was lost in thought and unaware, her beauty and grace and her easy light-hearted presence in the world; seeing her like that filled me with a naïve joy. Soon, I descended and located her beside a dry fountain. There was an air of nonchalant abandon about the grounds: the broken sculptures, the ruined tennis court, the unpruned and unwatered fruit and flowering trees, the star-tortoises that shambled about, and the jays and bee-catchers that shot through the air. In one small hedged-in area, the skeletal remains of a whale lay upon the earth, its great bones looking outlandishly prehistoric.

We walked back along the shore as the tide receded and sunlight gleamed upon wet sand and rays and beams shot down through a low cloud cover; the isolation and enormity of the scene were refreshing. Leanna collected raw agates and seashells as plovers scattered at our approach and terns dived like small blades into the shallows; bright blue and scarlet crabs dashed away from our path. Offshore, a dhow was plying its solitary way westward. Gone were the days when fleets of country craft anchored in the roads off Mandvi and the Kacch was one of the great marine stations of the Indian Ocean, terminus for much of the marine commerce that ran between India and the West and provider of passage for thousands of Moslem pilgrims to and from the sacred cities of Islam in Arabia. Now a deserted *quietus* had come over the contemporary landscape and sea. Those old routes between Muscat Zanzibar and Kacch were now almost without traffic and Zanzibar was no more Mandvi's most important market; most of India's ivory had once been shipped to this coast.

We arrived at the port just as dusk was settling. Many families were gathered on the beach in small separate groups to picnic or frolic in the waves. A playful and capricious mood hung about the place, and food-sellers had positioned their carts along the edge of the seawall. We entered the noisy smoky hubbub of town, where mosques and temples were emitting various calls to devotion and men were gathering outside those buildings: it was an important social moment of the day. When we arrived back at our rooms, they were shabby with coarse sticky dust caused by a change in the wind direction, and for days, dampness alternated with squall or tense gritty winds; then the fierce sovereign sun would reappear. Everything became grimy with sand or dirty moisture; a soft brown astringent powder covered my desk and papers. It was as if a shutter were opening and closing as the rains alternated with grainy wind and the sky discharged heat and clamminess and coarse sand.

When a remission in the monsoon arrived, Leanna came home that day saying that she had discovered a wonderful driver and car and that we would be leaving for Koteshvar early next morning: this was Razul, a suave young man who always dressed impeccably in a well-tailored gray safari suit and who drove his ramshackle brown-painted four-wheel-drive jeep with great *panache*. We set off early on the following day laden with water bottles as the elderly vehicle lunged and lurched over narrow rain-eaten roads and quail and pigeon and rabbit dashed across our way. Flocks of goat or small herds of camel-cows with calves grazed the endless thorn-scrub that grew everywhere in the flat terrain. Now and then we passed a few hamlets of conically built dwellings with low thatched rooves, but rarely did we see any human being apart from an occasional child.

Long ago this region had been called *Tejasthan*—land of heat or splendor—and that same *tejas* still dominated today, for the atmosphere inside the car was intense and the air coming off the stony desert was superheated. It took about five hours, heading towards the northwest, to reach Koteshvar, a great Hindu pilgrimage destination on the edge of the Rann; in fact it was one of the five most important pilgrimage points in India. Once a famed and extremely populous Mahayana Buddhist site on the banks of the Indus, seismic shifts had reconfigured much of the ground and the fluvial system had retreated; now there were only the few ancient temples and the great lucid space of salt-marsh where shallow tides came and went. All that remained to indicate that Buddhism once held great sway and influence in Kacchi life were the small and remarkable rock-cut and pillared caves just to the east, near Syot, dating from two millennia ago, an area where the remains of a large town lay just below the surface of the earth and where many acres of field were thick with strewn pot- sherds and broken architectural elements from an unearthed city. Sindh, to the west, had been a strong Buddhist kingdom until the seventh century when brahmin kings had seized power.

We left Razul listening to a tape of Kacchi *raso* music and smoking cigarettes as he leaned against his vehicle. Having rung the bells and made obeisance to the deities, we went up onto the walls and circumambulated the precinct. The soft dun coloring of the stone and gentle pastel shades of the temple decoration—lilac and pink and yellow—gave the small for- tified enclave a serene aspect. The immense extent of the Great Rann sur- rounded us on three sides, glittering and reflecting the ardent light of a vivid sky, as if light were coining light. Here and there large painted storks glided past like ancient unearthly creatures, drooping languidly through the air.

We stayed there some hours and then proceeded on towards Lakhpat, formerly a conurbation and trading stronghold, now merely a great quan- tity of sand enclosed by a tall dark sandstone perimeter, interspersed with squat circular bastions. The remains of a mosque or the spire of a temple occasionally rose upward, but the place was abandoned and barren, more remote than anywhere else that I could recall visiting. Some ornately carved and domed tombs were the only intact architecture to be seen, with a small whitewashed Sikh *gurudvara*. We sat and rested from the crashing heat on one of the walls looking out onto the great open void of the Rann, now a thin sheen of mirror-like water that was bare of life or any motion.

"I do not think that I have ever been so removed from society and time as we are in this place," said Leanna. "It is so beautiful. Nothing moves; it just exists."

"What about Kalo Dungar?" I asked.

"That was too inhuman for me. That was an extreme, an edge; good for you, Kevin, but not for me. This is also an edge, but it is human. People have lived and died here; there was business and there were children. You go off to your isolated lifeless places, Kevin, but this is my greatest remove. It is a pity that we cannot stay here a while, but what would we live on?"

I lay down in the shadow of a crumbling wall, dumb with heat, and slept for some minutes as Leanna wandered off, returning with a handful of porcupine quills. We walked about hand in hand, seeing no one, and it was with sadness that we eventually found Razul and set off homeward. The simple purity and remoteness of Lakhpat was something that was unlikely ever to occur in our lives again; those few brief hours had been so vast, and yet so finite and inextensible.

"The world is losing such places," said Leanna. "Perhaps in innermost Asia there are a few remaining spots like this, but not many."

On the way home, the road—as we approached Mandvi—became horribly crowded with dozens of overtaking trucks, all competing for speed and vomiting out a filth of black slimy fumes.

"What a nightmare," Leanna observed repeatedly, as Razul swerved off the narrow road again and again in order to avoid another oncoming vehicle and as the vile stench from the large-bore exhausts belched through our windows.

That night we were both restless and unsleeping and went out onto the veranda, naked and perspiring, and sat there in the wet darkness listening to small discrete sounds of the sleeping town. How diminutive and irrelevant human life seemed then; even its vagaries appeared illusory. Large fruit bats were skimming past emitting thin needle-like squeaks; the tide was out, pools of water reflected a limp moonlight, and dogs were slinking along the road like shadows. Within the room a hot gravid air was churned by the idle spinning of the fan.

The ensuing day, I woke early and went outside to a yellow occluded dawn and spattering rain; wet sand, hazy listless air, and a tacky moist dust covered all surfaces. Sleep was onerous during this season, as if drugged with gravity and oil, and everything possessed a stale odor: clothes, bed linen, the rooms themselves. I closed the door quietly, leaving a naked Leanna sprawled upon the bed beneath the humming fan, and went to sit at the white plastic table where her agates were neatly lined up. Outside, the world slowly came to life beneath a leonine sky. All objects were varnished with a layer of thin oil, and a taint of ordure was upon the air. Even the schoolboys on their bicycles appeared unenthusiastic that morning. The tide was out, and human figures and dogs were wandering the flats; the dogs were playing and wakening, rolling and lolling on the sand, performing their many formalities and rites of hierarchy and territory. Flirtatious sparrows were nesting above our balcony, bringing bits of thread and straw in their beaks, happy and pleased with their work. Leanna soon joined me on the veranda, sleepy-eyed, a sheet wrapped about her as she told me her dream, something concerning embroidery. This weather was making her feel confined and restless, moody.

The gray wet air was busy with burnished pigeons and vagrant crows, and sitting there I realized how much happier I now was than ever before in my life, which was shocking: being with Leanna and being in this land. Previously, the natural solitariness of Indian life had enveloped and assimilated me to its lucid and satisfying haze, yet even though this was my place, India had never really taken me as its own until now, until we were married: it was if it had been waiting for us to observe propriety. We bathed and dressed and drank some tea and went out to the town, through the bazaar, and down towards the shore and walked westwards. Monsoon on the Arabian Sea was somewhat like Belle Ile in spring, a place that I had often visited in the past during youthful European summers, just off the coast of Bretagne; or it was like the Normandie of Marcel Proust and conducive to introspection and recollection. There was that same gray, derelict quality to the air. The vagueness of colorless light and a constant and ceaseless recurrence of endless tides and breaking seas along with an absence or slowness and solitariness of human life; all this disposed the place towards illuminating our irrelevance and lack of emotional efficacy. No achievement or resolution seemed possible for humanity in such a setting. Even vicissitude was illusory; the true inner tempo was without rhythm and like a single straight line. The ultimate solitude of the humane was visible today as we walked the shore; the atmosphere was so profoundly evocative and stable.

"Perhaps that is all love is," said Leanna, as we looked upon the varied grayness of air and white curling sea. "All that we might accomplish is a sharing of our singularity with one other person, and love is founded upon an understanding of solitude and its mutual fission."

A small dhow was passing, heaving gently through the seas about a mile offshore, plunging and breaking open the water in showers of spray and foam. As we turned to go back, an agile yellow-haired animal suddenly appeared on the dunes near us, somewhat like a fox, but with a long sharp skull and small triangular ears and thin curved tail. For a while it watched us in its vulpine way before slipping off into the trees. It was an extraordinarily beautiful creature, golden and preternatural.

On the succeeding day we set off again with Razul, this time to go northwards towards the border. Monsoon was still deepening, and there was no direct sunlight as small white cattle-egrets with rust-colored necks flashed across our way against a background of a dark vacuum-sky, making brief, vivid marks. As we went north, the climate changed, and we entered a terrain of dry stony plain interspersed with low black conical hills. Often we passed herds of young camel or buffalo and their shining calves, all healthy and fat with the new season. Closer up, towards the border, we drove past many charcoal burners who lived in isolated communities of tents surrounded by slow-burning circular mounds of heaped wood. All those whom we saw were dark-skinned, blackened by their work, and all of them—women and boys included—carried small sharp axes with metal hafts casually slung across their shoulders. The faces expressed a terrible and mean hopelessness.

Our destination was a group of monastic shrines that nestled in a fold of crimson hills. Someone whom Leanna had met in the bazaar had told her about the place, but on arrival we found it to be disappointing. The sanctity of the retreat had gone, and the buildings—harmed like so much else by recent seismic tremor—had been clumsily mended. We walked about enjoying the perfect stillness, and Leanna made some drawings; then we ate a meal in complete silence with two old cowherds who resided there.

As we drove back later in the afternoon, *nilgai* or bluebuck were visible on the plain here and there, grazing in small groups. There was an air of distance and vacuity about the landscape, of exhaustion, as if it had been fecund and busy once with community and livelihood, but now all had withdrawn and ceased. Only deer remained to supply movement to something that had become acutely static. We paused on the way—an endless narrow track that never seemed to deviate from the perfectly linear—for tea and respite from the vehicle's pitching. Leanna bought some mangoes in a village, and we halted at the next shrine and ate them, trying to draw our quiet and reticent driver into conversation, but he did not want to speak and just smiled and nodded his head.

Near Mandvi we reentered the monsoon. The road and sky became more and more drenched and gray, and soon we were driving through torrents of sluicing downpour. What had once been dry rocky gullies were now swollen and seething rivers. Boys were sporting in pools whilst their elders waded delicately through mud and refuse. A lot of dead fauna was drifting in the water: pigs, dogs, birds, and enormous quantities of plastic urban flotsam. Mandvi was deeply awash, and all of its life had slowed due to floods of brown silted water. The wild dogs became pathetic and shivered, crouching for shelter anywhere or crawling into holes. Leanna loved the disorder and fertility of this weather, its wet filthy chaos, and immediately went off to visit the bazaar, returning soaked and happy. She loved the humanity of life now and the fellowship generated by deluge, having abhorred the intensely sterile and burning heat of a few weeks ago.

There was soon no electricity, and that evening our rooms were lighted by stubs of candle stuck upon windowsills and on the floor. During the night I was repeatedly woken by thunder and a myriad of insect bites. The sound of water rushing off surfaces and of rain falling upon further water filled all of the hours with a seething.

In the subsequent days, everything became wet. Nothing was dry, nor could anything be dried; flies came inside in black droves. An odor of water was upon all things, as stale and decaying air hung about, and I missed the hot dry noons, the topography of mineral and flagrant light. One night I dreamed that I was on the moon and that there were stone creatures walking about like sedulous oxen in a waterless, powdery world. Dawns became hazy and stained with bronze shadow, the sun a pure white disc as the light sparkled coldly and metallically upon a receding tide. Many birds were in the air, brilliant white ibis and large egrets and sometimes a few storks, who looked weird and gaunt with their huge gangling bodies.

"You are not really interested in people, are you, Kevin?" Leanna said to me one morning as we sat on the veranda sipping tea from steel beakers and swiping at the dozens of flies that would cling to our legs. "You like to observe and watch what they do, but you are not actually concerned with how they live and feel, are you? Landscape is your domain, vacuous landscape."

I just shrugged and did not reply.

"You are not really Indian at all, are you?" she asked. "You just like to think that you are. This place is too heterodox for you."

"I am more Indian than you are."

"You cannot say that. It means nothing. This society is more complex than anything else that you have ever experienced. There is no more or less."

"The hours are longer here and the days are shorter," I said. "How about that?"

"Yes…. Time does go slowly, and yet afterwards I cannot remember anything. One has to succumb and not force our way through time like we used to in America or Greece. Here it just envelops us and there is no autonomy."

"Do you think that we shall stay here?" I asked.

"If we do return, it will be different. There is no going back now; something is different, and it is not just that we are married. Something has changed or shifted."

"Well, we must return at some point. There is my work and there is the house."

"You are so western, Kevin. I am not sure if you can stay here. I think that you have lost India and that the West is your habitat. India is your source, but you are a guest here. It is not your home; you have lost that, and you cannot pretend that this country is now your place."

I kept quiet, as I did not want to argue. Leanna was right, although I was not quite sure why. She was my home, and that was all.

"The days glide by here so mysteriously," she added, "so intensely and slowly, imperceptibly. Yet they possess such a richness and complexity of image and rhythm. It is difficult to actually recall what happened in a week, time is so dense and lucid. My mind works differently now, and I do not understand that: what to forecast or how to think."

"It is not that there exists no retrospect," I said, "but that time itself is dissimilar and such a view has less valence than it does in the West. India is much more feminine in that respect, constantly divergent and engaging."

Monsoon seemed to be passing, having paused only briefly above the Kacch; the strong commotion of sky was no more, and the solidity of air was diminishing. Crowds of dogs were out on the river flats again in the early morning, and rose-ringed parakeets were noisy as ever on the wires outside our rooms. A white sunlight glittered upon the tide. Once the really heavy showers had ceased, we ventured out again on our walks and journeys, and each day we began to swim offshore near the palace, where the sea was powerful and tumultuous, the water brown with sand. The combination of intense humidity and hot sea with a high salinity of air and water was intoxicating, and we became mechanical and tedious in our ways. Swimming was not like it was in the gelid, still, fresh water of Champlain in Vermont, unlike the vigorous and oceanic water off Belle Ile, and not at all like in the pure, limpid Aegean waters; here, a potent undertow and the force of persistently large waves and the heat and the density of everything made for unusual aquatics. One swam very hard and yet never moved: just to remain in the same spot required enormous effort. Not to be washed away or constantly submerged was all that movement could achieve in these conditions. It was very Indian: a lot of exertion went into remaining in exactly the same spot. Otherwise one would be lost.

Walking back along the shore where several of the turbines had broken and ceased to rotate, we often used to arrive back at the port by dusk, and the lighthouse would be blinking and flashing a pulse seawards. We used to halt and drink tea at a stall and sometimes watch the last mourners who had been attending a cremation; we always set off quickly then in order to avoid their grief and melancholy. The calls to devotion from the many mosques in Mandvi were mounting as we approached our guesthouse, and for some minutes the twilight came alive and resounded with various chants and cries; then they suddenly all lapsed as night came.

For the first time in my life, as we walked home then—in the sudden darkness, passing the vast hulks of careened dhows, Leanna beside me as we went hand in hand through the traffic and cows and pedestrians—for the first time ever, I felt that our being on earth was limited. All this must not only end for us, but it would also continue without us, and these wonderful and concentrated instants were thoroughly finite. Loving Leanna gave me not only a constant feeling of joy at the richness of existence but also of the imminently limited quantity of such a state. Death had never appeared as a threshold for me before but had seemed merely another condition or aspect of life. Now, being in love and being loved, I was undeniably mortal. Love of place transported us away from the temporal, but love of person fixed us irrevocably in time. Once, the multitude of phases had been so great for me and their details irrelevant, but now time had become unilithic, a vessel that would one day discharge us as it proceeded on a course of its own, embarking other and dissimilar passengers. I knew that I had to love Leanna and must never diminish that fortune; there could be no interim. I had never realized the value of time before, how valuable its days and months were, how profound its years, having lived like a spendthrift or wastrel for so long, only pleasing myself.

The tractors, camels, auto-rickshaws, landrovers, motorcycles, buses and trucks, cyclists, pedestrians, donkeys, camels, and ox-carts, the push-carts and automobiles, sometimes an elephant, and the great heterogeneity of people, the pastoralists and tribes-folk, the holy men, *saddhus* and brah-mins, all the profusion of noises and the voice of dogs and birds: these were the teeming innards of the day or a small fraction of the day's con-stituence of time and its relentless particularity. Beyond that, beyond the temples on the far shore of the river, was the ancient and stone landscape of Kacch, with its indigo and sandy rocks, its isolated and overwhelmed cities, its neolithic burial grounds and wealth of reptilian fossil life; its shrines and temples and inaccessible villages, its herds and lonely shep-herds, and the peripheral margin of sterile salt, the circumscribing Rann. Here we were, the two of us, dyadic among all this complication of life that did not even notice us and was not only unaware of us but uninter-ested in us. In marrying Leanna, I had gained my *nostos*, and the rest had no bearing any more. That was a strange feeling for someone like myself, who had always pursued a life of the liminal and extreme, both physically and mentally.

I had never before considered terminus as a condition of loss or con-clusion for my perceptions, and understanding of place had all been out of time and extra-ordinary. Now, with Leanna and marriage, I was locked into a state that was not infinitely persistent but that in fact would one day become final. Marriage had supplied an ultimatum, and human love was Faustian in this sense, in its craving to exceed. Now it no longer really mattered where I was—India, Greece, even America—for Leanna had become my truth and situation; and that, unlike landscape, was finite and its life restricted.

Some days later, we set off towards the palace for an audience with the Maharao, who had returned from Mumbai and Bhuj. We waited for him, barefoot, on an enclosed veranda at the rear of the building. He soon appeared, casual and gracious, tall and mustachioed, and we sat a long while, sipping *chas*, cold and fermented buffalo milk, discussing life in the Kacch and his recollections of Mountbatten and the Gandhis and of Nehru at Teen Murti in Delhi. Mandvi was his only remaining intact res-idence, apart from a flat and a club in Mumbai and a country lodge to the west: the earthquake had wrecked all his other palaces. He still stayed at one of the Bhuj establishments, the Ranjit Vilas, but much of it was rubble. Peafowl shrieked outside and insects buzzed as a mild breeze seeped in through the shutters and a lattice-work of screens.

"Our ancestors have taught us much," he said. "The British never understood that. They came with their plans and guns and we thrashed them at Anjar. They only beat us by bribery and subterfuge; they could never best us in the field," he laughed.

He laughed a lot during that first interview, his head leaning backwards and his eyes narrowing. He was a very big man with large bones, and he loved reminiscing. When I asked him about kingship in the future, he described himself as Humpty-Dumpty.

"We cannot be put back together again," he said. "I am the last of the Mohicans. Kacch will soon be independent from Gujarat, though," he added, "we are seeing to that. We are too different and too prosperous and we must be separate again. I am a poor man now," he smiled, "but I am still myself."

He was interested to hear news of his uncle at Dhrangadhra and of how the earthquake had affected the town and the residence. After two hours of talking, he rose and went to call his wife to join us. She appeared wearing a green *sari* and sat with us for a short while. Vivacious, light-hearted, and humorous, she was fascinated with Leanna. Afterwards, as we walked along windowless corridors on our way out, the Maharao paused beside a large glass case mounted on a wall where a panther was forever about to pounce. Above it was a photograph of a small boy with a rifle, standing over the fallen beast.

"My first panther," he exclaimed. "It had strayed into the grounds of Bhujiya fort."

We went down towards the shore, and I slept on the sand with a sarong about my head as Leanna patrolled up and down the waterline, combing the jetsam for shells and stones.

"He is so like my father," she said, as we walked homeward along the shore that evening. "It is uncanny, which makes me feel uncomfortable … because I love my father."

Mosquitoes began to be more of a problem at night, for the heavy turbid wash of the fan no longer succeeded in driving them off our naked skin. They seemed to particularly enjoy biting the soles of our feet, a sensation that I had never before experienced. Completely covering ourselves with coconut oil helped, and we would spend an hour before retiring rubbing the sweet-smelling liquid onto each other's bodies. These were rainy days in Mandvi. Squalls passed throughout the day, and at night, thunder and lightning would intermittently stain the sky with magenta, crumpling and flashing as the heavens deluged the earth with copious rainfall. The electricity would then go out, and the view across the river from our balcony whenever a thunderbolt exploded was of a white silhouette of temples, a far-off world that we could never attain. In a day the landscape about the port changed completely, becoming covered with a sheen of nutritious grasses, a bright perspiration of emerald color. It became a completely different countryside.

One morning, Leanna having become impatient and touched with *chagrin* once again, I called up Razul and arranged to be collected before dawn on the following day. We intended to make our way up towards Dholavira if possible, for many of the roads and tracks had been washed out. I felt nervous, as I had spoken so often with Leanna about the place, praising its beauty; what if she was disappointed and found the site uninteresting? We considered halting at Dhrangadhra and visiting the household, but decided to postpone that journey until later, when the weather was less inclement. Harshraj had written to say that he and his wife intended to visit Delhi and his two undergraduate daughters, so they were unlikely to be at home. Yet I longed to return to the town and to show Leanna about its ways and hills.

So we set out early, incense burning on the dashboard of the vehicle, our driver chanting softly to himself as we drove across the bridge and away towards Bhuj. The Maharao had telephoned the previous evening to invite us to tea that day, but we had already arranged this excursion and had to decline. In my mind as we drove along, I could see him pacing the cool dark passages of the palace, or alone upon the roof at night, hidden from the world by marble screens. There was something about that man that I liked, something untroubled and unique. He was like a giant plunged into time, submerged in days and nights, whom others were unable to clearly apprehend; they could only perceive him in worldly and momentary outline. There was a seclusion that adhered to him and gathered about his shape that I admired, a privation that in no way disturbed him and that he carried about with lenient pride.

The desert towards the Little Rann was coated with a varnish of fresh green. Initially, squalls of rain were passing over us constantly and Razul had to switch on his windshield wipers, which scratched and squeaked. Between Bhuj and Bachau, the road was crowded with heavily burdened cargo trucks churning clouds of foul black smoke. Once we turned north, however, and were away from the commercial route, we were back among herds of cattle and sheep, bullock-carts, and families of transhumant Rabari, whose camels were loaded up like castles whilst they walked behind the tall laggard animals. Small children and young goats and lambs rode atop the loads. Once we had crossed the thin causeway onto the island of Khedir, a sweetness and quietness was about the landscape, that same stillness which had struck me on my previous visit. This time, the region was touched by a viridian florescence, and when we reached the site, the great mound of a buried city appeared smaller, for much weed was growing upon it; the ground of its slopes was also pitted with deep rivulets where rainfall had cut away the earth. This was the first time in many years that the monsoon had reached up to this part of the Rann, and deep cavities were everywhere apparent where water had drained. All about the surrounding plain, large bodies of dun-colored pools reflected back a gray shell-like sky.

Razul carefully parked, and we walked over to the site office to greet two old custodians, one of whom remembered my visit with the *Rajkumar* Harshraj. Having sat for a while and drunk some water and allowed the stillness and silence to absorb us after so many hours of rocking and bouncing about on washed-out roads, Leanna and I set off towards the mound.

"It is such a pleasure to be away from human beings again," she said, "and not to have to listen to motor vehicles all the time."

The air was full of thousands of munias, cuckoos, and buntings, twittering and flitting about the light, and the tranquility of the region was like an invisible sphere into which we had entered. We paused outside the northern gate, admiring the smooth walls and their calculated incline. There was a lyrical quality about this site, something deeply human; the size and curve of the walls was distinctively civil rather than martial, and the coloration of great carved rocks that formed the gateways and entrances was of a yellow and purple fusion, giving the situation an aesthetic rather than severe aspect. Leanna wandered off on her own, and I sat on a large lintel at the highest part of what had formerly been a citadel. How different it was this time compared to when I was here before. Then I had been possessed by the place; it had been my Jerusalem. Now, nothing was the same, and that profound and overriding need to experience love of place no more impelled me. Previously in my pursuit of the ideal landscape, I had often ignored if not actively eschewed personal contact; even the perception of human life was something that I had frequently done my best to abjure. Now with Leanna intimately beside me all day and night, that trajectory had changed, which made me smile to myself, for I was inhabiting a completely different world.

As a migrant across the earth for most of my life, I had shifted back and forth between need for place and love of person: always between two identities or poles of consciousness. That oscillation had organized my life once my family had gone and I no longer belonged anywhere or to anyone. How odd that the alternatives were so much in counterpoint: topography or humanity. Although, if love is atavistic and we only return to our source—that first pre-conscious and pre-discursive condition— then perhaps the counterpoint is not so incongruous. Now, simple kinship with one other human being in the face of so much locative absence was sufficient for my apprehension of self and was completely satisfying. It was inimitably beautiful at Dholavira, and the great and unspoiled antiquity of the site continued to be near-transcendent, but no longer was the place as persuasive. I preferred to watch Leanna wandering about the slopes rather than gazing out across this mysterious geography. She soon returned from her walk with some unusually painted sherds and a handful of pink raw agates, and she had also found two small slingshot weights, perfectly fired clay spheres.

That night we slept upon the floor in one of the Archaeological Survey huts whilst the monsoon sparked and crackled and filled the air with water, spraying lightly into our room through a barred, unglazed window. In the morning, we were up before the sun and walked out to nearby fields, where we bathed in a pond next to a shrine. Our journey back towards Mandvi that day was long and stupefying, as we rattled and sped along the small rain-impaired ways and now and then halted in a village for tea. At evening, as we ate our tiffin on the terrace at the rear of the guesthouse, the sky pulsed with distant flashes, and as we made love and fell asleep, soaked with sweet and oily monsoon-perspiration, I realized how far upon a new and other life I had embarked.

"Here we are," Leanna said, as flies and mosquitoes attacked our legs and ankles whilst we dined the following evening. "Here we are in one of the most ancient spots on earth, where human civilization found a beginning, and yet we do not really belong to this landscape nor to these people."

"We belong to each other, no? That comes first."

"Where do we go, though, Kevin, apart from here? Do we really return to Cambridge? Would you want to go back to Greece? I am sure that you could find an appointment there."

Neither of us were able to answer these questions, which left us feeling uneasy and incomplete, for it was as if were conducting an immature and unreal life. During those days I realized how for many years we had only circled about each other in our separate lives and never really had the time to love, being so involved in our various works. The vicissitudes of the human heart sometimes took us in a direction that was not where we truly wished to proceed. It was like Swann with his tangential pursuit: the experience of rejection was actually necessary sometimes if one was to become fulfilled later, for sometimes there is more need for dismissal than for admission as the arc of passion moves through time. Yet only human warmth and affection can bleach out and eradicate dishonesty, that timeless need to betray and to be constantly avoiding real intimacy. I had never felt so attuned to another human being so completely and with such stability as I did during those days in the Kacch, without distraction and without constriction of any desire.

How green the world became, so verdant and fresh with cool gray windy skies that were almost autumnal. Gone was the fierce autocracy of sun upon desert. Trees swayed in the air and birds were blown by the winds; there was a mood of timely fruition to the days. This was a busy season for farmers, with plowing and sowing, now that the soil was moist and there was water in the tanks and wells for irrigation. Then there came the hoeing and weeding of fields and crops. At weekends, which began on Friday, the Moslem *juma*, the wind-turbine shore was packed with families and honeymoon couples. Fully clothed, they would play in the shallow waves, dashing in and out of the heavy seas. Crowds of young girls in blown *saris* walked with arms linked and roamed the beach in long lines, chattering and laughing as they made fun of the young men, who were busy with vigorous masculine games played on courts marked out upon the sand.

These were restless days, windy and noisy, and Leanna became more troubled by our future: whether we would stay in the Kacch or not, and whether we should try to establish this as our home. We began to think of moving to another part of town, somewhere more private and secluded, but I loved the view of the river, the sight of dhows being built upon the banks and the constant to-ing and fro-ing of tides and the birds upon the water and outline of temples on the far shore. There was a highly active visual space here that I found satisfying, but Leanna disliked the noise. Then as monsoon passed and the sun returned with an increasingly blue air, prediction and recollection became inseparable, for the days were slow and began to fuse and blur, and the nights were long and warm. Crowds of small white egrets would fly above our veranda at dusk in the intangible yellow light, and time merged into a force that was less consequent and impelling. In the hot saline trade wind, so much that once preoccupied us became indistinct. Like the rotors of the wind turbines, we circled, steadily and thoughtfully, without hesitation or acceleration.

Leanna visited the bazaar every day and spent time with women whom she had met there and with shopkeepers, or she would sit at the table on the balcony writing letters whilst I sat in our room at my desk and worked on my bronze-age women book. Sometimes we would visit the palace, and if the Maharao was there, we would pause and talk for a short while. Sometimes he merely waved at us from a window in his apartment on the second floor as we passed below on our way towards the shore and swimming. There, the wind would be lightly filling our eyes and ears with sand as the sea filled our mouths with salt.

Sometimes we slipped away from the shore into the deep privacy of the dunes in order to make love. We were like two complex pieces of silver then that hovered far above our bodies in space and that mortised perfectly, or like a two-dimensional substance that existed in an instant of sudden yet timeless fission, a brief unspeakable moment when the soul became visible. As love always refound the place where it had once ideally begun, the days now filled our life with unqualified and undifferentiated time; physical existence receded as we harmonized more surely upon an emotional and sweetly phenomenal plane. In the sky, gray was being replaced by a sharply hot amethyst blue; at times, a wild and fervent wind would blow as we walked home of an afternoon along the foreland coast, making speech difficult. Occasionally a young shepherd would appear with a herd of small black goats, a stick and water bottle slung across his shoulder, and he would shyly approach us and greet us, staring at us with candid disbelief.

Apart from an infrequent dog or slow incurious crow, we were always alone on that great exposed shore as the sea pounded and rolled in, its somber force breaking upon the sand. The energy of waves splitting open was contrary to the impetus of the wind, and it often appeared strange, as if a swift white fuse were being fired in a long thin surge. At times, small pink and purple discs began to materialize upon the sands beside the water, the rejected juvenile jelly-fish of the sea. On another occasion, two young men in sarongs once swam out to draw in a long blue net where several baby sharks were caught. Later, as we returned, we passed some

boys playing cricket. One day we walked westward from the palace where
the coast was narrow and the sea more rough and breaking much further
offshore, and for once we could undress and be nude in the sunlight without fear of anyone passing and seeing us. I soon fell asleep, whilst Leanna
read her book written by a journalist friend, about the war in Baghdad.
How lovely and distant and uncommon that day was, with no human
being nor bird nor dog in sight. I felt like Robinson Crusoe; the sea and
the air were so void, and yet brisk and forceful, as the place became more
than marginal and so beyond measure.

I always wanted to linger in the port as we walked homeward along
the seawall in order to observe the shipwrights at their work, tapping and
hammering, sawing and adzing the massive timbers. It was gratifying to
watch these enormous vessels rise upward from their keels, skeletal and
then substantial as the frames were planked. The world of shipbuilding
was a society of its own, ancient and exclusive, a culture that had existed
upon this shore for centuries, whose relations stretched for thousands of
miles across the ocean; for until recently Mandvi had been one of the traditional five ports of Kacch, trading with Asia, Arabia, and Africa. One
boat in the eighteenth century had even reached the North Sea ports of
Europe; even during the days of Dholavira, trade had extended as far as
to the Gulf.

Sometimes of an evening when Leanna was off wandering, I would
walk down to the port and watch the builders preparing their timbers,
cutting wood into shape with small chisels, occasionally preparing a completed vessel for launching. Perhaps ship owners would be there, inspecting and admiring their new craft; they often came with children, small
boys, all of whom wore crisp white *kurtas* and spotless white caps. The
beards of the older men would be clipped and stained auburn with henna,
and they would sit beside the hulls and drink tea with dignity and discuss
their vessels and future cargoes. The shape and lines of those ships was
satisfying to observe; there was something profoundly formal about their
volume, abstract with both purity and inherence. It was an integrity come
of many years, centuries of refinement and the experience of sea, ocean,
and wind, and also of wood, the forests of teak trees that were felled and
cut and fitted into these gigantic shapes. Leanna's paternal family had been
involved in shipping for generations, in Greece, the Levant, and America,
and she was dismissive of my delight in boats, for they signified work for
her and possessed neither romance nor aesthetic. In fact much of her
youth had been spent aboard a ship. That had been her home for many

years, so now the sight of a vessel and the prospect of embarkation only filled her with horror.

"I hate boats," she often used to say.

One evening as we strolled the pavement beside the river, I kept on glancing at her, for she looked unusually beautiful in a new pink *salwar kameez* and new gold earrings. The light was low and radiant and the tide had withdrawn, leaving all the craft heeled upon wet mud. I was aware of the men along the seawall eyeing her with curiosity and interest, wondering who she was: Leanna possessed such a mercurial and amorphous quality that evaded all definition, and her beauty unfailingly drew the gaze of those about her, for she carried herself with easy distinction.

"Consciousness is different here," she was saying, as we went up from the boats towards our guest-house. "Human qualities of awareness are so unlike how they are in the West, how they flicker and reflect. The temporal is different here, is so much larger and longer, and humanity represents itself with much greater variety and complexity; it has more room for expression."

"Also," I responded, "change is not such an important aspect of time as it is in the West. The possibility for change lacks potential, is perhaps even irrelevant here. Apart from the weather, there exists no anticipation for alteration in life; the same will always reoccur and there are no necessary progressions."

That evening was the night of the first new moon after the solstice, and firecrackers and a vociferous clanging of bells—as well as the usual cry of mosques—charged the hours. There was much chanting from temples, amplified by loudspeakers: this was the onset of the Kacchi new year, a most auspicious time. Later on during the night, I remained awake long after Leanna had fallen asleep, and I crept out onto the balcony to sit in the dark, listening to music from a tea-stand that was near the bridge, with its flashing pink and lilac light bulbs. The music was from the time of early Hindi cinema, racy and emotionally provocative. How I loved those quiet hours of rare stillness when the feinting wind paused and the tide hesitated and shady figures passed along the road in the night, with the gleaming river and temples and mosques outlined in the distance as the shadow of pariah dogs glided along the walls of the bank.

I used to worry then about my various unfinished books and how I was to conclude them, for they were large works that had already absorbed years of pursuit and intent. I was undetermined about whether we should return to the West and my university or if we should stay here, but how was I to continue without a library? Returning to the room and gently lying down beside the warm and redolent Leanna, my *angst* was dissipated. She was immediacy and all of existence, complete and astonishing, and the rest of life with its tensions and constraints fell away and departed as my sleep joined hers.

Sundays were quiet in Mandvi, a day of rest observed by Hindus and Moslems and pastoralists alike. Traffic upon the bridge was quiet as skeins of young gray heron flew across the trodden gold of dawn and waders browsed the tidal flats; a solitary kite frequently soared across the river. The sun rose in a haze of yellow, ascending into a swirl of nacreous cloud, and brash parakeets flew around the electricity wires.

"There is too much noise and business here for me," said Leanna. "It is too urban. Why do we not move somewhere and live among trees instead of people? I am losing all sense of time; the days are a blur. It is not time any more," she added, snapping her book down on the table as if to punctuate that statement.

So we went and ordered the Ahmedabad *Times of India* newspaper to be delivered each day. Leanna had once worked for Reuters, long ago in Paris, and having a paper each evening to peruse and to have a crossword to puzzle over after dinner became part of our routine. Reports of that year's monsoon in the south were dreadful: thousands had died from flooding and dislocation. In the north of Kacch, in the Banni where many Moslem *maldhari* herders lived, whole villages had been destroyed by the rains, and refugees were surviving beneath bits of plastic sheeting suspended from thorn bushes. They had lost everything: kin, cattle, dwellings, and stores, and they had nothing left but their sparse clothing. Many children had been orphaned.

We planned to make a trip onto the mainland and visit southern Gujarat, but I became ill with fever; once again great febrile spikes surrounded me of an evening. Those were days and nights of oblivion beneath a clicking whirring fan. My weightless body with its bones on fire, chased over by flies and mosquitoes, was intermittently drenched with perspiration or became shivering and icy cold. I was always thirsty, always longing for cold fruit, had violent black dreams, and was anguished, endlessly narcotic and malodorous. The noise of horns hooting, from trucks and rickshaws, became nightmarish, and there was always the whiff of sugary feverish sweat about the room. My head clanged each time I moved, as waves of enervating fever came and went like metal sheets squeezing my body between rollers, or like great skimming bats of darkness bumping into me. Lassitude dominated every minute, and a twanging-hissing was in my brain. Sometimes I was encircled by leopards during the night, waiting, their warm salty breath close to my face as they stared and watched, crouched low in their particularly feline way: thin-lipped, hungry, preparing to feast. In turn, I watched them, with the pain of solitary observation, for nothing could be said.

The moderate cadence of the sufficient moon moved all the world forward, and suddenly I awoke one day and marveled at how wonderful it was not to be crushed by fog and sweat. Time was no longer aleatory but specific, and I could plan the hours. Sparrows had come into the room and were flying about the beams of the ceiling. What a relief that was, to be human and motive again, and to lie there listening to their tiny voices.

Soon afterwards, Leanna returned from the bazaar one afternoon saying that she had met a most amazing fellow, someone who had his own mosque; this was Momin, who was to become our close friend and associate in Mandvi, and for us, he became the poet and soul of the place. Slight of figure, dark, youthful in an uncomplicated way, he had unimpeachable and meticulous manners. He enjoyed speaking about his family and how much he adored his many nieces or what his sisters were doing, and he would often present us with his latest work, penned in Urdu in an elaborate and beautiful script of red ink upon large sheets of rolled paper, objects of great precision and fineness. He would often come in the early evenings and join us for tea, translating whatever it was that he had been writing.

"Lives, not on earth but in the sea, around which days and worlds drive on…. Whose souls have preceded, long before their dust, into a light beyond the sun…. Where life glows and wanders toward noon, saying, what shall I do without a way: there is no more time to know."

Those poems captured Mandvi for us, its inaccessible and peaceful world of ships and antique ocean, its mosques and temples and shrines and its birds and animals, its lovely old mercantile houses and the slow civility that inhabited them. They were part of the process by which the Kacch gently became our flesh, how its earth entered into our heart. Yet for me, Mandvi was inextricably bound up with Leanna and her presence, and in my mind the two were inseparable.

The friendship of *svelte* Momin and the imagery and tempo of his poetry—his graceful company as he sat upon the balcony on a plastic chair or at the rear of the building upon a concrete bench among the cacti and date palms, sipping his lemonade and telling us about his life and ideals—all this crystallized our being in Kacch. He was that primary catalyst about which deposits or signs began to form. For him, ethical conduct constituted everything: from the point of view of kindness or generosity and without adherence to any dogma or belief. His family had arranged for him to marry, but he had resisted and eventually refused. It was his easy ability for friendship, the eager curiosity that ran through his life and drove him on, that led him to give much if not most of his time to others, listening and talking. He had a great capacity for healing and care and never hesitated to give away large amounts of his fortune. Outwardly simple, yet discreetly compound and sophisticated, he possessed neither self-interest nor ambition, for Momin was an Ashraf *pir*, a *sayed* or descendant of the Prophet, and his lineage was sufficient for him. His sister was also a hereditary saint, a prophetess who lived surrounded by her *murids* or followers, in the large house next to their shrine, the *dargha*. In all of her life she had never once left the building.

Leanna began to spend much time at the *dargha*. In the company of that place she discovered a community that soothed her inherent restlessness, and the days became more manageable. "All knowledge of the arts is a revelation from heaven: and captive, all of nature is compelled to confess the mingled power of melody and love." This was engraved upon a slim silver collar that Leanna now wore constantly, which had been given to her by Momin's sister as an amulet. For me, it was curious to observe how aniconic monotheism could be so conceptually fertile in its poetry; this was very different from Western traditions of the art.

Still the remnants of monsoon hovered undisclosed, a few drops of rain splashing down in the evenings; the land became green and enriched in contrast to the stark granitic terrain of some months ago. Leanna, in a new maroon *salwar kameez*, set off one morning to visit Momin at his school on the outskirts of town: an establishment for boys who had been made destitute by the earthquake or by the great floods of the succeeding year. I had been to the school a week before with her, and the unearthly beauty and purity in the faces of those boys was stunning; they were completely lacking in any sense of desolation or anguish. In their presence I felt humble and tainted by my ambition and misgivings.

Once we dined at the house of Momin, and as we arrived, passing through several heavy gates and crossing courtyards, all the women—the sisters and aunts and nieces who were preparing the food and cooking—scattered like starlings at our alien approach.

"You must shield your face with your hand and look downward, when you come here," Momin instructed me, laughing. "Never look at them. It is improper."

Within his rooms, whose walls were tiled and curtained in bright azure blue, we sat and talked about his life and family and the world of the Kacch. Education was his passion in life and dominated all of his days, and he was zealous in that pursuit. As the youngest son of the family, he was caught between their formal traditional ideals and his own liberalism and generosity. I often thought about Momin, for he seemed to own an intricate destiny, and I wondered what lay ahead for him in life, what trials and tests; it was as if he had assumed enormous tasks, but lightly. His geniality and warmth were but one aspect of an elaborate and highly involved time on earth, and he appeared to bear great burdens with a reckless nonchalance. Towards the end of the evening, a daughter of one of the Mandvi ship owners came and sat with us. A recent graduate in medicine, she was about to open her own clinic and practice locally. She and Momin spoke about England, where she had studied, for he was soon to be setting off towards London in order to try to raise extra capital for his school.

As we walked home late that night across the main square of the town, one of the municipal buildings was gaudily illuminated with colored and flashing lights. The marriage season had begun, and rites were occurring nightly in the brightly lit hall, sometimes with the simultaneous union of dozens of couples. Well-dressed women in much finery were thronging about outside, and a sound of drums and chanting, of piping and of cymbals maintaining tempo, was audible from within. Young men, clothed in heavy red turbans and embroidered jackets, were visible inside, and the square was pervaded with the scent of thick incense. Leanna wanted to enter, but I held back from the nuptial threshold, feeling invasive and indecorous.

I awoke late the next day, mosquitoes biting my feet, to a light mist of rain. Leanna remained sleeping, curled up with a pillow across her head. She had been up during the night, edgily patrolling the darkness, deeply curious about the marriage rituals of the previous evening. Upon the river ibis and stork were pondering, and flocks of small blue flycatchers dashed across a blustery sky. There had been wedding guests staying in our hotel that night, and they had repeatedly woken us with their songs and laughter. Small twin girls, daughters of our host, were preparing to set off towards school, chattering nonsense as they went downstairs and laughing like tiny birds.

A train of large military vehicles was passing on the road, full of men in battle dress. As we were close to the border, this was not an unusual sight, and they never halted in Mandvi. A boy was doing handstands far away on the other side of the river as a companion watched. A man pushed a cart upon which a large grapnel anchor was balanced, fabricated at one of the Moslem smithies on the other shore and bound for the shipyards; two camel carts plodded past. There was a Scottish quality to the light upon the river that day, northern and autumnal, as avocet paced the margins and white gleaming rays of light fell diagonally from a hidden sun; long slender cranes glided above the water.

Thus our lives ran on in a channel as days became months; how domestic and civilized we had become. Dhows, *kotiyas*, began to appear upon the horizon, making their way to port and running in with the wind. We had looked at various houses both inside and outside town, but nothing really captivated us. Momin had promised to show us a place, but that had not yet occurred and we had forgotten to remind him; I wanted to stay in town, but Leanna was more inclined to village life. Mandvi must have been such a spectacularly lovely settlement once, before earthquakes obliterated its fortified walls and bastions, with its ships and minarets and its many diverse elements of society—the tribes, castes, and sects and the heterogeneity of seafarers—and with its many shrines and old commercial and patrician houses. Now the population was out of correspondence with the buildings, and although the old perimeter walls remained, bungalows, shacks, and camps had sprung up everywhere and corrosive modernity was arriving, tasteless, disproportionate, wasteful, and unseemly. Only several hundred years ago, India had been the wealthiest country in the world and famed for its opulence; now that condition was returning, and in a few decades, India and China—Asia possesses half of the world's population—were likely to outstrip the West in production. What would happen to the abject and destitute then, I wondered; would they no longer exist in such crowds? A potential for disorder and violence lay there, something that sectarian politicians could manipulate.

That day Leanna, with a large bag of sweets and another of glass marbles, went off to visit Momin at his school. I stayed at home, feeding sparrows on the veranda ledge, reading a recent study of Indo-Aryan origins and working on my own book; they were quiet, reserved, and impersonal hours. She returned that evening from the bazaar, happy and shaking a newspaper at me, her lioness smile full of delight.

"Ten centimeters in Mumbai.... We shall soon be deluged once more."

She was right, as the days became increasingly cool and lightless and a fine capillary rain descended. All the roads and ways became muddy and filthy and a dampness crept into our rooms again, into the books and linen and clothes in the steel cupboard. Confined, Leanna became tense, pacing at night, absent-minded.

"Why do we not visit Jakhau?" she asked, as we reclined in bed one evening. "Momin says that it was once a fabulous port."

I switched the light off and we lay in the humid darkness conversing, listening to music coming from the radio at the *chai*-stand.

After working awhile the next morning, we set off with Razul and his clattering vehicle and headed up the coast through well-irrigated and fertile land with many groves of date and coconut palm. Soon we were back in the desert, flat stony earth with small purple convex hills in the distance and no villages in sight. The day was overcast and gloomy, damp, without light or shadow. The harbor of Jakhau port, which was deserted and without trace of living humanity, was immense and held deep water; a naval fleet could have found shelter there. Rows of godowns and warehouses were forsaken and abandoned, their doors and windows wrecked. A broken tanker, thick with rust, lay at anchor. All about the port in a landward direction, salt-pans extended for miles; here and there great mounds of filthy salt were heaped up, and a narrow rim of chaste essential blue shone on the horizon where rain had gathered and liquefied the alkaline crystals. Flamingoes were browsing the marshes, their pink plumage a startling touch of color amidst the endless desolation and neutral whiteness of the salt flats; a few unhurried pelican were on the wing.

It was an eerie, bleak place, ghostly and peripheral, with an end-of-the-world air about it. Off the coast, islands of mangrove were visible as a dark and vivid green line where sullen heavy swells of the sea opened and closed. In the harbor itself the sea was running, splashing and breaking onto well-made granite quays. We walked towards where many short dark masts were ranked, pennants flapping and flicking in the cool circuitous wind. The dereliction of the place was ominous, and along the shore, near where the fishing fleet was beached—dark black tarred hulls drawn up as far as the eye could see—the sands were covered with huts made of sacking and bits of plastic sheet tacked upon frames of driftwood and spar. Not a single human being nor any birds were in sight, and yet the place was copiously littered with detritus, the various disjecta of a fishing community: bones, lines, bits and pieces of marine timber, items of worn clothing, ash, and excrement. Apart from the dozens of aligned fishing vessels, all was completely neglected. Hundreds of bow lines ran ashore from the boats in a mass of tangled rope towards huge rotten iron grapnels half-buried in sand.

The filth, disorder, and desuetude and the many broken and decrepit upturned hulls—large and once beautiful vessels now in a state of decay and desiccation—troubled Leanna, and she stayed close to me, fascinated by the sight. There was something grandly sublime in the quietness and dereliction and somber weather. We had entered another system of life where human beings were unnecessary, and all that remained was a melancholic reminiscence of humanity. The sound of waves constantly lapping upon the underside of hulls and of the wet wind clattering through the rigging was loud and overwhelming. If we spoke we had to shout, not that we said much, as the foreboding and extraordinary beauty of the place overwhelmed us.

Leanna was wearing a *dupatta*, a long muslin scarf about her head of blue and green and crimson, and she looked peculiarly different, older and more introspective. Her beauty was always ephemeral, profoundly and constantly transforming, and she always appeared dissimilar depending on the time of day; hers was a mercurial and protean beauty, amorphous, vital, and quick. Here in Jakhau she had become someone unlike the daily Leanna whom I knew and loved, and I could not intercept her mood nor its undisclosed silence. It was a startling experience for me to see her looking so amongst the hundreds of black hulls with their broken paraphernalia. For once I wished that I had a camera so that I might record the moment: this quiet prophetess amid her ruined ships, musing on their desolation. Somehow the place had transferred her into a vision of a woman whom I knew intimately and succinctly but whose ancient spirit I had never previously recognized. Briefly and for an instant, perhaps without even really being aware of it, we were closer then than ever before, yet in a way that was unspeakable.

Leanna began to collect shells off the ground, large, weird, swirling cones of hard umber-colored nacre. Once, suddenly in the distance, a young woman with a baby in her arms appeared and then immediately vanished. She wore thick gold studs in her ears and a scarlet *sari*. We wandered about for an hour or so more, speechless, meditative, and then refound Razul, smoking inside his vehicle, and set off homeward through showers and windy squalls.

The next day we walked to the palace gardens again and called upon the Maharao, but he was absent and on tour somewhere. So we walked out to one of the pavilions perched high above the dunes. It had been severely smashed by age and earthquake and fragments of carved crimson stone lay about on the grass. We sat and watched the white breakers bearing in onto the shore below, coming out of the great universal vacancy of Indian Ocean.

"You can see the weather moving up the coast from Mumbai," said Leanna, pointing to seaward where shadowy squalls were obviously approaching.

We were there for a couple of hours, surveying the landscape and birds—greenshanks and sandpipers—and talking about ourselves and the future, what we wanted to do and what we should do. Setting off down the path, once a small road but now fully overgrown with babul and khejri, we passed some slim young camels grazing on the new leaves. Leanna walked up to them, and they responded affectionately and with curiosity, which pleased her.

"If we live here, Kevin, we should have a camel to help with the shopping."

"I think that we had better have a small motorcycle," I said.

Soon the rain began to pelt and we were walking through deep ochre puddles of water. Wet birds, wet ponies and donkeys, even the camels reappeared, soaked and bedraggled and not as cheerful as before. The grounds became a transparent sheet of gray water, and it was a long walk to the road. We were thoroughly drenched by the time we reached home. The electricity was out and the rooms were stale with humidity, without fans to agitate the air. We bathed and then retired early. That night, I rose during the small hours and went out to the rear of the building, where all was wet and the sound of dripping crammed the moist black monochrome dark. The Mandvi lighthouse sent out a circling beam every half-minute, a long thin creamy ray that gleamed upon the sodden air as it spun around, pulsing slowly.

Soon the sunlight became sensibly hot again, and days rose yellow and distinct from the far shore, as slow and perfect storks flew their erratic and careful way across the water and hundreds of pigeons circled about the Jain temple. Momin called several times whilst we were out on our walks, leaving messages for Leanna to join him at the school whenever she could; then he sent a written message to invite her to his house, as his sisters wanted to tattoo her hands and arms. This delighted Leanna, and she set off the next morning with smiles and a box of sweets, leaving me to spend the hours at my desk going through a palm-leaf manuscript of a much abbreviated *Mahabharata* that I had discovered in the bazaar. That evening she returned happily stained, patterned with henna upon forearms and fingers, and we set off arm in arm to walk towards the port, taking the shore path through the boatyards where dozens of *kotiyas* were waiting for repairs or cargo. Teak was lying in piles everywhere, and men and boys were finishing work, smoking cigarettes or drinking tea; some were in sarongs and were bathing in the river. Young casteless *adivasi* girls and women were gleaning wood shavings from beneath the boats to take home as fuel.

We walked out along the breakwater to the west of the harbor, where the stones were wet from the breaking seas. The place was shrouded in precipitating mist, and one solitary fisherman was at the far point beneath the light, casting for small sharks. A few tiny shrines had been built into the walls where incense and dishes of oil lay with old photographs of deceased mariners. Out in the channel, three young men were dragging a long, fine-meshed net across the tide, slow and difficult labor, as they were up to their shoulders in a murky current. It was a spot that I had spent much time at when I had been in Mandvi decades previously; then, there had been a busy customs shed on the shore, which was now empty. Looking back inland—at the anchorage and town with its many minarets and spires, its tens of loitering ships and the long turbid swells of the whitening ocean running in and uncurling—one had a sense of how ancient a port Mandvi was and of how wealthy it had formerly been. Thousands of ships had come and gone over the centuries and seasons, loading and unloading, exchanging stores and lives with the Gulf and East Africa, even with China. It was no wonder that the Maharaos had been famed for their luxury and abundant assets.

"So much of desert Kacch is without perspective and appears only two-dimensionally," said Leanna, as we huddled against the seawall beside an old bronze cannon keeping out of the spray. "That is why time is so different here. Being in Mandvi, we are constantly caught between many simultaneously contrasting worlds, neither marine nor terrestrial, as if we were part of a fabric of varying time or some grand reticulation. The tempo of life here suits you, Kevin," she added. "This is a pedestrian land; everybody has a pace which has not altered in centuries, even the sailors. You can maintain your own measure here, unlike in the West."

"There have been so many ports and harbors in my life and they all stay with me," I said. "I think about them often and still experience their details constantly. Is that not odd? Boston, the Piraeus, Stave Island on

Champlain, even the southern China of my childhood, and my youth in Wales and Scotland. So many havens and seafronts, the sound of a quay, and here we are once again where the sea confronts urban humanity. They become vague as time recedes," I added, "but the sounds are always identical and the sensibility the same. Waves lapping on stone walls, the splash of mooring lines or the cry of sea-birds soaring and diving, twittering; the sound of marine engines and of waves driven by wind and tide and breaking open, I know it all," I laughed, "just like my body. These sounds are in my ear and never depart, and the odor of maritime vessels and nautical life."

A launch was attempting to drag one of the dhows off the mud where it had grounded. Lines ran ashore and also to a smaller vessel which repeatedly gunned its motor and ran into the waves, bucking up and down on the current. Other, lighter craft were moving about the windy port, some by oars.

"I love the livelihood of sea-people," said Leanna, "their silence and their kinship. They are so unlike land people in their reticence and dignity. Perhaps because their emotions are constantly caught up by and attuned to the mood of the sea, and that mood can sometimes be lethal and deadly. It is not a lazy life."

"I feel level and attuned here," I told her, "deeply at rest and without motion or impulse. It is rare to feel such equilibrium in the world and to be without movement and so fitted. You are very much part of that, you know."

She just looked at me for some seconds and nodded to herself, as if remembering another occasion.

Returning homeward, we made our way among the cows, dogs, goats, and buffalo of the town. At one point we passed two prostitutes with a tiny baby slung in a shawl; one of them held a monkey on a chain. Their *saris* were ragged and stained but bright, and their faces were uncannily beautiful, eyes heavily outlined and made up with *kohl*, with large gold discs in their ears and nostrils and heavy bands of silver upon their ankles. There was an air of lewd predation about them, however, of impudent desperation. According to Momin, Mandvi was renowned for its easy ways due to so much shipping, and Leanna often came home from the bazaar and described the whores and transvestites, *hijras*, whom she had seen, but I had never before noticed them.

Momin came to dine with us that evening, along with a companion, one of the teachers from his school. We had asked him many times to join us for a meal, but he had always prevaricated, avoiding our hospitality, for we were the strangers and could only be guests, and it was improper for him to accept our generosity. He spoke about the intractable corruption of politics and told stories about Mandvi life. He also spoke about contemporary poets in India and how important they were and how he respected their contributions to literature. Poetry in India was different from how it was in the West; there was no question of innovation, only of perfection in form—that was the sole artistic virtue.

That evening Momin's manners were immaculate and undemonstrative, and his companion was witty and urbane; they made an elegant couple. She was a young brahmin woman, and as the evening drew to a close, they both spoke about their affection for each other and how impossible that was unless they fled to Bangalore or somewhere else far off.

"What about my followers if I leave?" he asked. "Marriage is a problem."

She dared not tell her father, although her mother and sisters knew, and he could not inform his family, so they were trapped into dissembling. He asked me why I loved Leanna, and I told them that she was my home, my only equal, and only she in all the world truly knew who I was. "She is pure and unmixed," I said, "and not caught up by modernity." This made them smile, and they nodded knowingly.

The next day it was still intermittently pouring as monsoon continued to hover about the land. Leanna read Cervantes and wrote letters in the morning whilst I worked on my notes; we set off for a walk towards a village near to the palace in the afternoon. The lanes were deep and wet and ran through cultivated fields, and the hamlet, when we arrived, was awash with mud. We turned back almost immediately, haggard and soaked but satisfied, and returned home in a soft lemon-colored light. The little twins were playing downstairs—a girlish form of indoor cricket—with one of the house-boys, chattering and shrieking and running about. The owner of the guest-house was performing his evening *puja*, burning incense before the household shrine and tinkling a small silver bell to summon the deity. That evening a messenger arrived from the Maharao, inviting us to join him on a visit to one of his estates the next day, which we accepted.

Early the following morning, we met him outside one of the old city gates and drove off in a small gray car, the royal pennant fluttering at the front of the vehicle as the driver rushed impetuously through the country lanes. The Maharao was in a happy and witty mood, telling us about the landscape, the villages, the trees, and the names of the mountains. He spoke of his lack of progeny and how the line—in which he was the nineteenth—would cease upon his death. A nephew would inherit, but that was different. The sanctuary—our destination—had been established by his grandfather as a reserve for game; he had been extremely fond of his grandfather and told us many tales about him. His Highness's own father had gifted him the land when he was nineteen years old, and the tank there was the first reservoir to be built in Kacch and had been stocked with crocodiles. Pragsar was to become an important site for us, and we returned many times after that day. The lake with its great sleepy reptiles and many aquatic birds, the ruined cottages, lodges and plantations, and the placid hills about with their well-kept tracks and outlooks: a serenity and composition had gathered about the place, as if all of the Kacch was encapsulated there. As we walked, the Maharao carried a small sheathed spear with him.

"In case of panthers," he laughed, "for there are still several who inhabit the area. One only crossed in front of our car just last week. You know, if we really engage with time," he said, "and desire to create something out of time and direct our life in a way that is unlike any other life, pursuing a vision that is immaterial and unworldly and seeking to make that in a fashion that is beautiful and extraordinary, then life is valuable and finite. We are not simply passing through the days seeking to live and enjoy time, but using time for its service, for what it allows us and provides in terms of experience. Life is very different," he added, "if one has such a plan. Vision," he repeated, "vision, that is the only true action for a man. You have to believe, or you are nothing and cannot exist."

"There is a word for that in Greek," I replied. "It is *pothos*, and means this unconditional zest or vision which some people possess and which rules them."

"That's it," he said happily. "That is true."

We walked back to the lake, where one of his staff occupied him with business. For a while we sat with them in a small wooden hermitage, listening and watching, but then we wandered off alone. We halted on a small mound above the lake and observed a pair of pied kingfishers diving for food and what appeared to be some uncommon cinereous vultures across the water. A few spotted deer strolled the hills and one or two adult *nilgai*. For a while it was as if human-time had passed and Pragsar had withdrawn from the world; neither inimical nor harsh, yet not hospitable to human beings any more, the landscape kept to its own hidden and unpeopled tempo, of scrub and stone and light and shadow. Returning to the lake after an hour or so, we paused to watch a water-snake struggling with a fish that it had caught. The Maharao then took us to a shrine that was central to the reserve, a small temple nestling in a hollow. As we went, he pointed out the numerous spots that he had enjoyed as a boy and youth, telling us sportsman's tales. The shrine was where the Maharao habitually used to pray, and we sat for a while with the priest and two young *pandits*, cross-legged upon the ground beneath an awning. The priest looked strangely like the Maharao, and Leanna commented on this.

"Oh yes, of course," he exclaimed. "We were born on the same day in the same year."

The priest then performed a short rite for us, sitting before a stone that was covered with pipal leaves; praising celestial rivers, he chanted mantras and poured a steady libation of milk upon the rock as we sat gathered closely about him. Before we left, we descended by a short passage into the rock to one side of the shrine, to where a low subterranean hollow ran beneath the spot. Just discernible in the gray light and within the hill was the original, much older sanctum where a stone *lingam* was visible in the gloom about which the earth had been swept. That was the first point of worship—and there must have been a snake there once—from long ago, the above shrine having been built recently. It was strangely moving, as if we were glimpsing through a dim aperture into the innards of the soul of India, at an unveiled Mahadeo, abstract and profound, one of the basic pretemporal forms of this culture and its place in time. For me it was one of those rare instants when I felt that I had touched or perceived something about the land, some nerve that vibrated with an ancient and genuinely ingrained tempo. Now and again in the dawns I would occasionally feel actually and fully present, located in more than the spatial, and briefly, I felt a similar moment then. The stones of Elephanta or Kanheri at Mumbai also—occasionally—could touch me in the same acutely terrestrial manner.

As we sped home that evening, the little car darting through showers of rain, the Maharao told us more stories about his forebears and the land itself and of family rituals that were no longer performed. There was something about this man that was inimitable and peerless, isolated in time and ancient with experience. His speech had an unusual precision and vocabulary, was exact and yet humorous, and his energy was ceaseless. Most of his life now, he told us, was spent on tour, visiting villages and temples. He was obviously very fond of Leanna, and he questioned her about her experiences and family, curious about what we did in the West.

"I lost my passport in the earthquake," he said. "We shall not be traveling again."

Afterwards, when we had returned home and the Maharao had sped off, waving a hand through the car window, after we had taken tiffin and Leanna had settled into the swing on the terrace with her book and newspaper, I thought through and recalled details of the day. There had been a poignancy to the hours, as if they were not to be repeated; their richness and density were to remain forever unmatched, and that view of the terrain at Pragsar when we had walked alone together stayed before me. Sleep came like an axe that night, sedative and oblivious, we were so exhausted, and we both lost consciousness as soon as we were horizontal. Even the wailing and barking of the raucous dogs did not waken us.

The fluent wind of those days filled everything with fine sand; books, clothes, water and food, fingernails, everything, as the desert reclaimed the monsoon. Along the shore where we walked of an evening, no human life was apparent except for an occasional shepherd with a stick slung upon his shoulder; the ruined shrines and abandoned mausoleum were the only sign of erstwhile humanity. In the far distance, the gargantuan wind turbines spun like wondrous statues, vestiges of a foregone civilization. The sea would be booming and exploding, driven shorewards, as Leanna combed the fringe for shells and stones, unusual objects with which she would adorn our veranda and walls. Those were pure and windy afternoons, and I recognized their rareness, for to be so alone with Leanna was both exciting and exotic, and I knew that it would not last, that these exclusive days possessed an absolute quality not to be regained once we had passed through them. I felt that this time was being granted us as a special gift, that our love was being sanctioned by this award and that we were allowed to be sole and unsurrounded in this remote and deserted world only briefly. There was no color to this place, the gray ocean, the dun sand, the pale sky, nothing chromatic was to be perceived, which only highlighted the isolation and solitude that we now tentatively possessed. Those months with Leanna were the happiest days of my life, balanced, equable, untarnished in their quiescence, and more intensely vivid than any other period I had known.

In the evenings after the thin blonde light had passed overhead, to be followed by a sudden radiance of roseate air in which droves of small white egrets shot by above us, we would sit upon the veranda in the dark, listening to old cinema music from the tea-stand, enjoying the emptiness of the night and watching the interminable traffic passing on the bridge:

profuse forms of humankind so distant from how we lived and so much more sophisticated in their subtlety and simplicity and age. That view was rich in its expression and effortless disorder, indelible and adamant in its untimed patience.

"I wish that we could live at the shrine of Pragsar," said Leanna, as we chatted on the swing, the darkness perched about us and perforated by bats. "Something happened to us there," she said. "I was changed."

Soon after that, we visited the Banni, a low alluvial region to the north that opened out onto the Great Rann. It was a desert tract of almost four thousand square kilometers where the light glittered like an empty mirror and any sensation of life appeared abstract and linear. Once Moti Banni had been a rich grassland or *rakhal*, "an extensive meadow" of "luxuriant pasturage" where the people lived mostly on milk and exported their *ghee* southward to be exchanged for their few other needs, like clothing. They were not cultivators, but pastoralists who bred stock more for sale rather than for grazing and milk production. Now Banni was an area of growing penury, often tormented by a lack of rain, and the mining industry was encroaching upon its natural terrain. Still, however, there were four head of cattle for each human being in the area. Up there, the culture of human life was Sindhi, unlike the coastal life to the south, and people would speak of family and kin and locations across the border.

At Hajjipir, site of an important midwinter *mela*, we halted for tea but did not stay long, for the poverty and destitution of the village were distressing. With Razul, who covered his head with a handkerchief, I visited the shrine of the *pir*, the interior walls of which were festooned with many tiny infant cribs, votaries left by childless parents. We soon set off once more, and as the road ceased, we made our way across the crusted sand, following in the tracks of other vehicles. At one point we stopped, confused as to our direction, for we were trying to locate a village that Momin had described, from where many of his orphan boys had come. Leanna and I walked off for a while whilst Razul refilled the radiator from a bottle of water and smoked a cigarette until the engine cooled. There was an extraordinary silence upon the place, a nothingness that was audible in the dense hot air, with only the sensation of a slight breeze passing over the earth and now and then the unusual cry of an unseen bird. That quietness was stunning, intrinsically beautiful, and filled me completely in a way that I had never before experienced. Even now it remains with me, silent and unmixed, unmarked and pure, without disturbance or sign and just the odor of space; the sheer unqualified beauty of that region was spectacular. Usually the motion of air itself is audible, but on that day there was true silence. Razul hooted from the car, and we returned. Soon afterwards, we came across a narrow metaled road, much of it crumbling at the edges. Driving for hours, we sometimes halted for water or tea or to give a lift to a solitary walker or to simply rest from being thrown about in the lurching vehicle. I was happy to return to Mandvi that evening, for it felt like home, familiar and comfortable, replete with recognition.

"Do you know, Kevin, what makes me sad here," Leanna asked as we sat at tiffin that night. "I have said this before … the sad thing is that we shall recall so little of these days."

"You said the same thing at Lakhpat, when we sat on the walls looking out at the Rann."

"It is true. I knew then that most of the day's experience would be soon forgotten. So much of our lives receives such dissolution and we have no recall of time and phenomena, just a few details here and there. I feel sad about today in particular, with its lack of any active experience and yet its vast reality, soon to be lost from recollection. Rarely do we perceive the elision of time in such a manner. What is there, really, what do we keep, I wonder?"

"I think that only human love and affection maintain us. Love is primarily an effort to remember, a striving to be reminded of what has been lost. That is why the desert was so wonderful today, for it reminds us of the potence and initiation of nothing. Death or loss is the beginning of how we become discrete and hence how we are able to love."

"Last night I dreamed of a falcon," she said. "It was in the palace grounds, and we were walking along one of the paths. It was before us, leading us on, flying away as we approached, further and further, pausing, until we caught up with it again. It was gray and amber-colored. I wonder how long it will be before I have forgotten it."

"We are so fully unaware of time and its actual efficacy and production, its increments and sedimentation, even its true sentiments. I also wonder what the future holds for us, you know. Compassion is really the only decent way to live; then the cycles will always unveil themselves slowly, revealing their patterns as consciousness struggles towards metaphor and lucidity. I do not think that we recover anything; there is reception and there is discrimination, and that is all. Without love we are lost."

"Well, I think that a lot of memories are actually specious and do not represent anything historical. They are merely dynamics of our psyche provided with imagery and are rear projections of a present system only."

"Perhaps, but that sounds like a solitary state to me and ungiving."

"Do you think that Momin is ever lonely?" she asked.

Late one afternoon, when Leanna did not return at her usual time from the bazaar—she must have gone to visit Momin—I walked across the bridge and along the far shore as the sun went down into the earth behind Mandvi. Work on the ships had concluded for the day, and young men were bathing in the shallows—sluicing themselves from brass pots—and washing clothes. I sat on a plank outside a hut and watched the business of the other shore, the town. Traces of the former walls, bastions, and gates were still visible, and here and there a thin vertical line of minarets or palm trees inscribed the twilight. A mingled sound of car and rickshaw horns came across the river and a noise of dogs barking. Mandvi never really rested, was never still even during the smallest hours of the night; its life constantly swarmed and brimmed over into the world.

There were several ships on the sand flats, propped up by stocks and looking massive and gigantic as tiny figures moved among their ribs. They were such remarkable vessels, artfully and slowly constructed, and without a straight line in them apart from the keel. The sun settled downward in a vapor of low cloud and humidity. Youths began to pass, clean and dressed and on their way towards town; several of them greeted me, obviously restraining their curiosity from lingering. There was a buzz of pleasure in the air that evening as if a fair or celebration was to occur, synthesizing further life. Then I remembered it was Independence Day, *Svatantradivas*, which was why all the vessels wore flags at their stem and stern.

As *muezzin* began to raise a cry in the incipient dusk, I set off, and for the first time ever I felt that Mandvi was within me; it had come inside, and now I could replicate it wherever I was. The place itself was not important, for its valence was internal; I had it. It was Leanna whom I now adored and wanted, and I walked quickly and hurriedly, for I could see that the light was on at the guest-house and her form was visible on the balcony, moving back and forth. When I arrived, she was wearing a new outfit and her hair was down; she sat at the table writing in her journal. I bathed and changed into a sarong.

"You must go and telephone Dhrangadhra," she said, looking up at me. "Can we not go there soon?"

I could not make a connection for some days, and so we continued our habits and walks about Mandvi, visiting the palace and going down to the shore to swim, walking home in the soft twilight when the sea was halcyon and it was as if monsoon had departed. As we returned one evening, I kept on glancing backwards, for the light was especially beautiful, opaque and grainy and numinous. The complicated rooves of the palace looked as if they existed far off in paradise, appearing distant and serene and immaterial among the trees. I continued turning as we went, feeling that something was beginning to pass away from us, something that we would never be able to perceive again. It was as if we were passing through invisible and temporal gates and a period of great benignity and tranquility was closing. The palace would hover for an instant in suspense and disappear, and we would never be able to return.

It was late by the time we reached town, and the light was already weightless, with a yellow lucidity that soon turned to sudden pale cerise. Men in immaculately starched and creased whites were arriving outside the main mosque in anticipation of evening prayer. One woman, completely veiled in a black *burkha*, greeted Leanna in a sweet and familiar voice.

"Hi," she drawled, almost lasciviously.

"Oh, that must be one of Momin's sisters," Leanna smiled mischievously.

Down in the port itself there were the same fishing vessels beached upon the mud and heeling. Men were teasing out and folding green nets in preparation for work.

"Monsoon must be over," I said, "if they are putting out to sea at night. The winds have ended."

That evening a messenger arrived from the Maharao inviting us to join him on the following day whilst he was on tour again. He arrived early the next morning, tooting for us outside the guest-house, looking raffish and debonair. His driver revved the engine and took off like a racer as soon as we were in our seats, the royal pennon flapping vigorously with the impetus. Leanna and the Maharao talked constantly as we drove through the landscape along narrow stony roads, swerving to avoid cattle and camels. I watched the land go past beyond the windows.

"This was once lion country," the Maharao was telling Leanna. "Even Europeans came here to shoot. Long ago there were also rhino, but that is before our time. My great-grandfather remembered them."

The terrain was gentle and open, without the usual thorny vegetation; green undulating moors reminded me of Scotland or parts of Wiltshire.

"That village and its buildings and land was given by my ancestor," the Maharao was saying, "to the masons who built the palace for him.

Their descendants live there now. None of this is any different from when we were young," he added. "Perhaps some of the trees are slightly altered."

Leanna informed him that we were planning to stay in the Kacch and live here permanently if we could find the right place.

"That is good," he laughed. "We shall make sure to give you some land if you stay."

We paused for food at a village of one of his *thakurs* or landowners, where the Maharao addressed a meeting on the subject of separatism, Kacchi *Rajya*. At the end he beckoned me over and introduced me, asking me to say a few words to the audience in Sanskrit, which I did, in metrical Sanskrit, the only form of the language with which I was familiar. The Maharao's world was that of the land and countryside, for the towns, Mandvi, Bhuj, and the rest, were not part of his life any more. There, he had been displaced by the new business classes whose interests lay in enterprise and profit; it was the landscape and its people that were his world, for the urban manifest a different approach to the apprehension of time and the material conditions of life. As the civic became more pervasive and powerful, his basis was reduced and his knowledge of the region was disregarded if not disdained.

After another long swift drive, we halted at one of his lodges, where he left us, and we continued on into the town of Mata-No-Madh, where at the temple of the tutelary deity of the region, the Devi Ashapura Ma kept her residence. His Highness was the first servant in all of Kacch to her. The temple had been wrecked by the earthquake and was now being completely reformed, and masons were working on sculptures that covered the building's fabric of red sandstone. Their work was intricate and exquisite, detailed and refined, as they tapped away with small pointed steel chisels. The image of the deity herself took the form of a large stone, adorned with minimum paint and possessed of four gleaming black eyes. It was an impressive sight, and on leaving—after we had made our obeisance—I purchased a little wooden icon. Outside the temple, a group of drummers—five young men with large martial-looking drums—were sitting upon a carpet beside a shop and beating complicated rhythms together, each taking a turn with the lead. A fife player, an older man, soon joined them. It was the sound of the desert, of night, of *kshatriya* life, repetitive and tragic, and that *raso* sound haunted me for days with its ancient monody born of space and solitude and longing.

As we drove homeward, the moon rose full and tangerine across the land, throwing out a sphere of virtuous light. It was rising much more to the north now compared to when we had arrived. How all of Kacch had changed since those days and presently wore a thin cloth of green, even in the most barren and rocky areas. The two of us had also changed, but in ways that were not obvious; our mutual levity had shifted, as well as our understanding of the nature of action: how we conducted and affected life and when it was appropriate to merely wait.

The next day was Leanna's birthday, so we set off towards Pragsar and walked up to the lake, where we paused for a while in the sun and observed a few crocodiles and white-bellied herons; there were many rollers and bee-eaters about the air. After the bustle of Mandvi, it was pleasant to be within a landscape without human beings and merely among animals and trees and rough bare terrain. Leanna and I were happy that day, leisurely walking about those mauve hills hand in hand.

At the Maharao's high point—"the turret," as he called it—we drank some water and halted again to watch the great panorama beneath us. There were a few tortoises about, tediously making their way across the grainy earth. How the world receded from that prominence, the plain and range of black hills, and below us the lake was a bright celadon stained with the shadow of passing cloud. Buffalo were grazing in the meadow of a far shore, and herons and storks were visible as white marks beneath us upon the water. For me, that moment and spot marked the midpoint, the fulcrum, stasis, or equilibrium of our time in Kacch: all else would only ever be radius. There had been many similar instants, but that day, the view was central, both in time and space, and as a pair, as a human couple, we were constelled not only within it but coeval with it, for it was to remain a focus for us. In our hearts we had both arrived home and had achieved something mutual and indelible, not with ourselves but with our place.

We left after a couple of hours, going down to the shrine to visit the *pujari* and to drink some tea, chatting with him and his wife beneath the blue canopy that covered the sanctum. Only a week previously, there had been two panthers who had been playing and pranking on the roof of their hut one afternoon when he and his wife had been sleeping, and they had been terrified. He spoke of his life—being then in his seventies—and showed us photographs of his father, who had officiated at the shrine before him. When his wife brought the tea, he told us that when they had married he had been forty-one and she had been fourteen. Later, back at our vehicle outside the gates to the sanctuary, we discovered Razul asleep with his feet out of the window, snoring softly. We set off towards Bhuj, where I had to go and meet the curator of the palace museum in order to obtain a book—a calendar of Kacchi festivals—whilst Leanna went to prowl the bazaar. Bhuj appeared lively and almost elegant after Mandvi, and its streets seemed broad and affluent.

"We have become terribly provincial," Leanna observed, laughing. "This is actually exciting."

That evening, back at the guest-house, I went into town to collect a jacket that I was having made. When I returned, Leanna was out on the terrace walking up and down holding a small packet. The Maharao and Maharani had called and had sent their driver up with this gift, which she had waited to open until I returned. Inside the manila envelope was a coin, a *dhinghlo*, a sixteenth of a *kori*, from the mid-nineteenth century and minted by the Maharao's nominal predecessor, Pragmulji II. Leanna was profoundly touched by the gesture. There was something infinitely empathetic and humane about the Maharao, decent and civilized and considerate of detail.

"He is such a careful and delicate man," said Leanna, examining the coin and trying to decipher its worn impress. "He has an unusual charisma," she murmured.

Even though the monsoon continue to spray us with rain and the roads were not yet dry, we decided to visit Harshraj and his wife at Dhrangadhra. I had spoken so much about the family and the region and its buildings that Leanna insisted on going there; her restlessness had returned. I finally managed to telephone him—as the lines were generally not functioning—and we set off one early dawn in a thin wet fog. Dogs were howling as if they were mourning as we rose in the dark to bathe and dress and drink some cold tea before departing.

Driving across Kacch and over the Little Rann was long and tedious, as the road deteriorated as we moved eastward. Once off the island and into Saurashtra, the landscape distinctly changed, becoming flat and verdant with streams and rivers and much agriculture. I began to feel displaced and nostalgic for the black hills and that hypnotic terrain that I loved. We halted at Halvad so that Leanna could see the old palace, but the giant gates were firmly locked and we merely walked about and around the lake. All was just as exquisite as before and yet still sadly in a state of advanced collapse. I wondered if Harshraj would ever raise the funds to restore the place and turn it into an art school. In one more hour we were at Dhrangadhra, and how strangely familiar it seemed: it was as if this was all within me already and there was no experience taking place. He and his wife were exactly the same and the city palace had not altered and it was as if I had never been away, everything was so immediate and close. The dogs gamboled about, and I remembered how happy I had been when I had been there before, something I had forgotten. That evening, as we walked off towards the south of the town into open country, a small herd of wild donkeys appeared and watched us go past, and some *nilgai* were visible on the hillsides; a solitary wolf appeared, and the dogs had to be leashed.

I rose early the next day and sat quietly in the large courtyard, talking with Harshraj about his family and about our life in the Kacch. Soon children began to appear, singing and chanting, and we retired inside the old building. The thick walls and deep thresholds, the low beams and dark rooms and the lattice-work of the former *zenana*, separated us completely from the surrounding urban world. Harshraj went off to work, and I took Leanna about the town, showing it off to her. At the main palace, all the trees that he had planted had grown, and the buildings had been restored from the harm of the earthquake. It all felt deeply familiar and strangely part of my life. We visited the masonry yards where the various works continued to be produced, and the place was littered with lions and deities and urns; the tap-tap of chisel upon stone was memorable, shifting me between years.

Leanna was fascinated, for I had spoken so many times about Dhrangadhra and my sojourn there had been such a test for us, a trial. At the villa where I had stayed, we pushed open the gates and tentatively entered. All was deserted and quiet except for peacocks that strutted and the clattering of bats in the trees, but the vultures were gone. Baddhu Singh came out, and suddenly the whole family was there, affectionate and curious and shy. They were captivated by Leanna, having seen her photograph on my desk years before. Very little was different, except that the rowdy younger son had grown into an earnest youth and the elder daughter had been married off to an officer in Bhuj and had produced a child. We sat down at the swing upon the terrace and looked through an album of photographs of her wedding. At the back of the book, there were two pictures of myself, taken there outside the building. How disorienting it was, to be so suddenly cast back and for Leanna not to be present: I had completely forgotten what her absence was like. Leanna just stared at the images, perplexed that she was not represented, as if she had been inexplicably erased or removed.

In the afternoon we walked out to the hills beyond the lake. Little had altered in the landscape, although it appeared more prosperous and the view back towards the palace was now obscured by the plantings. We returned and slept a while and bathed and prepared to go out with the dogs again when the telephone rang and the Maharaja's office called to invite us over for an audience.

On the terrace at the back of the *darbar* hall, he was sitting on a smart new swing, watching some of his staff play a ballgame. He seemed well, insouciant and humorous and in better health than when we last spoke, and we talked at length about the *Mahabharata* and my books and of Sonia Gandhi and her family, and he told us tales about Pragmulji, his nephew. He was utterly charmed by the vivacity and glamor of Leanna and soon ignored me altogether, favoring her conversation. Once again I was struck by how odd it was to return and to be so recognized and equable with the life of Dhrangadhra. It was as if I had dismissed that period of my life and yet it had firmly adhered to me.

When we departed the following day, we were forlorn to say goodbye to Harshraj and his wife and to their enchanting household. I realized that I did not know this man very well and yet I felt close to his understanding of the world, such was his deliberate wisdom and his studied understanding of things. The clarity of his speech and thought was unusual, and as with the Maharao back in Kacch, it was a pleasure to merely sit and converse with such a person. There was a special art and dignity in that careful verbal process, and I was sad to make our farewell. Driving homeward, Leanna and I both snoozed in the car, only wakening when we were across the Rann. How wonderful it was to be back in our landscape and among those people once again; it was a relief to be among our own dust and to perceive those low tapering hills upon the horizon. I realized how much I loved this land and actually needed it for my sense of well-being: it was the earth in my heart, and these people were our familiars, just as the terrain was theirs. We unpacked and bathed and Leanna immediately went off to the bazaar in order to reconnect herself; she was extremely happy to be home. That evening we walked across the bridge to the other side of the river and watched the tawny sun settle behind the town. How naked we were that night as we slept, and how completely at rest.

Some days later, we met up with the Maharao and took tea with him on a terrace overlooking the sea. There was no humidity, and a great clarity was about the day. He was astute as ever, sensitive and generous in his conversation, and talked about the White Eagle School, where he had briefly taken us one afternoon some months previously. It was an establishment that he patronized, and he spoke of another similar school in Gandhidham and his ambition for its development. He also spoke about his uncle Dhrangadhra and about how only he and the Queen of England were the sole remaining members of a particular Order, and of how the uncle was the most long-lived prince to sit upon a throne in India, having acceded to the position as a very young man. There was much affection in his language that afternoon as we chatted, sitting out in the sunlight, the trade wind softly flowing across us and blowing sand upon our feet.

For a moment I had the impression that I would never see this person again, and a great sorrow came to me. Mentally I captured his image, as he sat there gesturing with his large hands and throwing his head back as he spoke; in the distance the amethyst sea was breaking open and unfolding upon the long flat shore. He was a unusual and rare individual, similar to Harshraj, for both men thought at length before they spoke and then spoke carefully. Both were deeply compassionate of human experience and practiced an active humanitarianism, not surrendering to cynicism or pessimism about the dilemmas of social life in India. I often wondered if the Maharao felt any sorrow in his life despite his steady lighthearted demeanor, if there was some unspoken solitude come from his inheritance and the life that he had enacted. All of us possess some unopened, inconclusive wish that we carry within us through the years, something that has been put aside as we make our compromises in the world and delimit our emotions and desires. In our exchanges, we often do not receive all that we once aspired to, and that sometimes leaves a small trace of silence, an occlusion that we are aware of but do not actually register or apprehend. Like a grain of sand within an oyster, this becomes cased in time and opalescent as a pearl, representing a small interior grief that is never to be addressed.

After that interview, I remember walking along the shore, westward and alone, leaving Leanna prone upon the sand with her book. I went a long way, going further and further into solitude and quiet. A few gulls passed, but that was all. Then a large hawk-eagle of orange and gold underwing suddenly flew slowly overhead. For an instant it was as if that bird assumed my consciousness, assimilated my identity, and I too disappeared as it glided off along the shore heading inland. How strange, I thought, for it was as if my soul went with that bird, and what remains now as I write this is but the empty shell of my being, a hollow tunic or moth. Something of my spirit joined with that winged creature as it flew so intently towards the Kacchi desert.

The rest of life would be easy, simple and uncomplicated, for my purpose was complete now, and all else would be level and unstrenuous. I had fulfilled my work and my spirit had moved; the rest was impossible to know, but it had imparted reasons, and in response my knowledge had achieved a fruitful and full state. Marriage was mine, and at last I was free of the ghostly imperatives that had previously baffled me. It was as if the sun had come upon the day, dispelling shadows, and in those shady and darker areas all wisdom resided, displaced and revealed by so much absolute brightness.

On my return to Leanna—still at the palace shore some hours later—she was assembling a tall sculpture of two life-size figures fabricated of items collected from the sand: driftwood and seaware and objects discarded from ships and fishing vessels.

"A wedding couple," she said, laughing. "The King and Queen of Kacch on their marriage day. This is the veracity of supernature. Do you accept ... if I am yours and your desire is mine?"

III. Bidhada: Our Home

As I walked on the soft pink earth mile after mile with Leanna, a great sun arched above and threw our shadows about us. We paused now and then in the shade of a banyan to drink some water, with only a few birds in the air and no other sign of life. That was my sole joy, being lone in the world with this woman and being with her in the Kacch. Only two places on earth have captured me in this way: one was Kacch, and the other was in southern Greece, in Lakonia, the province of Sparta. It is something that I cannot explain, for no other environment possessed the power of exciting and thrilling me in that way. Certainly, the overtly visual was involved, for something about the perceptible form of topography in these two places affected me profoundly, unconditionally, if not morally, but it was more than the visual; another force was at work. It was not simply an optical response to linear shape, for the formation of the two landscapes was different. The earth, the dust, and the stones and the avid light of Kacch entered far into my being and caused a love unlike any other. This continues to possess me even now as I write and supplies a necessary sense of belonging to my daily consciousness; yet it is as if Leanna herself were the actual medium and real location of such passion and the tissue of language between soul and terrain.

She and I did return briefly to the West to put our affairs in order before we returned to Gujarat. I taught for a term and worked on my book and rowed in the annual regatta. We visited some old friends on lake Champlain in the north, staying with them on their island in a beautiful red wooden house surrounded by cedars and pines and the sound of cold green water lapping against the rock shelf. That was the only place in America I had ever really loved. Then we leased out our home in Cambridge and swiftly returned to India. We had found a small modernist bungalow designed by the Mumbai architect Anand Pandit, set in the grounds of a refuge near the town of Bidhada, called Jalaram Bag, not far from Mandvi. It was owned by a retired Jain businessman, Mr. Shah, who was devoting the rest of his life to good works and spiritual exercise: his days revolved around the planting of trees throughout the region and also in a practical regime of meditation. Curiously, reforestation had been one of the most significant activities of my father, a Scotsman, when we had lived in southern China during my childhood. The Bidhada house was exquisite, small and round and surrounded by a large grove of date palms. Our new young son, Maxim—named after Leanna's paternal grandfather—attended the nearby Jain school. We had a motor-scooter, which Maxim called Hanuman, and a flock of cautious sparrows and mynah birds that Leanna fed each morning and that soon became an integral part of our household.

Her father was Greek and my father had been British, but it was our mothers, both of whom had been born in the sub-continent, who were the ones to truly inform us, leading us back—in time—to this situation of India: for there is something beyond all apprehension in a mother's love which forever contains a life and is unspeakable. The love of a father concerns action and language and the achievement of things, whereas a mother's love is without frame and interior, defining identity at a primary if not subliminal level. Certainly, Leanna and I had found each other in life and then found the Kacch and settled there driven by such force, and our former migrant and itinerant existence came at last to rest in that motherland.

For us, walking together had always been a paradigm of companionship, an activity where we recreated ourselves as conjoint souls in pursuit of the non-ephemeral. That peripatetic behavior where one crosses an open landscape on foot, that uncivil mobile state, was how *homo sapiens* had dwelt upon the earth long before agriculture appeared and before all neolithic settlement. It was an external condition deeply ingrained in the human psyche and prior to other experience—like fire before its domestication—and preceded any fixed or sedentary life. I am not sure how far the atavistic reoccurs within human consciousness, but walking for me has always remained a means to retrieve that fundamental identity, *vis-à-vis* the natural world, a consciousness that is most true. One of the initial acts in both the Hindu and the Greek Orthodox marriage rite takes place towards the conclusion of the ritual, when the bride and groom take several—typically seven—paces together, hand in hand. Walking is the proto-activity for the newly wedded pair, the original form and emblem of their joint life where soul might reveal itself.

Like the celebrated twig that was taken down into the depths of a mine and left overnight in a cavern, which, on being retrieved the next day was discovered to be heavy with mineral encrustation upon its limbs, crystalline and substantial; so too does love find adherence in the passage of time shared, the sequence of days and nights physically bound and coherent, where a man and woman offer up and exchange an unspoken momentary vision. I remember that when I first met Leanna long ago in Cambridge and we began to make love together, she would never stay and sleep through the night with me, not initially.

"Sleeping with someone is far more intimate than making love," she used say. "It is a complete surrender, to be with someone like that when one is unconscious for so many hours."

In sleep and in walking, those mysterious deposits occur as we admit another unutterable world into the silent recesses of our life, where the crystals and jewels adhere and receive their physical mass. The gifts of the earth are only offered during such instants.

Conversely, what binds a people together as a community, as an *ethnos*, is language, not just in terms of vocabulary but also in terms of metaphor. The crises occur when signification shifts—for whatever larger reason—and then the dissimilarities in words become conflictual: people fight about meaning and kill to secure those statements. Violence becomes the order of the day within a community, as in Ahmedabad or Mumbai. For every word has its dirt, just as light causes shade, and the accumulation of dirt—what a term excludes but implies—leads us into contest and dispute: boundaries as pure abstraction emerge or dissolve, and it is upon these walls that we struggle and clash. The mystery, or obscurity, is how words become obdurate and less fungible, what informs such sclerosis, and what is the nature of the larger or containing body that effects such change? This modification that, occurs in language—in terms of inclusion and exclusion, a response to some more enclosing or immuring pattern or media—supplies a palpitation to time as history, and I think of history as just one of the many metaphors of time. There are the eons and cycles, the *yugas*, solar and lunar time, and agricultural or migrant time, which concern climate and rainfall; people receive their apprehension of time differently as the temporal manifold is always various and never simplex.

Just as implicit in a fluid compound are the planes of crystallization and solid form, so too for language, forms exist as the possible metaphors surrounding a word both in potential and yet derived from physical and material locality. Exterior causes can effect an alteration in this charge, and it is upon these margins—these are the walls—that opposition takes place. The art of liberty is one that essays to alleviate such resistance in order to maintain a maximum porosity of terms: humanism, in other words. Tragedy occurs when we are no longer inclined to interpret and insist upon a single meaning. Some would say that strife, *polemos*, is a condition, if not a necessary condition, of human life, and that the function of the state is to compete on a level of maximum violence to effect junctions there: junctions between the meaning of words. Only the invariance of love can make things commensurate, the plea for kind and that humanistic ideal of reasonable curiosity germane to what we are not. In other words, if we are to survive, we must abjure the certitude that truth is exclusive; speech and language are only devices, creative devices, and rarely function as statements of matter.

It is our facility for memory that permits us to enter into a love affair and to be loving. If we are unable to recall love received, then we are unable to love: there is only this simple transmission or equation, for the experience of emotion is in itself an unconscious recollection of past events that are being reactivated as inconscient memory. Obversely and sadly, it is the recollection of violence sustained that similarly fuels our capacity to commit a brutal act, when we communicate our suffering to others. If we can forget the horrible deeds performed during Partition—in Kashmir and the Punjab—or when the Nazis retreated from parts of occupied Europe, or what happened in a particular camp long ago: then the impulsion to punish cannot exist, unless conditions are so appalling that one must voraciously struggle merely in order to remain. Yet how is it that we should forget? Does this mean that one must not speak of horrors witnessed or experienced and permit silence to heal such wounds, if it is only silence that can fully embalm our lesions and injuries? This is a silence that gangs and fraudulent politicians seek to split apart, seeking to exacerbate the cleavage.

Spontaneous and uncreated love is rare if not impossible: that is, a love that is not informed by antecedence and the causative impetus of preceding time and that simply coheres under appropriate conditions, heedless of historical weight. For human love only fulfills historical process, is part of an unfolding career that exists prior to our own lives, and it possesses a potential to continue long after we are deceased, if we have loved. We are caught, and perhaps it is only the uncommon chance—if such a thing exists—that provides us with a moment's freedom; for the weightless and insubstantial tissue of love is nothing but time, and obversely, the cycles and spheres of time are informed and constellated by acts of love. In love we transfer our narrative or story towards another narrative that is structurally similar or ideally equal: that is all. This would include love of place. The force of narrative is paradoxically such that it is always and only compelled to seek its own closure out of time, and we are caged by the necessary abstraction of those invisible words.

In India, because of the lesser importance given to material objects, particularly in traditional and non-affluent regions such as the Kacch, emotional life is totally unlike emotional life in the West. In the latter society, identity is always founded upon—if not attached to—material conditions: consumption and advertising play crucial roles in the construction of a persona, and the *self* is essentially based upon an adherence and inherence of *things*. In India, due to the lack of *matériel* and the scarcity of goods, the etiology of an individual's emotional stature derives more from kinship relations than from physical relations.

Thus there is less individualism, insofar as the nuclear unit is not as singular, and there is simultaneously more affection and human warmth at play in social exchange. The household is composed not only of a married couple and their children, but incorporates the various uncles and aunts and grandparents and cousins who are attached to that marital unit; there is no concept of a solitary individual who pleases his or her self and whose identity is constituted generally by the purchase and display of goods and who lives with little plural responsibility. Identity here is composed of kinship affinities and emotional connections rather than via an appropriation of object-things that reinforce a sense of personal classification. Thus ideas of value in their generation, transmission, and reception are unlike the social values produced in the West.

Looked at it from another point of view, as there is little shopping to be done in the Kacch—although a large and fashionable supermarket has appeared in Bhuj recently—there is not the relationship with the *object* upon which Western individualism is founded. As the market in Kacch lacks what are known as consumer goods, these objects that in the West—thanks to advertising—formulate what composes an individual's self-conception do not exist. Certainly, with the arrival of the cell phone and the small motorcycle and especially with the advent of the household television set, this system or structure is beginning to change in form; virtually no village is presently without a television. Yet human personality, and not just rurally but also in the emergent towns and *bourgeoisie*, remains principally and firmly based upon kinship relations: an individual is defined by his or her groupings and not by objects. This is thoroughly unlike Western idioms of identity that are firmly grounded on the acquisition and possession of things, where personal conception and hierarchy are composed materially rather than socially. Plus, traditional Kacchi society was typically non-competitive and non-acquisitive, being founded upon a hierarchic constitution; it was also a social order where marriages were not simply arranged but almost destined. In non-metropolitan areas, due to the disposition towards kinship rather than to individual livelihood, there is of course virtually no recreational sexual behavior, unlike in the West.

Thus the complexity of Kacchi society is not only due to its many ancient historical currents and the diverse order of its constitution—the various clan, caste, and religious groups—but also due to its sophisticated kinship structures. Marriages of course are always arranged, and out in the villages, this can require many years of time between the moment of initial betrothal—which sometimes occurs in childhood—and before an exchange of dowry is fully complete and the bride finally crosses her new threshold. Some communities still practice child marriage, but discreetly, as this is legally improper nowadays. There are few rare exceptions among the rising and educated or professional middle class where couples do marry for love, but this is not promoted, and inter-caste marriage is unusual, as it means matrimony beyond one's natal or religious community. The only civic unrest that occurred in Mandvi in the twentieth century was occasioned by a crisis caused by the discovery of a Moslem youth courting a young Hindu girl. For the latter group, this was wholly unacceptable and in fact dangerous. In Kacch, adulthood for a man begins with marriage, but for a woman this transition is marked by the birth of a child, particularly a son.

It is thus the kin-group which dominates communal life, unlike what obtains in much of the West, where the idea of the mobile individual is paramount. In contemporary Kacch, the social unit is the extended family, not the singular being: a person only flourishes within a conjugal family group, and nowadays this extends to cousins in East Africa or the Gulf or to fraternal kin in North America: to all the members of a band as well as to those further social groups from whom brides and grooms are received. Often in other parts of the South Asia, these kinship formations of caste succeed well in burgeoning industrial economies, where they perform as fraternal capital supplying dynamic infrastructure to new capitalist systems, a phenomenon which has transferred to migrants in Britain and North America.

There is more love, in other words, in India, and love that is unrestricted; nor does the phantasy of required romantic love preclude strong emotions of attachment. Marriages can be and are arranged because the sustenance of love is not laid upon a phantasm of illusory individuality, itself founded upon a near-autonomous series of object-relations. Love in the sub-continent—or much of it—is a very different story therefore, compared to what is heard and seen in the West. The two forms of narrative are entirely dissimilar and unlike in how they combine living bodies, for apart from such stories the human frame does not actually exist: anatomy without language has no destiny whatsoever.

Thus the emotional life of the Kacch differs markedly from what obtains in the West. This is also the case for much of modern India, although the Kacch, being far more conservative and orthodox and having only a small and non-consuming middle class, manifests this paradigm more succinctly and inflexibly; this is changing, however, with great rapidity. Not so long ago, the bicycle was seen as a middle-class vehicle; then the lightweight motorcycle began to dominate the roads; now it is the small automobile that is the cynosure of rising status and acquisitiveness.

In a book that I had written some years previously about human migration and walking, I attempted to portray human affection and its pursuits. In that book I focused on one particular model of the feminine as being key to the entire formulation of Western love, that of the *femme fatale*. Such a psyche perhaps exhibits the purest form of consciousness— almost animal-like in its original integrity and pre-morality—without the accretions of complex language. I suppose that historically this is due to such individuals—both men and women—being severely inhibited at some point early on in their cerebral development when the natural evolution of emotion became barred. Needless to say, it is my firm presumption that the feminine takes all priority in the formation of any love, and here, the idea of the *femme fatale*—in my book it was a woman—was the primary metaphor. Naturally, this is an image which could actually be applied to both men and women, to the male and to the feminine; for by the feminine I do not only mean *woman*; I mean a kind of agency, not an active biological person.

For me, the model of the *femme fatale* is a picture of emptiness and of living void. It is the zero or naught which can be perpetually moved among any series of ciphers in order to change the quantities concerned. If metonymy is the nature of how such a psyche functions, there is little access to metaphor in such a state; for such a life is only and necessarily serial, constantly attaching itself to things or other persons who are themselves the subject of things. For those kinds of people, and not only women in particular, sexuality and the sensual charge given to the human body is greatly controlling: therein lies the wealth of a corporeal economy whence value is created, via the creation and privileging of pleasure and genital sensation. As with Don Juan, the emotional market of such a person is one that desperately and repetitiously seeks to find a single value in a life that is destitute of all valence. One could describe Don Juan as a *femme fatale*, someone who is frantically seeking for just one dependable and substantial sign; he is a pure and unresting phenomenologist, an hypothetically presocial man.

Love in India is different; there is no *femme fatale* in that culture—although by India I suppose that I actually mean the Kacch and perhaps Saurashtra—and the absence of such a void is substituted by the extraordinary complex patterning which large and extended kinship structures provide. Human life is extremely different in that part of the globe in comparison to the West. Leanna remarked on several occasions how there was never anything at stake for Kacchi men; there was no performative necessity by which their masculinity was driven—as there is in Greece or France, say—and Kacchi masculinity nowadays evinces far greater emotional range than anything that is to be observed in the West. The same can be said of Kacchi womanhood.

In all these pages so far I have tried to trace how—given the nature of the *femme fatale* and the vacancy of an individual—if weight is not available to objects and to things and to consumption, then landscape and its topography become active in the organization of identity. Love of place is perhaps the only truthful fortune for the alienated Westerner unless he converts—and that process is mysterious—his disaffection and estrangement and retrieve what is his inheritance: the unique and rare contact with another human being upon which all life and optimism is founded. This is the ideal type for humanism itself.

In other words, for those who have lost their original kinship formation, through migration, schismatic modernism, urbanism, or through subjective loss—the affinity and affiliation of family, the tissue that envelops the personal and that creates a persona—there exists the possibility that place, terrain, or situation can supply the prime metaphors leading to desire and expression. These, by filtering language and speech, enable an individual to became aware of his or her self, so granting a concomitant sense of efficacy in time and the world. For the individual is a fine illusion;

it is a false mirror and only projects a quality or aspect of *trompe l'oeil* upon the screen of a human soul or *psyche*: that is something, in its abstraction, that is akin to the infinitely proliferating idea of a market economy, which is so implicit and paradigmatic for the modern West.

Cattle feed upon grass, sheep and goats browse and forage for shrub and vegetation, camels graze upon thornier and more desert-like but palatable plants: so an environment imposes conditions upon those who rear such animals, and it is not simply landscape itself which generates metaphor within a language but also the means of production by which a people thrive or survive therein. The system of living itself is causative of metaphor, myth, and of language, and one can even posit that geology ultimately affects literature and that a respected landscape possesses a humanizing quality in itself.

There is a hill, a small mountain, south of the Banni area of Kacch and the Chari Dhand marsh, called Nanamo. It is a former volcano, about which much cultivation and herding takes place, and for those who dwell in the region is it a focal part of their panorama. For distant mariners at sea, however, Nanamo stands out like a great beacon—what MacMurdo, an early traveler to the region and the first British resident, described as a giant sugar-loaf—powerful in its definition and remarkable distinction, providing them with an indubitable bearing.

For me, love has always been of a similar mettle. When one is close and within its vicinity, it is not obvious and its being is not conspicuous. From afar, however, when one is alone upon a wonderful sea or ocean, love appears as the organizing principle of all one's mental field: palpable, thoroughly evident, and the principal landmark to all transitions.

Part Two

IV. Dhinodar: Gifts of Friendship

Kacch is a region situated in the far west of the Indian sub-continent and is divided by the seventieth degree of longitude; the Tropic of Cancer bisects it laterally. There are three low ranges of hills that run in an east-west direction, from which water drains northward on the upper slopes and southward on the lower sides. It has been described as "a strange semi-island … on the Arabian Sea between the Kathiawar Peninsula and the Pakistani province of Sindh." In my tattered nineteenth-century German copy of Arrian—one of the earliest writers to describe the terrain—Kacch is entitled Cilluta Island. In Urdu, *kaccha* means raw or wild; it can also refer to the untenanted terrain on the sides of a river.

About one hundred and eighty miles broad at its extreme and a maximum of fifty miles in depth, it is bordered on one side by the Great Rann, a salt desert that presently occupies what was once the lower courses of the Indus river, and on its eastern side by the Little Rann, also a tidal salt waste. Farther beyond the Great Rann is the frontier with Pakistan. Excluding both Ranns, Kacch extends for more than twenty thousand square kilometers, and two million years ago this was beneath sea-level. The word *rann* would appear to come from Sanskrit *irina*, a desolate place. During the monsoon—if it arrives—these arid tracts fill with water from the Arabian Sea and the Kacch becomes effectively an island; this slow ingress of sea-water along the coast augments the increasing desertification of the inland territories. The Little Rann is crossed by a single causeway—built in 1968—which runs to mainland Gujarat from the point of Surajbari. Nomads, travelers, merchants, pilgrims, refugees, itinerant warriors—including the British and perhaps even the Macedonians of Alexander—have all made tracks across the Kacchi sands.

There are three strands to contemporary life in the Kacch that I am portraying and twining together in these chapters as a circumstantial *schema* to my years there with the wonderful Leanna: the geographical, the temporal, and the social. Firstly, there exists my own sense of the remarkable and marvelous and the great pleasure that I have found in that landscape, its varieties of culture and ancient domain. Then there exists a trajectory between the traditional and the modern, where both human society and its physical environment change in time: a shift marked by a varying regard being paid to the natural world and its valuation. Lastly there is a corollary, for life in the Kacch in the past and present is founded upon the phenomenon of migration. The movement of human beings across a terrain—typically on foot—is for me always a founding source of native consciousness. If one removes the imprint of human culture from a psyche, then, hypothetically—for this is of course not possible—all that remains is weather, solar and sidereal time, and landscape; reproductivity is there, but that is simply corporeal and animal. It is the elementary submission of this book that landscape is the founding pattern-maker of human culture; that is the first cast to lie upon the human mind.

There are remains of urban settlement in the Kacch that date back to the third millennium B.C.E., the most spectacular of which are at the site of Dholavira to the north-east. That region is also rich in fossils from the Jurassic age: shells, reptile bones—even dinosaur eggs—and traces of former verdure and fish, and there, Neolithic microliths can be picked up from the ground. Walking about Kacch, one has a sense of dry wilderness that has not altered much in thousands of years; it has merely been traversed on foot by small successions of migrant peoples. Apart from Indus Valley objects, the earliest cultural artifacts that have been discovered come from Andhau, near the town of Khauda, on the eastern edge of the Great Rann. These are six memorial *stelae* from early in the Common Era and are presently to be seen in the new Museum of Bhuj. Upon these stones are eroded inscriptions written in Prakrit—a Sanskrit vernacular— which commemorate a brother, sister, wife, and son. They were erected during the rule of Raja Rudradaman, and each inscription culminates with the phrase *lashti upapita*, "this stone was raised," probably by Buddhists.

The present-day Kacchi language is more colloquial than Gujarati, being in essence a dialect of Sindhi; it is very different from Gujarati, although the script used is presently Gujarati, which is itself derived from Sanskrit *devanagari*. However, a great many people are unable to read a book, and literacy does not flourish beyond the towns; thumbprints often stand for legal signatures. Gujarati became a medium of education only in the twentieth century.

Kacch has traditionally been a land apart and separate from mainland South Asia to the east and north; because of the Great Rann, it is distinct from the Sindh to the west, a province that since Partition has become part of Pakistan. Until fifty years ago, the only extant road ran between Bhuj and Mandvi, and transport was by bullock cart along tracks or across the desert by camel or pony. In the nineteenth century, there had been a direct sea link between Kacch and Mombasa, and until recently, to visit Bombay, one took the steamer from Mandvi. Up to the second half of the last century—because of long-standing maritime traditions—the Emirates and other Gulf states were both culturally and physically closer to Kacch than Delhi; Karachi used to be the nearest metropolis, and it was only in 1965, after a failed invasion of Pakistani tanks into the Rann and a subsequent war situation, that the ferry connection between Bombay and Karachi, via Kacch, was halted. After that, there were soon terrific communal riots in mainland Gujarat, and the tension between India and Pakistan was only slightly defused after much UN and European pressure; this brought about an accord, made at Tashkent in 1966, concerning who controlled the Great Rann.

The Kacch is dry and stony and frequently a bleak wilderness devoid of moisture, the ground being typically a russet-colored sandstone; temperatures can rise to forty-nine degrees Celsius during the hot season. Only about fifteen percent of the flat land is cultivated, and during the rainy months, the dehiscent earth becomes vivid with a bright green sheath of thin vegetation that soon—in a few weeks—dries to a delicate golden brocade that in a breeze shivers vivaciously like running water. The territory is generally flat with volcanic outcroppings, large hills that rise up perfectly conical from the plain, and here and there low undulations appear at the edges of ridges in a basket-of-eggs topography. At the present, there is a mean annual rainfall of thirteen inches, but this varies, for the monsoon—which arrives in July and usually continues into late August—might not come at all, and great hardship and destitution then visits the land.

Then thin starved cattle are to be seen everywhere, trudging wearily, and villages are somber and serious in mood. Water is thus intricately associated with prosperity and the production of wealth in the Kacch. Its lack is an immediate cause of famine and migration, as happened during the second half of the 1980s; although the worst recorded drought and famine occurred at the turn of the twentieth century. The number of years of scarce rainfall has doubled during the last hundred years, compared to the figures from the nineteenth century, and droughts now follow a tri-ennial pattern: this means that many seeds that once could lie fallow for a year or so can no longer remain dormant. Nowadays, however, drought does not necessitate famine and death.

Due to the dismal rainfall and also to the increasing salinity of groundwater, there is little tree cover in the region; only scrub and acacia are common. Recently there was an incursion of charcoal-burners from Rajasthan, who systematically decimated great areas of *prosopis juliflora*; the stench from their slow-burning fires would linger for miles. This plant was introduced by the present Maharao's grandfather from Mexico to sup-ply the terrain with shrubbery and the people with fuel, yet its root system was so voracious that it swiftly overtook the landscape, often to the exclu-sion of native plants like the *acacia nilotica* and the piloo or *salvadora persica*, and now it cannot be eradicated. It also can choke the course of water runoff, so that when a well-set monsoon deluge does arrive, there can be terrific flooding, causing death and much injury. Reforestation is a major political issue in the Kacch, and the Forestry Commission wages a constant struggle to replant areas, for trees maintain the water table and sustain a plethora of microclimates. Without tree coverage, there is only increasing desiccation and a diminution of bird and insect life, which includes the bees, which are crucial for pollination.

Also, since the terrible earthquake of 2001, the provincial government in Ahmedabad has encouraged industry—especially mining—to invest and build in the region. This has led to an increasing consumption of poor groundwater resources and to the rapid increase in land prices, as land itself became commodified, and hence a concomitant illicit encroach-ment upon public space has occurred. The Banni, formerly one of the most munificent grasslands of Asia, due to a falling water table and to the invasive effects of the exotic *prosopis* mesquite, and due to the construction of dams to the south that catch the superfluous monsoon—so preventing a leaching of alkaline soils—has now become sterile and saline, and its villages are often on the verge of dereliction. Only in the Banni did I wit-ness real economic hardship: a serious lack of decent nutrition and the mental indifference of misery.

The history of Kacch is usually a matter of traditional account, as lit-eral records are rare and events in the past are impossible to fix. Past time possesses no social certitude, and different communities possess different founding narratives. The stories of the Moslems, for instance, concern the land to the west; the mariners' tales of social organization relate to the Indian Ocean peripheries; Hindu reports of the past look eastward or north and recall events that occurred in those directions. There do exist twentieth-century Gujarati historians such as Karani or Sampat, but given the dearth of early data, historiography is often a matter of invention and the legends of oral tradition; there is little written literature to supply the present with a hypothetical antecedence. The Gazetteers did provide some evidence of historical process, but their sources were at times unfirm.

There are historical sites more recent than the Bronze Age, as with the walled *giridurg* or citadels of Rohar or Kanthkot, which date from post-medieval times, but they are rare. We sometimes visited Rohar, perched high above the desert plain, and wandered about the wreckage of what must have been a wonderful palace, now totally abandoned and made derelict by successive earthquakes. There were deep open cisterns where cobras lived and tiny lanes that threaded between the ruins of what was once a flourishing town but were now only inhabited by mongeese and mynahs. Hordes of colossal bats hung from the ceilings and arches of broken rooms. Such places are deserted and near unknown, and few Kacchis would ever visit them; no one ever seemed to understand why such formerly rich strongholds became so neglected. Mutable patterns of land tenure, natural disaster, new forms of rule that usurped earlier systems: it does not take long for nature to reclaim what has been discarded, and once human life moves away without a written tradition, recollection is not persistent. We recently heard that a Punjabi businessman had purchased the hilltop site of Rohar and was going to develop it: an instance where the prospect of tourism or the new middle class hunger for status does actually lead to a conservation of historical or natural resources.

At Kanthkot, one early afternoon, we walked about some of the extensive ruins. It was truly a gigantic site, an enormous flat hilltop that had once been fortified, and its walls ran for several kilometers along the edge of a plateau. Along with the fortresses of Gadhsissa and Bhujia, it had been one of the three impregnable places in Kacch. The last earthquake had wrecked what remained of two temples, one dedicated to the Vedic sun-deity Surya, and another a large Jain temple. The walls, spires, and sculptural elements now lay scattered in pieces upon the hot earth. There were many ceramic sherds lying about the ground, and one had the sense that we were at rooftop level and that the dwellings and palaces lay beneath our feet. Near the main gateway to the fort, there was a deep narrow avenue leading uphill, along one side of which an assembly of dozens of hero stones were standing in row after silent row. Carved into the dark brown stone, images of the deceased, fully armed and mounted on horses and sometimes camels—along with their *sati* wives—were aligned, their gaze fixed forever upon those who were entering the stronghold. Such was the nature or material of historical record, these anomic stones, rather than any written account, expressing merely thin bare inscriptions beneath the graven portraits.

How a society recalls its social past—particularly when the society is as variform as Kacchi society—is not always obvious, particularly if few written reports exist. Often it is the case that the past is continually reformulated in order to support and sustain whatever group is presently dominant. Holy men, *gurus*, saints, and *pirs* have played a significant role in the competition that occurred over the years between rival sects seeking to appropriate the authority of antiquity, and such figures recurrently constellate a resurgence of verbal transmission concerning *itihasa*, "how it once was." This phenomenon was always confusing for us whenever we tried to ascertain the story of a place, for different people would tell us diverging tales and often with great conviction.

Human knowledge is such that a spoken or sung tradition is sufficient to maintain social patterns of *gotra*, clan, or *jati*, caste-group, and the present is laterally organized rather than temporal in its suspension. Genealogy or affiliation informs the primary ground for such information. The Rabari, for instance, possess myths of generation that propound descent from a deity or hero, and the past has no linear structure but is organized more as a horizontal reticulation of meanings that support a present existence, like landmarks upon a territory. This is not so much a case of either fiction or truth, but of mnemonics affording a modicum of conceptual reality and enabling life to proceed: rather like the metonymy of the zero cipher in mathematics. Human beings require conceptual perspective if life is to not become centrifugal, and it does not really matter whence those vanishing points are derived nor where they are situated, so long as there is coherence and process is facilitated: veracity concerns integrity rather than formal proof. Historical course or series dominates Western terms or reception of identity, whereas kinship patterns are more pronounced in the Kacch; neither system possesses a thorough solution for the human predicament but is simply a fruitful medium for patterning the vacancy by which conscious life is surrounded and encased.

History in the Kacch is not linked to questions of property or land tenure, nor to definitions of ethnicity, for unlike the recent European centuries, there were no such forms of contention at work. Until the mid-nineteenth century, the *kshatriyas* dominated the current of recognizable time with their culture of conflict and contest about standards of rule. Knowledge in those cases was more a question of emotion or proclivity than logical and evidential fact; the socially true was of greater import than the rationally or demonstrably genuine. Historical reference is thus partial and never collective, unlike the historical and consecutive order that is said to prevail in the consensual or more synoptic West, where sequence receives so much priority in social explanation.

There are physical artifacts, however, that do actually signify events in time, like the *stambhas* or *paliyas*, the many hero stones that are found at shrines or about temple precincts. These often date from the late eighteenth century, when thousands of Kacchi warriors fell at the battle of Jhara near Lakhpat. On some of these carvings there would be a woman holding a baby, an image that fascinated my wife. I used some pictures of these stone pillars—taken from Leanna's photographs—for the cover of my book about women in the *Mahabharata*. A highly formalized heroic code governed human life in those days, and a *kshatriya's* existence was in accordance with such ideals, ideals that were typically propounded in song, the warrior epics that were modeled after the Sanskrit poem *Mahabharata*. Even in Bidhada I had heard on certain wintry evenings in the year the descant of a wandering bard who accompanied his voice with a cheap metal *vina* that he plucked whilst his wife or mate would keep tempo with small brass cymbals. He would be sitting on the ground at a closed-up *chai*-stall and usually sang of the deeds and exploits of Ramdev Pir, a Rajasthani epic tradition that merged Hindu and Moslem devotional elements.

These hero-stones, along with the many ancient temples and shrines that dot the landscape, as well as the remnants of gateways and bastions that can be found in towns and villages, give the Kacch a rare visual if not romantic quality. There are many abandoned forts and, as with Lakhpat and Dholavira, large and deserted cities that today are full of sand and inhabited more by owls, snakes, and porcupines than by human beings. The extensive and massive walls of Lakhpat, several kilometers in circuit, today surround only a few old houses and tombs: the rest is emptiness, looking out upon a bare and deserted Rann. The vast site at Kanthkot in the east is similarly wild and deserted, a place where the sand drifts about ancient walls and cattle bones. Certainly, one should not idealize that heroic warrior past too much, for it was often a time of lawless predation, cruelty, and rapine, what in modern terms would be considered a period of gang warfare. MacMurdo spoke of how in his time every village "has a chief who acts independently, and who lives only by his own predatory excursions." Violence was a way of life; hence all the fortified towns and settlements with their great walls and ditches and gates, and hence the proliferation of stone monuments commemorating the valiant dead warriors and the bearing of arms. Nowadays—as it does in Scotland—all this appears captivating and romantic in retrospect, chivalrous, picturesque, and evocative, and yet the reality was, I surmise, somewhat apathetic, rude, pitiless, and brief, as well as being often deadened by large-scale opium addiction.

What caught me and consistently drew me back to the place of Kacch was primarily the visible aspect of life there. I was immensely attracted by what I saw, for the situation resonated strongly with my literary work, and only later, when we had begun to make friends, did I realize how extraordinary and wonderful the people were as I grew to love them. For many years in my written work I had struggled to create a naturalist aesthetic, a poetics that would continue the traditions of Hesiod and Virgil, of Theokritos, of Spenser and the English renaissance poets and Milton and the later Romantics. My poetry reflected landscape and the figures of men and women in a natural and uninhibited world where the cycles of life were governed simply by movements of light and shadow, a world that had nothing to do with modernism and the urban irreligious. This was a view comparable to what John Constable had depicted, a vision that many British landscape painters had once discerned in rural Greece, beginning with the Dilettanti and then Edward Lear and continuing down to the Neo-Romantics, including Ben Nicholson. I was trying to temper a similar aesthetic for the present time and produce work of a quality analogous to what was once similarly admired and pursued by the Concord naturalists of New England. This is not some prelapsarian nostalgia, but a question of distinct *georgic* taste and critical judgment.

For a while I had secured some reification of this imaginary ideal by living in the Peloponnese of southern Greece, but that old Levantine world had rapidly succumbed to the expansion of the European Union, and now only elderly people lived in the villages, or less than orthodox foreigners. In the Kacch, as I made my way down from Bhuj towards the coast during that first visit so many years ago, I realized that I had found a territory that I had long been only aware of in poetry: here was an actual reality. I was instantly enamored of those villages with their temples and stone spires or the minarets of small mosques, surrounded by fields where yokes of oxen drew ploughs and harrows; of the various flocks and herds out upon the plains and the low hills with their mysterious and solitary shepherds; of the fords that used to appear during the rainy season where cattle would be driven across at evening, homeward to be milked; of the pollarded ashok trees that edged the fields; of the wild dogs, boars, and *nilgai* which roamed freely, and the many large raptors, buzzards, eagles, and kites; of the veiled *kshatriya* women and their children who would wash and do their laundry on the edge of streams as they gossiped; of the thin wandering holy men, the *saddhus*, and the occasional temple elephant decorated with colored chalks; of the sails that would appear off the coast as fishing vessels made their way back towards harbor and the great dhows being built or caulked upon the sands at Mandvi. Above all, I was captivated by the general pedestrian life that followed the slowness of draught animals and by the daily progress that observed an agrarian and festal calendar.

What had been a mental outlook and a carefully constructed system of metaphors drawn for literature suddenly became actually present, and there was no further struggle to maintain and refine an aesthetic that was necessarily exclusive. Here among these hills and tracts my ideas could stray freely, lightly, and most feasibly, and at last I could work with experience rather than simply ideals. The visual experience of words—of western pastoral poetry based on an ideal Hellas and the Sanskrit epic—in the Kacch became for me an audible experience that was visible and immediate.

Kacch had first entered to my life in the early eighties when I visited Bhuj and the seafaring port of Mandvi. I can still vividly recall the train crossing the sands as dawn came upon the world: the carriage was deserted— it was winter—and I was alone in a compartment except for one other man. He was a tall, lavishly mustached, and sumptuously turbaned fellow with great gold bosses in his ears. I had been sleeping on an upper berth and woke to his singing, a long rhythmic chant, the kind of song that I now know well as a desert song or *raso*, a monodic narrative about a hero and a lover.

I spent some time wandering the town of Bhuj, which in those days was small and uncluttered, although its extent had long transgressed the bounds of the former defensive walls. Some of the old gateways with prodigious spiked doors still stood, and here and there a squat isolated tower remained along with traces of old masonry. Then I had taken a bus down towards the coast and Mandvi, and I remember seeing small camps of Rabari families: men in vermilion headdress and *kediyun*, short tight white jackets, and the women in decorated black and alizarin; they had camels and flocks of sheep and goats. That was my first image of those wonderful pastoral people.

Like almost all inhabitants of the region, the Rabari long ago migrated into the district; their origins are probably Sindhi, and they came, some centuries ago, from Baluchisthan via a northward circuit through Rajasthan, where many of the clan still live. Presently, about ninety thousand Rabari are dispersed among three separate and endogamous social groupings: the Vaghadia of the east, the Dhebaria, who are more centrally located, and the Kacchi Rabaria to the west. Each zone possesses various subgroups. The Rabari have become modern icons of pastoralism, and it is their meager but often spectacularly gorgeous image that for most people—Indians especially—captures the wild and remote sensibility of Kacchi life and desert. It is a picture of the nomadic and transhumant, the migrant and sparsely beautiful, unconcerned with the urban materialism of a twenty-first century. It is their picture that fits well with the Romantic view of the dignity of nature and its moral purity: they are the old Arcadians and true to earth's promise, who are featured on tourist postcards.

If this present century fails in its systems, they will be the ones to inherit the Kacch, for only they truly know the place. Their textiles and embroidery are remarkable works of art with an incredible syntax and grammar of design, and they have drawn much attention from the West. Some of rarer pieces have been acquired and are now held in museums and private collections. The term *rabari* is said to derive from *raha*, outside, and *bari*, way: they are "outside of the way," meaning that they embrace a life of the wilderness, apart from the sedentary, fixed, and civic. Yet how much longer can that uncivil aesthetic and moral code continue? For I wonder what will happen with the next young generation of Rabari, the teenagers who have access to television and who see what happens both in India and beyond. Will this generation continue to dress in Rabari style and wear the heavy jewelry and old-fashioned outfits? Will the women undergo the painful tattooing procedures? The motorcycle, the cellphone, and the cool image of tight denim jeans and printed *faux*-Versace shirts possess great allure for the young, yet these items of inescapable modernity necessarily bear with them a simultaneous dissolution of social habit and a liberation of social practice.

Mandvi—established in the sixteenth century by the first Jadeja

Rao—on that first occasion when I visited it so long ago had instantly filled me with amazement. I felt as I crossed the bridge over the dry Rukhmavati that this was the place that I had been seeking for years: it was like a sudden and unexpected homecoming. Herons, hieratic cranes, and ibis strolled the mud, and on one shore a whitewashed temple thrust up a spire from a grove of banyan trees as hundreds of pigeons flew about the air like small dark particles. Mandvi then was strongly cosmopolitan and the people so miscellaneous that I was simply amazed by the life of the port and bazaar. Kacch is one of the most socially diversified societies of contemporary India, and Partition had passed without serious trauma or disorder as Moslems continued to live in the region as they had done for centuries. Often the quays of Mandvi and the tight narrow lanes of the bazaar were interspersed with exotic Muscatis, Omanis, and Somalis, and also with strangely powerful looking *Sidi* women who were descended from Africans who had long ago migrated—usually under conditions of servitude—to Kacch and mainland Gujarat and the Sindh. Further upriver from the Mandvi shore lies the site of a former ancient port at Nani Rayan, where many ceramic artifacts and Roman coins have been unearthed; that had been the town before the river silted up and before settlement moved closer towards the sea. Mandvi still remains an old-fashioned waterfront built up on either side of a quiet tidal estuary with the *bhadela*, the Islamic shipping community, resident on the eastern shore at Saleyah and most of the Hindus dwelling on the western side of the waterway. Commerce has dissolved over the years due to a shallowing of the estuary, yet ship-building is the present font of prosperity. Those huge vessels are constructed without plans or drawings and with only rudimentary utensils, the adze being the most common implement; even the long iron nails that fix the planking of the hulls are forged on the spot over small carbon fires. Big electrical saws, however, are nowadays used to cut the boards from great baulks of imported Burmese and Malaysian teak. Once smuggling used to bring much wealth to mariners and ship owners, but as the Indian economy begins to produce more consumer goods, this activity has diminished. I was fascinated that the huge wooden dhows could still ply the ancient trade routes following the monsoon winds—from the southwest in the summer and from the northeast during the winter—although most of these vessels presently run with diesel motors and use sails only for balance. The development of Dubhai in the seventies drew a great wave of young Kacchi male immigrants to that coast and caused a concomitant reexpansion of Kacchi shipping that continues to flourish today.

Modernism has brought even more of the giant steel windmills to the Mandvi shore, monoliths that are increasingly titanic in their stream-lined form and turn languidly yet forcefully in the trade winds. There presently exist other such banks or wind farms along the coast, and I sup-pose more will appear in time, their enormous white rotors spinning ele-gantly like kinetic sculpture. They are apparently extremely profitable but require huge initial sums of capital investment. Now, in the quiet narrow lanes of Mandvi, port trucks loaded with enormous cargoes rumble their heavy way, and sometimes convoys of army vehicles head towards the frontier in long, sinister caravans. A myriad of auto-rickshaws, *tum-tums*, spew out a high-revving noise and masses of dark, oily exhaust. Yet there are still storks who live on the lake at Mandvi, and small flocks of tall and nonchalant flamingoes—stunning in their flagrant pink plumage—con-tinue to browse the shoreline and cross the air in slow unearthly flight patterns. It is this odd concatenation of the sublime with the rude that stamps Kacch with its present amalgam of imagery. One is overwhelmed by the splendid and yet simultaneously appalled by the harshness of the twenty-first century as it infringes upon this wonderful geography and society.

Thirty years before, when I had visited Mandvi as a young man and first looked upon those tidal flats patrolled by small egrets, as large wooden ships lay heeled and at rest along with many smaller fishing vessels, my singular and impassioned soul had been easily rapt. Having grown up sailing in various parts of the world, the maritime scene instantly caught my fancy, and I had determined to stay. Many of the old mercantile build-ings along the seawall were finely designed and constructed of pale sand-stone in almost vitruvian proportion. Sadly, few of these remain in any state of order today, and the many similarly fabricated *dharamsalas*, hos-tels—for pilgrims to Mecca and for mariners—are now also in complete disrepair and disuse. I used to spend afternoons down at the old port observing that detailed nautical world, drinking tea and chatting with boatmen and captains.

One large vessel had put in on its way up from Bombay towards the Gulf—Muscat, I think, was its destination—with a cargo of water buffalo. The vessel had sprung a leak in heavy seas and careened against a seawall, where at low tide the crew worked on recaulking the seams; the animals had all been offloaded and were tethered at various points along the break-water. One drowsy afternoon under the shade of a giant banyan tree as I watched their labor and thought about their routes and passages up towards the Gulf and thence down towards Lamu and Mombasa and back, I entered into conversation with the captain of that boat. I had once in my youth sailed with a dhow, a *bhoom*, along the East African coast, and now this captain asked me to join them aboard the vessel and sail the rest of their passage towards the Emirates. I foolishly hesitated, for I had to return to Greece, where I then lived, to meet up with a colleague in a month. Also, at that point in time I had become ill with a nasty spike of malaria, and a day or so later I was on a bus bound towards Bombay with a vile fever consuming me and soon flying back towards Athens, where I ended up in a clinic. So the chance of a voyage vanished as the winds changed; it was a fortuitous moment that I always regretted, one of those occasions in time when the compass needle temporarily ceases to point and directions merge with new possibility. I always longed to fulfill that offer, however, and to sail those routes to and from the Gulf, or to follow the route down towards Mombasa, twelve days away with a good wind: that has remained as one of my oldest phantasies.

The second time that I visited the Kacch was at the turn of this century, when I had been staying at Dhrangadhra two hundred miles to the east with the Jhala family. Twice I had driven over the causeway from the mainland to the Kacch and gone to visit Dholavira with my friend Harshraj, and again, the Kacchi environment seized me with its pure startling beauty and rare antiquity, and I had not wanted to leave. That region where we drove had been terrifically hurt by the earthquake; whole villages were leveled and even now are still in ruin. I recall thinking how middle-Asian the district seemed, that it was no longer sub-continental but something far more ancient: lavishly turbaned men with richly dyed beards, rumbling and lurching camels and bullock carts, and women with indigo-stained arms, their *saris* drawn across their faces as a veil. The dust, smoke, and disorder of the villages and their lack of any semblance to the modern was to me intimately fascinating.

When Leanna and I put the West behind us and fully returned to the Kacch, we were accompanied by our little son. On one occasion, along with the child, we arrived in Bhuj on a blazing hot afternoon when the mercury stood at well over forty degrees Celsius; it was late June and the heat was narcotic and stupefying. We stayed at a familiar guest-house that nestled up against the walls of the former palace, the Prag Mahal. Parts of the older palace still existed in pieces, and here and there a few walls with carved oriel windows stood in fallen dejection. The later edifice, built in the nineteenth century, had been devastated by the recent seismic tremors, and shivered pieces of it still lay about the ground. Brilliant green parakeets whizzed around the broken towers and rooves, and bodhi trees grew up from among piles of debris.

We soon moved, first back to Mandvi and then to our lovely house on the edge of the village of Bidhada, sixteen kilometers from the coast and just off the Bhuj road close to the great Jain temple of Koday, which was made only of white marble. There we lived in an exquisite bungalow, perhaps the most perfect architecture in which I have ever dwelled. The building was surrounded by many acres of fruit trees, dates, mango, and chikoo, and it was in that wonderful little round house—modeled after the traditional domestic design of a *bhunga*, a circular mud-built structure with a roof constructed of foliage, usually palm fronds—that we really came to fit ourselves into the world of Kacch and become resident rather than visitors. Our daughter was also conceived beneath that roof on the hottest day of the year, one afternoon before I had to go up towards Delhi for some consultancy work on a new film version of the *Mahabharata*. She was a modest and most beautiful, compassionate little girl whom we called Manki, a name that the Maharao had suggested, meaning "glittering" in Kacchi, but glittering in an intellectual sense, from the verbal root *man*, to think.

In those days we frequently journeyed out into the countryside for many bumpy miles, traveling on our motorcycle for hours and hours, sometimes even during the swishing rains of monsoon, as the four of us hung onto that little vehicle negotiating tracks and uneven roads. When the monsoons actually settled on the area—and that first year it rained far more than usual—we remained at home and read our books and listened to the hoarse cry of peafowl and black ibis or to the dogs, and in the winter to jackals, barking throughout the nights. Sometimes we used to drive out towards the shore temple of Ravalpir, perched on dunes close to the sea, where the shrine was dedicated to the Jakhs, seventy-two horsemen from Byzantium who were supposed to have been shipwrecked off the coast several centuries ago and who had arrived with one woman. There are several Jakh temples in the Kacch, usually situated on hill-tops and always filled with stone images of those men on horseback and their single spouse: alien and silent statues placed upon a ledge or floor. Adjacent to the shrine at Ravalpir was the tomb of a Moslem *pir*, and devotees would often be sitting outside upon the walls, watching the shore and its tranquility and sometimes enjoying a holiday picnic.

We would often go there of an afternoon and walk the vacant littoral.

Ospreys would be about, and sometimes slender and shy flamingoes would be sauntering the shallows; my wife and son would collect shells whilst I swam or played with the baby. I loved the solitary world of that shore, its cordial desolation and monochrome intensity as the ocean unrolled upon the sands throwing up weird jetsam, the detritus of ships and empty marine space. Sometimes if we walked far we might encounter a larger group of flamingoes; those tall shocking-pink birds were almost supernatural in the way that they quietly moved, completely ignoring our presence as if we did not exist. Then they would simply rise into the air, effortlessly taking the breeze, and sail off as we approached. They were extremely beautiful but completely elusive and ephemeral, unobtainable in their dignity.

That little Bidhada house—surrounded by jacarandas and frangipani where sunbirds used to nest and play and the throaty bulbul and drongos constantly called, with its marble floors and central staircase—we appointed with items of sculpture picked up from stonemasons' yards or discovered among ruins and dilapidated temples. I even had a couple of pieces that I had long ago brought from Harshraj's yard at Dhrangadhra: a small warrior torso that I had uncovered from a heap of rejected carvings and a fine sandstone horse's head. That house enveloped us, and our residence there was unlike any other time in my life, as the seasons turned about and the grass changed color and the trees dropped their fruit and then blossomed when the sun returned. Winter was perhaps the loveliest time, with serene pure skies of sapphire and thin dry sunlight and low exacting shadows. Life seemed to gently pause during those days as time merged with time as if there were no transitions and the light ran out in long translucent ribbons.

Love of place and love of person have always been inseparable for me. Insofar as these two experiences supply us with a primary ground for all thought and metaphor, they are the foremost retaining conditions of life and language. Sometimes in the small hours before dawn, I used to rise and go out upon one of the terraces and listen to the soft night air, the noisy chattering owls or the breeze moving among the neem trees and rattling the date and coconut fronds. How life appeared to be shooting past then like so many swift arrows or javelins, and how impossible it was to resist that motion, let alone to secure just a few instants for the purposes of memory. I realized that those days—the nights and hours—were something extraordinary and would never be equaled and certainly not regained; each minute possessed an acute poignancy because it was so ephemeral. I wanted to seize and secure everything, to imprint myself with the experience so that nothing would be lost and forgotten when once again we moved; for—as Leanna always remarked—almost all of human experience is soon lost into an oblivion of forgetting, and we recollect virtually nothing, as the past is no longer legible. Usually in our lives, the beauty of what exists in time does not strike us nor affect us, yet there at Bidhada as we kept to that house, I was precisely aware of our riches, of how we had arrived at a place that fitted immaculately with the intellectual and aesthetic system of belief that I had spent decades formulating, refining, and expressing. What a fine sensation of joy that was, and yet it was qualified by so much transience: it could not be grasped except in the few images that I managed to temper and preserve for memory's sake or in the perceptions borne from acts of writing and rewording of experience. I used to love watching Leanna as she walked about the grounds with our little girl, for it was as if I were witnessing a scene from some wonderful tale that no one else observed.

The Bidhada house—with its trespassing rats and mice and its small snakes in the kitchen, two of those tiny cobras our son Maxim kept for a while in a box as pets—became our complete world whilst we explored the land and made acquaintances and our first friends. That time allowed us entry onto the threshold of domestic life in the Kacch, a world so separate and dissimilar to what we had absorbed from the West. It was home in a way that I had never before experienced, surrounded by gardens, flowering trees, and birds. Our son became a close companion to one of the men who took care of the orchard and grounds, and they were inseparable, wandering barefoot about the groves all day, tending to the irrigation and pruning and gathering *nimbu* or coconut for drinks: this was Bapu, an elderly *kshatriya* of the Jadeja clan. Max and Bapu built what we called the Tortarium, a pen made of stone in which we kept a collection of tortoises of various sizes and age, bringing them home from our walks or journeys and feeding them expensive cucumber. Sometimes Bapu would appear with a new member for the *ménage* that he had found in the grounds, and Max would be delighted. The name of Kacch itself in folklore is said to derive from the shape of the province, in that it is similar to the shape of a tortoise, a *kachbo*.

Guided by sagacious Bapu, Leanna discovered a large old tamarind tree to the north of the house where a family of demure owls lived, and she often spent afternoons beneath its shade; there was a ruined cottage nearby where she used to sit outside and read or write or merely watch.

I sometimes used to walk the domain at night in the dark, often pausing outside that cabin in the small hours before dawn, loving the deep stillness of the air and the many delicate sounds of palpable blackness with its discreet nocturnal lives.

It was only through our contact with a few uncommon people—those who became our close friends during this time—that *all* our comprehension of Kacchi life developed. There was, on the one hand, a world that we viewed and observed and occasionally participated in, and on the other hand, there were those several companionable and really considerate individuals who made these engagements and connections possible for us. During these years I learned so much, not only about the region but also about the nature of friendship, about the possible exchange of emotion and amity between those with whom we had little geographical, historical, or experiential community. All this, of course, played itself out upon a scene where change was rampant and often brutal in its force, and all of us were acting during that brief time fully aware of what was vanishing, as we attempted to grasp or secure a few instants that would reassure us that all was not soon to be lost. It was an unusual time, emotive and receptive and generous, and for me, a most wonderful and thrilling period of human association.

Leanna and I struggled not on a daily basis with our exertions to formulate some kind of identity for ourselves whilst living in the Kacch, but on an hourly basis; for every minute was an endeavor to come to some terms with ourselves and the details of a resurgent self-awareness. In America, when I first went to live in that country, I had gone through similar efforts towards trying to comprehend my social environment, but there, my mental energy had been directed towards trying to understand the architecture and literature and painting, the history of the country and of its family systems and what it meant to be Bostonian.

Whereas in the Kacch, what Leanna and I experienced on a much lesser and diurnal basis was more a question of emotion rather than of knowledge. We were always in search of a feeling of pause, a sense of rest, of tempo that had relaxed momentarily so that it could be shared with others and mutually received: instants when our persistent marginality would dissolve. This was not complicated, but it was profoundly enigmatic. Returning homeward one day from one of our long surveys with Razul, he had played some music on the car radio, and suddenly and briefly I recalled the vivid feeling of connection, of being at one with both place and society. Such instants were rare, when those seemingly inflexible boundaries collapsed and the invisible borders that separated us from our larger social and historical situation were lost; for then there was some brief joining, some conjunction of emotion as we shared a sense of moderate pleasure in the song and melody. Anxiety faded away as did incomprehension, and later, whenever we would hear such music again, that tenuous experience of community and concord returned.

During that early period when we were striving to fit into our new world, there were two men who became our special patrons in the Kacch, who extended much particular kindness and hospitality to our days, months, and years in that region; our friendship with them was of a different nature from our friendship with others, and it was thanks to their introductions that we were able to gently and discretely slip into Kacchi life. The first was His Highness the Maharao, and then there was Mr. Shah, a retired Jain businessman and our host at Jalaram Bag. Both were autochthons, born solely of the Kacchi terrain and with virtually no comprehension of Western culture or place, their minds being formed and colored by their own topography and world.

Since the sixteenth century, Kacch has been an integrated polity ruled by a royal court from Bhuj, although the British East India Company arrived formally and forcefully in 1815. Kacch possessed its own mint and issued silver and copper specie, and at Independence, Kacch was one of only a few states to be still fabricating its own coinage. In 1947, Kacch was one of the senior-most of the hundreds of princely kingdoms that existed within the new Indian state and was ranked—according to British *imperium*—with a seventeen-gun salute. There are only a total of four Maharaos in all of contemporary India, and nowadays they have no formal political power nor official standing, but only status. Pragmulji III succeeded to the title—for there is no longer any throne or jurisdiction—in 1991 and now lives principally at his palace on the verge of Mandvi. We would often visit him and his Maharani at Vijay Vilas and sit and talk in the shade of one of the enclosed terraces, sipping chilled *chas*. He would be barefoot and stylish and regale us with stories about his predecessors and boyhood or his reproval of contemporary moves in diplomacy. Sometimes the Maharani would join us, and occasionally we would take a meal together in their great dim dining room.

A prudent and subtle man, the Maharao presently spends much of his time on tour about the district, maintaining links with a few old landowning families, the brotherhood or *bhayad*, who were at some point in the past founded by cadet and fraternal elements of the royal line. There is a movement at present among these people in the countryside for Kacchi *Rajya*: for Kacch to become politically distinct from Gujarat and to be governed from its own capital at Bhuj rather than from Gandhinagar, the administrative center near Ahmedabad, and the Maharao spearheads this movement. Ironically, this separatist ideal is now beginning to appeal to Moslems due to the prejudice that obtains on the mainland against their community. For centuries the rulers of Kacch had worked in close alliance with the *bhayad*, the lineal association of *kshatriya* chiefs of the Jadeja clan, and great power was originally dispersed among these eminent figures, until the British lion arrived and usurped the Indian tiger in 1819.

Up till then, Kacchi polity had been divided among a threefold grouping: there had been the approximately three hundred and fifty *khalsa* villages subordinate to the one ruler; there were about four hundred villages divided up amongst the domain of the *bhayad*; and then there were about one hundred *thanodhar* villages that were distributed among temple and such possessors. Income for these administering bodies had come not only from the land holdings but also from the levy of customs duty on both terrestrial and coastal transports. The East India Company initially cultivated a more feudal system, favoring the *bhayad* until the latter part of the nineteenth century, when the English began to support a more singularly potent and central Maharao. By the time Pragmulji acceded, however, influence had again shifted, and the landed political force had been supplanted by the new strength of mercantile and business groups with their more corporate chieftains and, of course, by Nehruvian democracy.

The Jadejas, the Maharao's clan, had migrated eastward into the region from Sindh many centuries before the present. Once, rule in the Kacch had emanated from a fortified town called Virani, which had been in the west of the region in the area of Lakhpat, and in those days the Indus had still run in its old course and there was no Great Rann as we presently know it. Nowadays there is great charm and natural beauty to that extreme area, but it is essentially a poor and deserted place where isolated Jaths live with their camels and flocks. In time, as the various chiefs increased in power, rule became more central and widespread and was refounded at Bhuj, traditionally in 1549, when the Rao Khengarji drove a metal stake into the earth, still be seen to this day. This was the family into which the present Maharao was born.

Pragmulji III, who is probably the last Maharao of Kacch, was born three years later than L.D. Shah, in 1936. He became a good friend to us during those years that we spent in the district, and I spent many a genial

hour in his company discussing contemporary India and listening to him
recount details and stories from his long life in the territory. Now in his
seventies, the Maharao speaks about time giving him the slip. His mother
passed away in 2000, and a year later the earthquake struck the region;
he has one remaining brother, whom he completely and absolutely dis-
owns. Nowadays, since the Maharao no longer holds any formal political
position, his life is concerned with the Jadejas and their coherence in a
situation of gathering and unscrupulous modernity; he is also sincerely
engaged with the public aspects of Hindu practice, and in this latter role,
Pragmulji actively maintains the *Rajvada*, the traditions of royal princi-
pality, which he received from his ancestors during childhood. He also
plays a leading part in many temple rituals in and about Bhuj, at Mata-
No-Madh, and at a few other sites where Momaya Ma, the tutelary deity
of the Jadejas, resides.

Before he became Maharao, Pragmulji had worked for ten years in
the pharmaceutical industry, living first in Delhi and then in Kolkata.
When he came to the *gadi* or throne in the early 1990s, Pragmulji had two
specific aims: one was to ensure the greening of the Kacch and an increase
in forestation, and the second was to promote Kacchi *Rajya*. These have
been the two lamps that he has persistently held before himself since that
moment of *abhishek*, his coronal anointing.

He is a tall, strong-boned man who sways with altitude as he walks.
His wife, the Maharani, comes from a family whose former dominion was
in eastern Bengal, at Tripura, an ancient region just to the south of where
Harshraj's wife had been born. The Maharani and her husband had first
met in Delhi and were married in 1957. She was always charming and
engaging with Leanna and me, asking me about my various works and
about my book on the Sanskrit women of the *Mahabharata*. The Maharani
possessed a light-hearted elegance, and even in a cold pouring rain she
managed to maintain an easiness of spirit and bearing. I recall one such
day when we had been invited to the sanctuary of Pragsar and the monsoon came down, turning the paths and tracks into deep glossy mud; Pri-
tidevi in her green *sari* and delicately heeled shoes was thoroughly genial
and smiling, whilst we were cursing the weather. She and Pragmulji must
have been a astoundingly handsome and companionable couple when
they had been young and first in love, and photographs of them from
those years still emanate a certain romantic sensibility.

In the old days of Kacchi monarchy, the king would have had two
wives, one who had been chosen by his father and one chosen by the

mother. In practice, the groom would not attend at the marriage ritual itself and the brides would be wedded to his sword, which had been sent to the bride's household; only later would nuptial rites be performed at Bhuj. The prince would not visit his wives on their marriage night but would allow them to determine between themselves as to who would be the first to enjoy their mutual spouse; it was the girl chosen by the father, however, who became the senior wife. In the eighteenth and nineteenth centuries, one of these wives would usually be recruited from the Jhala clan in mainland Gujarat, to the east and one from the house of Sodha in Sindh, to the west.

Pragmulji had grown up into a sanguine world of ceremony and ritual, both Hindu and courtly. That microcosm of display rapidly vanished after Independence, and yet the impress remains today upon his being, and he stands profoundly Hindu in spiritual matters and is precise and careful in social manners. It is difficult today to comprehend what such a ritual life must have entailed for a royal youth, both intellectually and emotionally, but one can just apprehend that old order now by the style with which he bears himself, always with a sense of occasion and dignity and with a motion of grace towards others, especially women and guests. Such moderate *politesse* is unusual nowadays, especially in its lightness and ease. The Maharao was always very gentle and engaging with Maxim and often spoke to me about the importance and nature of well-conducted paternity. He commissioned a specially made boy's spear for Max with his name engraved on the blade, complete with a beautiful sheath, and promised him a sword when he was older. He also had a lighthearted and amiable way with Leanna, and they would tease each other frequently.

We sometimes spoke about the situation of princes in India, both in the past and the present, for even when British command held sway, much of the sub-continent remained under direct rule and about a third of the India had been ostensibly governed by more than six hundred princely states.

"Change is the nature of life," His Highness used to say. "Everything changes, and there is no utility in lament. We must behave decently and kindly, that is all. I am not a serious man, you know."

Yet he was seriously Hindu; that to me was his mainstay. Pragmulji's knowledge of Kacch was unique, and I learned much from his conversation and in his company. This was a knowledge that could not ever be replicated, although members of the *bhayad* attempt to maintain those habits and practices a little longer into this new century, but it often appears artificial or sentimental. Pragmulji knew the Kacch and each of its villages in a way that I do not think anyone else will ever apprehend, and this knowledge was tempered with a gentle sagacity and shrewdness. He had grown up surrounded by staff and court, but in his early years he also enjoyed the unusual experience of having not only a father and grandfather, but also a great-grandfather to advise and train him. Four princes at one time, all in their different palaces at Bhuj: that was a period in his life that Pragmulji often recalled when we were sitting together at Vijay Vilas, in that open room at the rear of the building overlooking the grounds, with their empty ponds and the lawns being trodden by peafowl and foxes. Of all those mentors, he had been closest to his grandfather and spoke of Vijayrajji with affection. Curiously, it was thanks to Pragmulji that I understood the *Mahabharata* much more intimately and surely: it was through His Highness's illumination and demonstration of present *kshatriya* life that I comprehended the epic and heroic culture—as given in the poem—more fluently, for he *knew* that old reality.

As soon as Pragmulji had been born in the City Palace, the old Prag Mahal of Bhuj, his grandfather, who had been entertaining his kin—three princes from the state of Wankaner on the mainland—immediately took to the road—the only road in the Kacch then had been the narrow unpaved highway between Bhuj and Mandvi—and went to feed the newborn child with its first intake of worldly fare. Then a delighted Khengarji, his great-grandfather, who was then ruling, caused the jails to be opened and declared the boy to be his ultimate successor, something that could not be altered.

My most vivid recollection of the Maharao came from a ritual in which he and the Maharani participated, at the Rudramata temple on the outskirts of Bhuj. Maxim and I attended as guests, arriving early and wandering about the decorated precinct. Several thousand people were present, and at the beginning of the ceremony, we followed the royal couple as they made their entry into the large courtyard, through a crowd which was showering him and us with flowers and chanting, whilst a small lithe old drummer—a Garasia Jath—beat out a powerful rhythm. It was a hot day, and the noise and heat and compression of cheering people were overwhelming. The Maharao was patently happy as he slowly proceeded, glancing around and followed by one of his staff, who showered notes of money upon the crowd. His dignity, nonchalance, and his pleasure at the occasion was obvious. In the Sanskritic ritual world, a sacrificer must always be accompanied by his spouse, and the Maharani gracefully stood at his side throughout the prolix rites.

At first the couple performed lengthy *puja* at the shrines to the side of the main temple, sitting cross-legged on the stones as a priest led the ceremony. Then, inside the temple itself, the ritual went on for another hour: an hour of heat and perspiration in a small dark area crammed with devotees—mainly Rabari women—where the air was dense and heavy with clouds of sweet moist incense. The agile and simian drummer was busy all the time, beating out a short, intense, and insistently loud rhythm. In the mature days of the early nineteenth century, according to the carefully detailed travelogue of Marianna Postans—which remains even today, two hundred years after the *Random Sketches* were written, one of the best books about the Kacch—a buffalo had been sacrificed in the courtyard at this point in the year. Now the focus of the ritual was the covering of the statues of the deities—Rudramata and her three sisters—with *patri* leaves and then catching them in a shawl as they fell off the stones. As we all crowded into the sanctum of the temple, the concentration of noise and heat and proximate humanity within that small dark airless space was overpowering. I felt transported back to some royal office of long ago, and it was as if the twenty-first century had suddenly receded and was no longer present. Those were very pure and colorful moments, powerful in sensation.

Afterwards, everyone sat around on the steps outside, exhausted by heat and noise, whilst the Maharao himself attended the drummer, who consumed a ceremonial meal on the ground before him as an emblem of their relationship. The tired couple then departed in their automobile whilst Maxim and I remained for a while, somewhat dazed by the procedure that we had just observed. I knew that we would never witness such an event again, that this sudden glimpse of a beautiful and ancient world was probably not to reoccur and such instants would soon become extinct, for that world was already poised in crepuscular light. I shall always remember the Maharao as he was on that day, as he delicately made his way through the crowd and then carefully performed the service: there was a strength and a force of belief in it all that had no need of material effort.

Jagdish—our latest driver, as Razul had gone to work in Bhuj—was waiting outside the temple grounds, sitting on a wall with a newspaper in hand. He was engrossed by the news of bombings in Ahmedabad, and Maxim and I strolled past him along with the exiting crowd. We made our way to the left and stood within an old *chattri*, looking down upon the multitudinous people, observing their laughter and happiness and colorful holiday spirit. Suddenly I felt a tap on my thigh and turned to see a beggar crouching low beside me; in fact it was an old and disfigured leper who was touching my leg with the stump of his hand, for the fingers were no more. Only once before had I seen a leper in the Kacch, a dirty young fellow in the bazaar at Mandvi, and I had made a point of following him in order to give him rupees. Beggars were rare in the Kacch, and usually I would make a small offering, but for lepers I always gave plentifully. Theirs was perhaps the most awful and sorriest of lives, for no shred of hope remained to them and no one wanted to participate in their destitute pollution. Sadly, I knew that no matter how much I gave, some voracious predator would probably steal it from them, yet nevertheless I always offered what I could even though it was hopeless. The memory of that suppliant figure, so crushed and deprived by life, with his ragged uncleanliness and ignominious impoverishment and the near mindless anguish in his eyes with their outcaste stare, minutely qualified my images of that day.

We accompanied Pragmulji on other ritual occasions when his non-secular position was called upon, as when he would officiate at the annual *Nagpanchami* festival, or, after good monsoons, at a thanksgiving rite at the Khengarji dam or the Vijay Sagar, when all the old *thakurs* would appear and there would be a drummer along with the usual customary paraphernalia. Maxim always loved those occasions, was fascinated by the ceremonies.

The last occasion when we met with the Maharao was out in the east of the province in the Wagar region, at a Rabari *mela* at Ravechi, a temple that legend associates with the Pandava heroes of the *Mahabharata*. On that day, after many long hours of driving towards the place, we encountered Pragmulji in a small room next to the main village temple; he was discussing Kacchi *Rajya* with an assembly of men who were sitting at his feet upon the floor. Outside, the day was extremely hot and aromatic and the atmosphere of the fair was heavy with dust and noisy with the sound of thousands of strolling people—families and children—and the clamor of loud recorded music that issued from the many stalls where bangles and cheap jewelry and plastic toys were on sale. There was one booth that sold camel equipment, and there were several cutlers, vendors of knives and various kinds of tempered blade, as well as many sellers of iconic materials, pictures and models of deities. Beside the temple of Ravechi-Mata was a small tank where turtles basked and waited to be fed with food by the pilgrims; the pond was covered with lotos flowers, and it was odd to see so much water in such a desert setting.

The Rabari were outfitted in their gaudy and embroidered finest, and the young men especially were like peacocks on display, such was the beauty of their brilliant festival clothing, their studded shoes and their shawls, waistcoats, and bags. A tremendous happiness was about the place, filtering the heat and the dust and noise as crowds of families wandered and laughed. The scene was like a picture taken from the Wessex of Hardy, such was the purely rural tone of mirth and communal enjoyment. Ravechi was at the edge of the desert on the way towards Dholavira, and it was a dry and treeless spot with no shade, yet the day was genial and genuinely pleasurable, with much humor and singing and the eating of casual and special meals.

Once again there occurred one of those rare occasions where we were far removed from modernity and its bounding and implacable lines of commerce, and as we drove homeward that evening—for hours and hours along the thin sandy roads—I felt that something was visibly vanishing before our eyes, that a beautiful and harmonious and antique world was fast disappearing, crumbling as if it were formed only of exquisite dust. It was not sinking away like the sun departing at evening, but that world was retreating and dissolving and its presence would soon no longer be visible. It would remain there, hovering about Kacch, but would not be apparent, and we were witnessing its ultimate and most lovely recession. Pragmulji was the touchstone of all that, and I admired him for not succumbing to melancholy at its imminent demise, for he always carried himself with such easy *brio*. I asked Jagdish later where the thick and bulky ivory bands that were worn by many Rabari women came from. "Oh, Sindhi," he replied, without hesitation. Now, elephants must have disappeared from the Sindh much more than a century ago, as did the rhinoceros, which once inhabited the Indus region. That frontier that had been rudely demarcated at Independence, separating Sindh and Kacch, had little reality for these people; it was something official and artificial. Many Moslem villagers living in the Banni region still have family members who reside on the other side of the Rann, and even today young men will still make that journey at night in order to rejoin kinfolk. For Jagdish, Sindh was merely local, even though the iron wire of an arbitrary border now made safe travel impossible: that frontier is only a theoretical line for them but is made dangerous because of army patrols. As Keki Daruwalla wrote, describing a young woman who had crossed the Rann in order to be with her lover: "For her it meant just a shift in dialect, a smear of Kutchi added and a little of Sindhi sandpapered away." The bracelets worn by the Rabari women that day signified an old connection of landscape, a former living tissue of earth where they had once resided and that had been drawn away from them by a rapacious modernity.

On another occasion one chilly February afternoon, Maxim and I, again with the ebullient Jagdish, had halted in the town of Rapar in order to find something to eat. Suddenly the press of the crowds—we were on the main street—began to move unusually, and we realized that a partially armored automobile of the Border Patrol Force was being surrounded and its uniformed passengers insulted and harassed; people were kicking the car and banging the roof. My reaction was to instantly leave, but both Max and Jagdish were keen to watch. Two young men had been apprehended by armed and seriously countenanced soldiers, and the vehicle was attempting to depart before the crowd became too large and aggressive. "Infiltrators," said Jagdish. "Sometimes they bring in explosives across the border."

That elegant world of Pragmulji, propitious, ingenious, beautiful in its colors and simplicity, was withdrawing from time; all that he presided over now was his great and unique knowledge. It was as if the deities were retreating, sadly and softly lamenting as they hovered, inhabiting the air above their territory, murmuring in low and somber *prosopopeia*, tones of sorrow and compunction. Indra and Rudra, those old and ancient divinities, were removing their affection as they were edged out by a trespassing human and technological world that paid neither interest nor solicitude to what was natural and terrestrial. In my mind's eye, I could observe those unearthly figures walking off into the dust of evening, going into the haze and dusk, not departing but simply fading from view, grieving for humanity's hubris and dismissal.

Pakistan was snarling away across the border—a completely unnatural boundary marked out by a bureaucratic Commission who paid no respect to human community nor to terrain—and terrorist bombs were being timed to explode in Surat, Jaipur, and Delhi, and there was soon the awful and dastardly attack on Mumbai. Not so long ago three terrorists had been shot by the police during an encounter at the village of Paya, near the Dhand. Similarly, titanic China was gathering strength to the east, uneasy about its limits, and America, who had never quite been an ally of India, was upsetting the equipoise of power in that part of the world with its belligerent clandestine policies in Afghanistan and the Swat Valley. All this made up for a containing vessel of time that was fractional and breaking. The small and traditional era that we had glimpsed at Ravechi that day and at other like places would merely leave its potsherds upon the earth, its bits of jewelry or a few illegible coins; its stones would gently fall down and fissure, and the happiness of all those lives, their extraordinary efforts and work of survival, would no longer exist.

Yet some invisible trace would continue to inhabit the region, as if the atmosphere itself were humming or the stars at night emitted a slight odor or perfume come from that time. A mild dust would cling and adhere about the transparent and spherical soul of all those myriad human days, as their thirst, their labor, their ideals, beliefs, and loves, all their detailed and gorgeous attire, all would vanish outright. Leanna and I had merely glimpsed it through a briefly open window. Pragmulji, even in his own words, was one of the final tokens of such society, and as a devoted Hindu he accepted this with mildness and ease. I am not sure if the Maharani did, for I think that this decline of a life troubled her somewhat and she remained faintly anxious. The Rabari themselves did not care, for they were not a conceptual people: like all wanderers and nomads, their sense of self was too strong and dynamic and there was never any question of doubt or hesitation, for they were naturally resilient and flexible.

"Nature," His Highness once said to me, "is the most powerful of overlords. Our human purpose is to complement nature, and to do that we must assist and protect it. We must blend with nature if we are to survive. Nowadays nature requires us to help it to preserve itself. In order not to perish we must consider ourselves to be only a small part of nature; man has often made enemies with man, and now he makes an enemy of nature. There is never any progress without peace," he added. "To live is to keep moving, and movement is eternal delight ... that is all."

Our second great associate and friend in Kacch who patronized us during that incipient time when we were trying to settle was Mr. Shah, on whose farm we lived and in whose company I traveled about much of the district, speaking publicly, listening, planting trees, reciting mantras, and visiting schools. I also spent many hours in conversation with Mr. Shah, just as I did with His Highness. These two men became our principal interlocutors during that early residence in India, and I grew deeply fond of their company. We first met Laksmichand Devji Shah years ago when we were visiting the area north of the port of Mandvi, when I was trying to gather material for my study of contemporary aspects of *Mahabharata*. Leanna had heard about the architecture of some small houses that had been constructed on his land, and we went in search of them one rainy Sunday afternoon on our way back from a *mela*. Eventually, thanks to Razul, we found the place and woke up our future host from his afternoon *siesta*. He sat on a swing drinking tea with us on the third floor of his farmhouse, telling us about his work, his ideals, and his life.

When Mr. Shah's family had migrated from Dhumra—a village west of Bidhada—to Bombay in the mid–1930s, the young boy had traveled by bullock cart to the port of Mandvi in order to take the steamer down the coast. In those days there were no metaled roads in the Kacch; there were only tracks that crossed the desert and ran from town to town. Then, economic life in the region was virtually pre-monetary, for there existed little cash, and goods and services were simply remitted or exchanged, each community being tightly bound by its own members. A great number of pastoralists lived in the Kacch during those years, and there were more kine than there were human beings. Partition in 1947 did not affect the area, except to establish a closed border that hindered those migrant flocks and herds in their progress of seasonal grazing. There is a deep nostalgia now among the Jath people of that region for the days when the border did not exist and they could drive their animals throughout the entire region; even Mr. Shah spoke about that earlier time and its unconstraint with wistfulness.

As a young man he made his way in business in the thriving city Bombay, working first in the grain trade and then in life insurance. His family found him a wife from another village in the Kacch, and they had one son, Suman, whom we always visited whenever we were in Mumbai. Mr. Shah returned to the Kacch only late in life, in order to organize the good works for which he is nowadays renowned.

Many of the present Jains in Kacch probably migrated into the district in the nineteenth century—if not earlier—from Rajasthan, when conditions there had been bad due to a prolonged lack of rainfall. Then those communities were not Jain, but they converted to Jainism when they settled in their new homeland. Before that time they had probably wandered into Rajasthan north westwards up from the Sindh. I noticed again and again, especially with old Jain monks, that they all possessed a singular and ancient visage: their faces were almost identical to the faces painted to illustrate early Jain literature, the pictures decorating the words and margins of old palm-leaf texts, illuminating the narratives. Those paintings, after the cave paintings of Ajanta, mark the beginning of the figurative tradition in Indian pictoral art, and it never ceased to amaze me when I met such people how their features had not changed in millennia. Mr. Shah was like that, for at certain times of the day, usually in the early mornings or evenings, his facial appearance seemed distant and unworldly, his countenance being exactly like that in the old illustrated texts of, say, the poet Hemacandra. It was always an uncanny moment for me to witness that timeless physiognomy of an ancient *pandit*.

L.D. Shah is today referred to throughout the district as a *Captain of Trees*, a title that the Maharao first bestowed on him, and since 1995, he has been running an organization called Koti Vrksh Abhyan from the date farm at Bidhada: his aim being to forest the whole region. Hundreds of thousands of saplings have been planted during this period and protected from cattle and famished goats by his celebrated tree-guards with their distinctive design. Hundreds of *smrtivans*—small fenced remembrance gardens or plantations—have been established, stocked with young trees, and Eco-Clubs have been introduced into dozens of schools throughout the province. All this is his sole achievement.

"Originally my plan was to organize the planting of *lakhs* of trees and to arrange for the irrigation of these," he said to us on that first meeting. "Now I only plant ideas; my work is educational and moral. Trees cleanse the atmosphere, like lungs, and India's population has increased about four times in half a century whilst the forested area has been reduced by five or six times. In 2006," he said, "at a village wedding of some friends, I sponsored a simultaneous marriage of a pipal and banyan tree. This led to great interest in tree-planting, and within weeks more than a thousand new trees had been established on the outskirts of the town."

Outside his office were ranks of saplings, and later, when we were staying there with him, dozens of boys on bicycles would arrive during the course of an evening to depart with these small trees and seedlings, planting them about the neighborhood. As a Jain who has retired from business in Mumbai, Mr. Shah—now often accompanied on his programs by myself and sometimes Maxim—devotes his time and much of his personal fortune to the greening of the Kacch. He is constantly on the move, speaking at schools and to the boards of the new industries that have come to the district.

"It is our duty to give back to society," he said at that first meeting. "I began in the village of Dhumra when I returned a few years ago and planted tens of thousands of trees. Now I operate throughout all the counties or *talukas*. Two years ago I distributed to every village school the essay "Letter Written In Two Thousand And Seventy," by the President Abdul Kalam. It is about diminishing hydraulic resources and how industry and global warming are vitiating the customary and conventional life and resources of Kacch. Since the earthquake," he said, "so many companies have come here, subsidized by the government. Only fifteen kilometers from Bidhada, a gigantic electricity generating plant is being constructed by Tata. Adani is building another similar factory five kilometers away on the same coast; it is being constructed by two thousand Chinese, and the coal-fuel will be imported from Indonesia. The Rabari village of Tunda Vandh is surrounded by these noxious giants, and the people cannot survive living as they have for centuries. It is a major tragedy. This is apart from the fly-ash and the carbon monoxide that will be produced and the acidification of the monsoon rains that is going to pollute and wreck our terrain and vegetation for miles. Already, the largest cement producer in India is situated in the Kacch, near Lakhpat. We do not need more monsters like that."

For years Mr. Shah has been organizing the distribution of millions of seeds to schoolchildren accompanied by printed instructions for the development of vegetable plots, and his teams have been visiting the schools and teaching the skills of kitchen-gardening. His was the first farm in Kacch to practice water conservation techniques by means of well-recharging; now more than twenty-five thousand wells in the district have been recharged. He has promoted water harvesting, by example and by demonstration, and his farm was one of the first in the area to employ drip-irrigation methods. He has written many dozens of articles for the regional and Gujarati press during the last decade, always pressing home the details of his one central point: reforestation is an absolute necessity. When Rajasthani bosses planned an invasion of charcoal-burners into the Kacch two years ago and they began to uproot the vegetation and denude an already barren and sterile landscape, Mr. Shah was at his desk for many hours a day writing articles and speaking on the telephone, trying to galvanize action against this scourge. A great deal of his time still goes into lobbying the Collector's Office and government departments in Bhuj, initiating awareness and always pushing for dialogue. He is one of the few genuine activists and philanthropists who operate in the district today, and the Maharao always spoke of him with great admiration and affection. I once wrote a piece about him for a Delhi magazine, which I entitled *The Green Jain*. Of all the people whom Leanna and I met in the Kacch, only he and Judy Frater, an American egalitarian and activist who works with Rabari artisans, were thoroughly tireless and unselfish in their boundless *largesse* towards the community.

"I have changed very little myself," Mr. Shah said to us one day. "I have myself done very little. It is like the story about breaking the stone. One man can strike a stone a hundred times and not break it; then another man comes along and with one blow strikes the stone and it cracks. My work is like that, and soon that other man will appear and my work will only then be seen as effective. No one really cares now; that is the sad thing."

Mr. Shah practices the modest Jain belief of steady attention to nature. A series of small and precise efforts, he believes, will be effective in the long run and his projects will develop their own grassroots infrastructure, operating with their own staff. The government Forestry Commission— like so many federal departments—is miscreant and ineffective and is actually jealous at times of Mr. Shah's accomplishments. Of the first thirty villages in the Kacch that he began to work with, twenty-seven of them, once the trees began to develop, went on to win *Nirmal Gujarat* awards for civic accomplishment; no other province in India has achieved such standards.

"That is how trees affect people's thinking," says Mr. Shah. "It is the will, not the technical knowledge that triumphs. Planting trees is the basis and origin of all environmental work."

The changes that Leanna and I witnessed in Kacch since the *bhokam*, the earthquake, are suddenly accelerating geometrically and out of control due to the Delhi policy of allowing industries an unconstrained development spree. What was once for me one of the most beautiful, harmonious, and naturally balanced regions of India is swiftly and quite visibly becoming an industrial and unruled wasteland. It is only thanks to philanthropic radicals like L.D. Shah and Judy that this might just be curtailed, but as he says, someone else has to break the stone. Koti Vrksh Abhyan has only arranged the planting and watering of tens of thousands of trees, particularly of varieties that require little sustenance and maintenance, such as *baiyonissa*, and in many hamlets there are now avenues of shade-bearing neem trees and ashok; ponds and tanks are surrounded by gulmohar and laburnum, and school grounds are pleasant and green places for play and rest. This is all thanks to Mr. Shah's passionate drive, and spurred by the initiative of Abdul Kalam, he has shifted his focus more towards school-children. Our friend Harshraj managed to achieve similar results on the family land at Dhrangadhra, where it was not so much the planting that was effective, but the protection and support of saplings once they had become established: the watering and also guarding of young trees from hungry cattle and goats—until they were tall enough to survive on their own—had been crucial.

"The real work," says Mr. Shah, "lies not so much in the actual forestation activity, but in making villagers conscious and aware of how crucial
the problems are and how they might be resolved. We operate with ideas
that are good for everyone, and these projects have been organized without
any regard for denomination or caste. Many Moslems and *adivasis* have
become involved in the process; we work with anyone who accepts our
help."

I was always impressed by the extroverted and enthusiastic modesty
of Mr. Shah and by how he conducted his life consonant with Jain principles of nonviolence, *ahimsa*, and *aparigraha*: detachment from things
and the avoidance of acquisition. Jainism is probably the oldest continuously living religious culture in India today, and it has always expounded
a deep respect for the natural world and its manifest and unmanifest souls;
in its origins, like Buddhism, it was strongly anti–Vedic or anti-establishment.
It is expected that a decent Jain will not only conduct the latter years of
his or her life according to *vanaprastha*, renunciation of the social and
material world, but will also work towards the betterment of living beings,
particularly animals and other creatures of the natural world, which of
course includes trees. The lovely land of Jalaram Bag, on the outskirts of
Bidhada, contains more than forty acres of orchards and gardens, all of
which have been grown from seedlings; it is a sylvan paradise, a small and
idyllic setting where the creation of a microclimate has attracted a tremendous variety of bird life and insects. Most of the date and chikoo crop is
given away to the local schools, and Mr. Shah supports many children
from impoverished families so that appropriate clothes can be purchased,
books acquired, and fees paid. Generosity is the mark of this man, a kindness without ostentation that is fused with great curiosity and a most judi-
cious acumen. He is an astute observer of human weakness and of man's
capacity for cruelty and simony, a practical idealist, yet one who has no
qualms or illusions concerning human rapacity and ignorance.

"Trees are vital and necessary components for the maintenance of
water-retention in the earth as well as being critical producers of oxygen
and inhibitors of carbon dioxide," he once told us. "They supply fodder
and fuel as well as material for house and tool construction. Although the
Kacch consists of mostly desert and arid terrain, if a well is sunk and irrigation occurs, what was once a barren and sterile topography becomes
fertile: mangoes, banana, cereals, all manner of crops can be produced by
the mineral-rich soil if it is consistently watered, especially by drip-
irrigation techniques."

L.D. Shah has proceeded with policies that instruct villagers how to harvest the rains more efficiently and how to replenish their old and shallow wells when the monsoon arrives. He has worked relentlessly for the establishment of nurseries and tree stations, and once the wet season comes, he distributes among the local boys thousands of small plants for them to cultivate; the concrete tree-guards that often protect these young trees can be seen in villages throughout Kacch. Presently he is trying to establish in each settlement an allotment of ground that will supply the local crematoria with sufficient wood, the necessary cremation of the human dead being one reason for the constant denuding of trees in an area. Contrary to traditional Indian practice, Shah insists that on his own demise his body be buried and not burned, and for many people, including his own family, this is indeed shocking.

Nowadays Mr. Shah's policies—and he spends most of each day writing letters and telephoning various government agencies from the Collector down—are aimed at generating interest in plantation rather than in the actual business of planting. For a committed naturalist, the sudden influx of so much modern business during the recent decade has caused a great many problems: contamination of both earth and groundwater with chemicals, the despoliation of landscape by uncontrolled mining, and the pollution of the air from exhaust gases and fumes. This moral cost outweighs the material benefits, but it is a cost that is generally ignored and there is presently a massive destruction not only of the natural *milieu* but also of human and animal communities. It is not merely a case of the past being romanticized but completely ruined.

Recently, Mr. Shah has focused some of his attention and resources on a small school project in Bhuj. It is a program designed to help the children of rag-pickers, a community who live in a *basti*, a rough camp in one of the suburbs of the city. They were a kin-group of ten or so tents where blue plastic tarpaulin rooves were fitted onto low mud walls, and he and I and a local teacher visited the place one day in the company of a journalist. The families had been there for eleven years, having originally come down from Rajasthan in search of work; their water came from five kilometers away and was carried each day to the site. Inside the dwellings, the sandy dust was immaculate and spotless, and the few objects were carefully and neatly placed. The people were so small, though, especially the women, and yet the children, whom Shah was trying to draw into the school for a few hours each morning in order that they might learn how to read, held such spirit and mirth about themselves. Although the parents had no formal government identity, Shah's colleague had arranged with the postmaster in Bhuj for them to open savings accounts in order to develop the habit of saving a little cash: each week they would deposit five rupees. Some days later, at Jalaram Bag, Mr. Shah came and told me that thanks to his efforts and to the fact that our photograph had been in the newspaper that day, the Collector had agreed to the establishment of several concrete tanks and a supply of water to be given.

"Gently, gently," he said, "we try and give to those who have nothing a little dignity and a sense of their own being. This is a pilot scheme and if it works, then we shall look elsewhere."

During the early 1960s in Bombay, Mr. Shah encountered the then little-known Jain *guru* and mystic who is nowadays remembered as Osho. Shah became a disciple, sometimes visiting Osho at his camps in the Himalayan foothills, and he has since led a life whose regime has been one of simplicity and the pursuit of sure consciousness, both in its transcendental aspects and in mundane and quotidian life. This dimension to the thought and ethics of the man is crucial and underpins his more orthodox views of naturalism, for Mr. Shah has always been an individual who has tried innovate regardless of convention. Osho—who is now deceased—was a figure of synthesis and calculated irreverence, very much in the antinomian tradition of a modern-day Dionysos or a Siva. He was a man of great personal liberation and encouraged his devotees to pursue a way of decency and analysis on their path towards gradual illumination. Realizing that the true nature of consciousness consisted solely in absolute autonomy, Osho urged his followers to become aware of the qualities of desire and constraint, as this promoted detachment: for only along that axis would a clear soul become aware of itself and engage its own conscious trajectory, where the transparency of life became persistently apparent.

Mr. Shah has thus combined traditional Jaina practices with a highly alert and dynamic green politics, as well as devoting his inner life to more unworldly pursuits: these three strands of his being are inseparable. He is an unusual man, and his small estate at Jalaram Bag has grown into a center for the redevelopment of Kacchi territory. Working closely with other philanthropists in the area, like the Schroff family and the Vivekananda Research Institute at Mandvi, Mr. Shah has for nearly two decades carefully tried to reform his natal environment into something both viable and salutary. Our entry into his cosmos amused us both, for Leanna and I were at first so removed from that world if not actually awkward there, and yet in a strange way we fitted and I grew to be extremely fond of Mr.

Shah and was always ready to listen to him. Often of an evening he is to be found sitting outside of his house beneath the trees, surrounded by young men and women, talking about how anything is possible, if only one could become aware of what it is that we really desired and about how little we actually needed.

"The beauty of the world only amplifies the beauty of the soul within it," he used to say. "What happens between need and desire is often just a great desert which we waste our transitory time in crossing. There is really only a visible silence where meditation can recognize its desired effect."

"What is that?" I once asked.

"That, Mr. Kevin, is the only truth, and I have come to believe that nothing else matters; yet somehow I need to supplement this, to go further, but I do not know how to do this any more. Once, I knew; now I am not sure. Perhaps I shall rely on you," he added, smiling at me in his quizzical way.

I have long admired this uncommon and generous man, because for me—and to a lesser extent for Leanna—he represented someone matchless in our experience. No one else in the Kacch is as dedicated a naturalist as he is, and I spoke with no one, nowhere in the world in fact, who possessed such mental vision and diligent and assiduous powers of illumination.

"There is nothing left for me now except enlightenment," he once said rather playfully, and laughed.

I often wondered if he actually meant that, for certainly in his regime of meditation and spiritual exercise, he was intent on only furthering that direction in his life, and we often spoke about the properties or worth of enlightenment, what it actually meant or signified, for this was never clear to me.

"Enlightenment possesses no quality and no requirement and is out of time," he once said. "This is the joy of disillusion. Enlightenment is beyond morality as it is also beyond life and death. The enlightened one is a perfect witness and there are no distinctions. To *be* enlightened," he added with emphasis, "is to *be* compassionate, to love and not censure. That is the only necessity that an enlightened one experiences. All suffering, unless it is physical pain or starvation, is organized solely by resentment. You know that, Mr. Kevin."

"Enlightenment is a degree," he said on another occasion. "It is not an absolute. It is that weightless and transparent condition that occurs when illusion and emptiness are in equilibrium and it is without gravity.

Enlightenment is not a state, nor is it a process and certainly, it is not a category; there is no other destiny really, you know, apart from that one human desire for non-boundary."

I often went with Mr. Shah on his programs, both of us speaking publically on issues related to reforestation and ecological education, and I grew to like this man so much, for his deep commitment and liberality and for his infinite humanity, for his careful awareness of the contradictory nature of human life and how heartbreaking poverty could be. He often supported young men and women in their educational endeavors, paying for courses and tuition, or sometimes he would even pay for a whole school or village to have a new set of clothing so that they could attend classes in a more respectable fashion. He usually did this on the occasion of his birthday in June. There was a gentle and unassuming greatness about him which I esteemed. Very often he would embarrass Leanna, for he always refused to accept a gift; the only possible item which he could not resist was a curious dessert or an uncommon and delicious kind of date. He particularly enjoyed the fruit of Iraqi date-palms, which she would seek out in the bazaar at Mandvi.

Usually I would join him of an evening, either in his office or sitting on the teak chairs that we would carry outside, or if it was winter we would walk about the fields. Sometimes we would just sit and watch the young-sters of the farm, including Max, playing at a game of badminton, for Leanna had set up a net between the eucalyptus trees and had purchased shuttlecocks and rackets. Or he and I would sit together with Mr. Patel—Mr. Shah's agent who ran the farm—discussing a project to develop cistern construction in the region. Mr. Patel's daughter was soon to be married to a young veterinarian from Dhrangadhra, a ceremony that Mr. Shah was to support financially.

He was a robust sort of fellow and always impeccably dressed in a sparkling white *kurta*, and he wore large heavy spectacles that were rarely removed; in colder weather he wore thick jackets and a hat, as he disliked the cold. Now and again I would encounter him of an early morning in the gazebo, where he would sit and drink his tea and read the daily news-papers—he wrote for some of them himself—after his morning yoga and meditation at the *ashram* next door. That *ashram* had an underground chamber, an amazing and luminous place, lined with marble and designed for the inward direction of thought and transcendental process. Even I found the place effective and often visited its deep vibrancy, and Leanna used to take Maxim there and later, when she was born, our little girl. As he grew in years, Mr. Shah has turned more and more towards that world of the spirit, struggling to conceive the greater situation of the cosmos, much inspired by his *guru* and the old Jain traditions. I spent many an evening in that office or at the gazebo talking with him about the similitude and substance of truth. He used to conduct periods of silence, *mauna*, initially for only one day a week, but it soon increased to two days, and we often discussed the impression that that practice would leave upon him; for only silence allowed him to be truly honest with himself.

"Death is not the opposite of life," he once told me. "There is no annulment that occurs; rather there is only a slight change in perspective, if one is true. You know, Mr. Kevin, existence will always support those who are in pursuit of truthfulness, for their aim is true. All that remains in the world is what we give to others; what we keep decays."

Now in his mid-seventies, Mr. Shah becomes less concerned with the Kacchi world and his plantations and more preoccupied with this non-material world towards which he feels that his being is soon to be directed. His arboreal work is concerned with only one *ashram* now, in Wagar in eastern Kacch, a place sacred to the nineteenth-century *guru* Jalaram. That part of Kacch is dry and sandy, and there are few trees in the area and it is close to Ravechi. There was about Mr. Shah a profound gentleness that always endeared me to his presence and company: those conversations and confidences I shared with no one else in life. From his boyhood on, he had seen Kacch change so very much, from a thoroughly traditional and rural livelihood without roads, electricity, concrete, and without much human movement, to this friable, fragmenting, and often filthy noisy modernity. This disturbed him, firing his interior world and mediations towards a struggle for a more transparent, lucid, and ultimate reality.

The Maharao had once been close to Mr. Shah, and they had frequently worked together on the greening of the Kacch; now both in their early eighties, these men see little of each other as their lives become more domestic and less outward, more attuned to the otherworldly. There were also many other individuals who were close to us during that early period when we were attempting to settle in the district.

Once, some years ago, when the Maharao had been visiting us for tea at Jalaram Bag one chilly wintry noon when we all wore sweaters or shawls, as he departed he mentioned that he was off to meet someone with whom he hoped to develop Pragsar as a resort. This was the professional naturalist who had been living for many years in central India at the game reserve of Kanha, Jehan Bhujwala, a scion of the last Parsi family in Bhuj. He was planning to develop the indigenous life and conservation of the Pragsar land.

"Pragsar," His Highness had once said to us, "is a place where time passes gradually. It is the least changed area here and remains as all of Kacch was fifty years ago. I have held the orchard for more than half a century, and now the government wants to seize it."

Jehan had recently returned with his English wife and their two children to the family home in Bhuj, a beautiful old courtyard-house that had been badly shaken by the earthquake and that had been casually repaired. There remained only one other house in the city of similar design, which was across the street in the neighbourhood called Camp and belonged to his aged aunt Roda Boatwala. Bhuj in those nineteenth-century days had been a small walled town in the desert with a water tank and its many *chattris* on the outskirts, and all non–Hindus had lived beyond the perimeter. Camp had literally been the vicinity where the British had first settled, an area extraneous to the old town walls; it was where MacMurdo had established himself and his force in the early 1800s and where Mrs. Postans had stayed; a small British church—dedicated to the Scottish St. Andrew—was still there, with its nineteenth-century graves. Pragmulji introduced us to Jehan one day out at Pragsar, that very rainy day when the Maharani had been present at the tea picnic. We had all been invited to view the remains of a dead panther that had just been discovered. Leanna and Jehan's wife immediately became fast friends and would often visit each other thereafter; he planned to build a lodge at Pragsar and to take in guests who would help finance his conservation project to support the diminishing panther community. Jehan had many years of experience at Kanha, in Madhya Pradesh, working to maintain the tiger population and the forest; he and his wife ran a small and now quite famous residence there.

Like Mr. Shah and the Maharao, Jehan had also sprung from the earth of Kacch, and his family—former businessmen in the community who first came to the Kacch as agents for MacMurdo—had always been close to the Rao's court. Although he had grown up and been educated in Mumbai and although the Parsis were originally from Iran—migrating eastward in the tenth century—his emotions were deeply tinted by the household that he had inherited in Bhuj, with its many prints, photographs, and paintings of ancestors and their engagements with the Kacchi Raos. He had frequently visited Pragsar as a boy in the company of his parents, and there was something about the Kacch that was embedded far within him, which he lightly took for granted, and because it was engrained within his body and psyche and was inherent to his being, he was not really conscious of that bearing. He was elegant and Aryan-looking, not dark nor in any way Asian in appearance, and was quiet and reserved but sure of himself, possessing a certain ease and polish of manner. The natural world was his passion, as were his children. His wife, Katie, was fair in an English way, tall and strong and intrepid and brimming with humour. She used to return to England each year for several months with the boy and girl and missed her family and village in Wiltshire when she was not there.

Jehan planned to reintroduce varieties of grass that had long ago disappeared and also to bring back certain kinds of tree that had once flourished in the area. This was to be one of the last habitats, if not *the* last, for the Asian panther, much as the Gir Forest region in southern Gujarat was presently the only locale where the Asian lion now survived. Whenever we saw Jehan, he always spoke about "the courts," for the Gujarat government had been trying for decades to acquire the many thousand acres of Pragsar from the Maharao and affirm it for themselves. Jehan's plans were pendant upon a decision, and he spent days at Ahmedabad in the High Court listening to arguments.

Once, Leanna and I had visited the Bhujwalas at their house in town on the occasion of the Parsi new year or *Pateti*, which had then fallen in August. The lintel of the front door was garlanded with a necklace of marigolds, and Jehan wore the ritual cotton undershirt, a *sudra*, with a rope belt, the *kusti*, and his wife was also well-attired in white. In a genial and festive mood, we had walked down the main street of Camp, an unmetalled and muddy track through what was primarily nowadays a Moslem area, where only a few days prior the police had arrested one of the bombers who had planted many of the explosive devices in Ahmedabad that summer. Jehan's old house was now next to the largest mosque in the quarter, and the call of *muezzin* would often fill his rooms. That day we were going to the *Agiyary*, the Parsi fire-temple, one of the few that existed in India and certainly one of the very few that remained in the present world. The building was well preserved and maintained, a square and red-painted structure set in its own sparse grounds surrounded by blocks of flats; it appeared Victorian in design. Inside, an elderly lady—his aunt—was sitting upon one of many brown lacquered chairs that edged the hall; there were old portraits hanging high on the walls depicting former Bhujwalas, men who had founded and established the temple. Now, no one but old Aunt Roda attended the place, there were no ceremonies, and someone had to be paid to maintain and tend the sacred fire.

Like so many things that have no more relevance to the present day, the *Agiyary* possessed a charm and a dignity. Like the Rabari peoples or the panthers or the Maharao himself, times had changed and modernity was crushing, not simply encroaching but devouring all that stood in its historical way or maintained any connection with the past. Unfortunately, conservation often only produced fossils of strange and hybrid artifice and failed to sustain life, which was no longer viable and healthy. That cool morning, wearing little peakless velvet *topis* on our heads, we circumambulated the smouldering hearth and lit incense in the darkened fire chamber where the silver altar, the *afarghanya*, was kept; then we sat around in the entrance hall, either chatting or trying to imagine how it had once been. Jehan and his wife were happy that the Bhuj press arrived, and they posed for photographs; Aunt Roda was in the *Times of India* that day. The children played and Leanna took pictures of them, and that was it: a small moment had paused and then reconfigured and moved onward, and we had exchanged something amongst ourselves that no one else in Bhuj experienced.

The Kacchi Parsis had left the district when prohibition had come in after Independence, and alcohol, their business, was no longer a feasible trade. In Mumbai, where they, like the Jains, were now mainly established, the *towers of silence* where the Parsi dead had been exposed for centuries for sky-burial had become defunct. As the vulture population of India had suddenly fallen and vultures had become virtually extinct, the dead were no longer being consumed by these carrion creatures, and the ancient method of disposing of the deceased could not take place. Solar-powered crematoria had been installed but with little success. Again, modernity smothered the ancient ways as it galloped forward towards a new system of relation with the natural world, where technology replaced a former reliance, and like the panthers, the Parsis were being intruded upon in their life.

Another time, we drove out to central Kacch one morning with our driver, the *kshatriya* Jagdish, and waited at a prearranged junction for the Bhujwalas to join us. Having met, we then motored on towards a small village and left the vehicles and set off to climb the mountain—in fact a big hill—of Nanamo. This was the hill that MacMurdo had described as a *sugar-loaf* because of its distinctive shape; navigators would use its silhouette as a mark, for at sea it was visible long before the rest of the coast came into view. It was a hot day even though the monsoon had been and gone, and our ascent with the children was slow and steep. I had little Manki on my back, and someone from the village that clung to the base of the hill had shown us where the path was: he was a mason and also took us with great pride to show off his quarry, where he removed heavy lime-stone blocks for building, using a mechanical wire cutter. His three children accompanied us in our ascent all the way to the top.

The hill was volcanic in formation, and the brow was a hollow with two elevations, once the edges of the crater. On one point there was a military signaling station, and at the other edge, which is where we went, there were some small ruined shrines constructed of dry brown rocks. Incense and matches and coins were scattered about on the walls, and the shrines were dedicated to Lord Siva. We settled there for a while, resting and drinking water, looking out across the plain of Kacch and its desiccated apricot-colored light; far beneath us, the land was presently dyed a mute green after the rains. It was a very ordinary moment, with the children pattering about and asking questions and demanding food; Maxim had found a scorpion, and they were all examining it. We sat and gazed about the place, which was neither spectacular nor amazing—the view was not like that of Kalo Dungar nor Dhinodar, another old volcano— and below us, villages and fields were discernible and the region actually reminded me of northern Greece, of Thrace, because of its modern cultivation and visual order.

Near where we were sitting, a dead hawk lay upon the earth being eaten by ants and flies; nothing remained for long in that sultry air without immediately decaying. It was a fine place for a death, however, and I quietly admired the bird. Below us, lapwings were audible from the plain beneath us, and crows. Although the situation itself was beautiful yet unremarkable, I felt that in our ascent we had established the ground for possible amity and future companionship, having performed something together that had revealed small particles of humility and modesty. Walking with people always had such an effect, stripping one of pretence and manner, and from the indistinct surface of life and endless time, we had managed to distinguish a few charming instants, raising them up from a monotonous and indifferent tissue of days and years and breaking the membrane of nature's impulsive repetition, much like fish poking their heads above water and briefly noting another world.

We made our descent a few hours later, and I paused at the car with Jagdish and looked back at the mountain whilst the others went into the village and wandered about tidy and clean lanes; then I followed them. In one or two courtyards there were young girls sitting on the ground at looms, weaving long and decorative shawls. I loved that sound of a shuttle, its soft hiss and thrum and the clack of the loom frame: it was a noise that had not changed in millennia, and it reminded me of old days in Greece and hot afternoons when daughters would be weaving inside darkened shady rooms beneath high ceilings and the sound was audible as one passed through a village on foot. Presently in the powerloom factories and mills of Indian cities, air-jets or water-jets are employed to blow the woof through a warp.

I could not find Leanna and the others, so I returned to the car and sat with Jagdish, who was reading a newspaper: more terrorist bombs had exploded in Surat. I gazed back at the outline shape of Nanamo, which rose like a *cabochon* stone from the ground, and wondered if MacMurdo had been up there on the top—for he had wandered all over the Kacch— and speculated about what he had seen from that height. The personality of MacMurdo fascinated me; he had been such an unusual man and had died so young, succumbing to dysenteric symptoms, and for long I had been in search of his tomb, which apparently was located on the edge of the Rann near Adessar. In those few seconds, sitting with Jagdish, my mind slipped away from the present to another moment, to a view that I knew in my heart from a time before roads and wires and engines, when life was pedestrian and defined only by sunlight and rainfall. The silence of the world then was something I could always hear, and it was perhaps one of the reasons that the Kacch possessed me so forcibly: I could not withdraw from that sensation, for it was always with me along with those shadowy and monochrome scenes that I knew so well. That was the world where I truly lived.

Our ascent of Nanamo had nothing of the extraordinary about it, and yet it reconnected me to that private and interior world that I inhabited, alerting me as to its constant and shining nature. Gazing up at the hill then, I was peering through time, perceiving those gray forms. For me it had been significant that the Bhujwalas had accompanied us and we had shared an unusual experience, a mutual sensation of something unsaid and unspoken, and we had been witnesses together. Such glimpses away from the present were a particularly pleasant and satisfying emotion that I was repeatedly aware of in the Kacch: it was as if we were briefly released from time and that moment was absolutely demanding and complete, being far more compulsive than anything present. That was the Kacch that used to come and go about us as we moved upon its terrain, expanding and contracting like an invisible envelope, capturing our consciousness with its lucidity, imparting something tacit and implicit that I could never define, but which Leanna occasionally pinpointed with words. It was a world that both Mr. Shah and the Maharao took for granted, which is what made those men so remarkable for me. They, like Jehan, possessed such a view, whereas I had to reconstruct it.

The Bhujwalas became good friends, and we shared many days and events and conversations with them. On one occasion, Jehan joined Maxim and Jagdish and me on a ride out towards the west of Jakhau; we wanted to explore the area, which on the map was blank and without indication, probably because it was adjacent to the frontier. Leanna and Manki had stayed back at Jalaram Bag, as it was too hot for them to spend twelve or more hours in a small automobile being heaved along bumpy tracks; in fact, during that season, the two of them rarely ventured out at all, as the days were exceedingly bright. Driving up along the coast road, we eventually entered into what was a desert wilderness, undressed terrain with here and there great broken plates of stone lying upon the sand as if the earth had recently been twisting and moving; they were in fact petrified coral, dating from when the Kacch had been submerged in ocean. There were few birds and no sign of life, and now and then we passed an old shrine, about which hero stones were ranged as if sentinel. Once we passed an abandoned and broken fort that rose up out of the waterless dusty earth in the distance, but it was too hot to attempt to approach it on foot.

Earlier that morning we had paused on our way to visit the old stronghold of Thera; it had been much hurt by the earthquake but was still captivating to the imagination and utterly deserted. We pushed open a massive wooden and spiked gate and slipped within to another world. There were dozens of peacocks upon the battlements in attractive silhouette, and the place was more of a large caravanserai with a central miniature palace—reminiscent in design to Rohar. We wandered its rooms and terraces for an hour, charmed by the antique solitude and the many carved columns and painted ceilings, which were everywhere coated with a thick and chalky powder, like plaster. In what must have been a former *zenana*, Max came across a canvas basket full of ancient correspondence in large and portentous script, the folded letters being formally stamped and sealed with a beautiful sepia impression. Outside in a tank beyond the walls beside which Jagdish had parked and fallen asleep, old brahmins were bathing on one set of *ghats*, and to the left on another side, women were laundering and young girls were collecting their daily supply of household water in large polished steel or brass pots.

Later that same morning, we passed—far out in the desert—a gigantic mine where machines were removing lignite from the surface of the hills, scouring enormous valleys into the landscape, one of which had filled up with water and was now a small steep lake where flamingoes were browsing. In that desolation it was strange to see such an unearthly structure, for the towers and high buildings of the place appeared almost futuristic and fictional. These industries were in fact like small walled cities themselves, with their own schools and clinics and settlements of row-houses for the workers, all of which were walled off from the surrounding terrain. An hour later, thanks to Jagdish's navigation, we had left that behind and were reaching a coast of mangrove islets where camels were visible grazing upon a far-off shore. Here and there upon the stony sandhills, little reed houses of fine, almost Egyptian, proportion were situated, and at a large stone cistern, several young women were collecting water. They veiled themselves as we halted and approached. Leaving Jagdish to his newspaper, we set off towards the sea. It was a terrifically fiery day and the air was thick and heavy with glare; the ground was pebbled and particular with a rough mineral texture. Far off towards our right we could see the shape of what appeared to be tombs rising up from the ground. We crossed a deep gully, probably the course of a river for the few weeks of monsoon, and entered an area that was littered with hundreds of stony graves, obviously from long ago. The sharp rocks marking the burials were of a dark umber brown, delineating the head and the rectangular form of interment. It was odd, to be in such a barren and inhuman terrain and to come across such a profusion of nameless dead.

The tombs, three of them, were extremely beautiful and stood on a small mound beside the gully. They were of slightly different fabrication and were obviously built at different times, the oldest being from about six hundred years ago. Made of large, nearly square baked bricks of almost a foot in measure, they were domed and niched and had once been plastered. Their solitude, architectural dignity, and great size supplied them with an air of distinction and resilience. Inside the buildings were the raised enclosures of the deceased, possibly ship owners or sea captains, for the situation of the mausolea dated back to the days when Lakhpat— which was not too distant—had been a thriving seaport. On the surface of the inner walls were images in white outline of ships, graffiti incised into the plaster; the crypts themselves were deep in dung and stinking with a foul stale odor of bat pellets.

The only sound came from a profligate wind buffeting the outer walls, softly booming as if replete with centuries and thousands of eventless and repetitive seasons: here time was merely residual. In places the dome was cracked, from a succession of many earthquakes, I presumed, and through one particular fissure, two curious mynah birds were peering down as the blade-like rays of sunlight sliced into the dim curved space. I sat there in the oldest of the chambers enjoying the limitless quietness and the extraordinary repose of the deceased mariners as they continued to navigate in utter silence. In fact I quite envied their rest and grand equilibrium; it was in such contrast to the slow and detailed turmoil of our daily human effort. Only I had crouched and crawled and made an entry into the tombs: Maxim was outside, sketching the elevation of the buildings in one of my notebooks, and Jehan was sitting upon a rock with his binoculars, observing a thin yellow jackal that had inadvertently drawn near and then halted, shocked at the sight of humans.

It was too hot to remain there long, and we soon set off back towards the car; this time we altered our way in order to pass beside one of the reed houses belonging to a Phakirani Jath family. For me, these were mysterious and admirable people, sophisticated in their abjuration of acquisition and property; if I had the time, I would have loved to study their manners and livelihood and to have attempted to participate in some small way in their beliefs. Each house was fenced off with a line of driftwood, and at our approach, everyone vanished inside the building. At one house a young man came and shyly offered us some water but would not enter into conversation and maintained a deeply modest reticence; he was literally wide-eyed at our presence and persons.

Jehan and I, usually with Maxim, made several similar rural rides in that sturdy diesel-powered vehicle of Jagdish. I enjoyed Jehan's easy company and his sincere conversation; his knowledge of the natural world, especially of birds, was remarkable and, to me, almost unlimited. I also enjoyed his tales about life on the reserve at Kanha, for that world was his paradise; only recently, there had been a tiger wandering in their camp, and on another occasion, he had watched from some rocks as a small group of wild dogs actually attacked and killed a leopard. He loved the life of Kanha, but he and Katie were worried as to how to educate their two infant children. Jehan also loved the Kacch and was thoroughly saturated with his family inheritance and presence there, and their house at

Camp was full of portraits and mementoes of past Kacchi life. We often
spoke about how tough it was in the Kacch, socially, physically, climacti-
cally, and yet of how wonderful and beautiful its life was, for both of us
adored the place.

Several times did we venture towards the Chari Dhand of Banni, the
shallow lake area of many square kilometers that was central to the desert
region, where in winter, when the ground was flooded, tens of thousands
of migratory waterfowl would settle. Selim Ali, the great early twentieth-
century ornithologist and friend of a previous Maharao, had written exten-
sively on the area and its avian fauna. We used to drive to the village of
Chari, which had once, according to local legend, been a port, and then
went directly north onto the flat frugal sand of Banni. In two very old
maps that I possessed, one of which accompanied my edition of Arrian,
the sea in former times came all the way into the Kacch and the Banni
terrain was then a long thin westward-running peninsula, so it is possible
that the tale of Chari being the site of a mercantile harbor was correct,
just as Dholavira and also Surkotada—another Indus Valley city of Kacch
which had reputedly also been a marine *entrepot*—had once been nautical
stations.

One of our first visits to the Dhand had been in May, when the temperature must have been in the upper forties; the air was so hot as to be
deleterious, like a drug or alcohol, and three hours outside in that ambience left one with little judgement or mental finesse. I recall Max's excitement at the mirage that surrounded us, when suddenly out of the vibrant
spirituous fluidity of distance, a herd of several hundred camels
approached us, led by a single man, one of the Phakirani; all were slowly
and rhythmically pacing, floating upon the quivering light. Such drovers
lived essentially on milk and nothing else, a little rice perhaps, and it was
always amazing to see their faces, their unworldly desert expression, when
they passed us and abstractly nodded. During the cooler half of the year,
especially after monsoon if it arrived, Banni became verdant and green
with luscious sweeping grasses, and cattle were driven for many miles to
feed upon its benison and to fatten on the rich verdure. Then the Dhand
became an exquisite aquamarine and turquoise lake frequented by myriads
of migratory birds, and its waters—like a small sea—stretched far up
towards the mountain of Dhinodar.

At that heated time of the year, however, small tornadoes of mordant
dust wheeled about us like guardian spirits of place, whirling and dancing
like *génies*. Despite the temperature, there were larks out there, and once

we observed a pair of large tawny eagles pausing upon the earth. Here and there were small volcanic hills dark with the shale of trap, and what few plants existed were halophytic, able to bear the hyper-salinity of the soil. Foxes, jackals, and sometimes wolves, even desert cats, managed to exist in that exquisitely silent terrain; certain animals—like the fox—only imbibing the heavy dews and the metabolic water of mammalian blood. Jehan loathed the present Chief Minister of Gujarat for his keenness to develop the Banni as an industrial district, for he loved that terrain with a gentleness and passion.

Friendship in the Kacch—when we were so foreign and alien to the world, to the people, their manners, and their calendrical order of time, to the customs of agriculture and economy—friendship then held a special premium for us. In the West we took our amity and companions almost for granted, for there were always acquaintances to be had and communities where one could participate and talk and share ideas, but in the Kacch, living on the margins of traditional and old-fashioned society, we were very much alone, even though we tried to become Indian. Leanna, who was far more outgoing and social than I and who craved verbal community, found this lack of company sometimes trying if not emotionally disturbing: she required those exchanges for her emotional well-being.

I suppose friendship is founded upon a mutual experience of narrative, something that concerns time and event and some identity of affect; hence the nature of ceremony, when emotions are organized and made socially mutual and so binding. Values that are often obscured or shaded become apparent in the course of friendship, and differences in value are then respected rather than ignored. It is not only the common that makes for friendship but the appreciation of that which is *not* shared, and in this case amity bears with it a responsibility and a deference, an acceptance of what one is not. There is thus something profoundly humanistic about the nature of such friendship, in its centripetal and yet diverse manner. We always crave an intense fusion of equivalence and unity, but that becomes rare as one grows older and moves through time, away from the easy porosity of youth. Our practical solitude in the Kacch, where we belonged to neither clan nor religious community and where our ideas were so different in their historical nature and formation from those with whom we lived, our emotional connections then were something that I learned to appreciate with both a slowness and a care; otherwise no comprehension was possible. This was the old and humanistic pattern of amity, not usually practiced in the West nowadays, where community is often only of likeness.

Living in the Kacch taught me much about solitude in life and about how we lose our experiences and memories and yet continue to constantly reform ourselves. I find this paradoxical, and yet I am always amazed at how little we recall of situations and events as even the good things vanish: like love and affection and one's apprehension of truth, even our visions do not remain irrefrangible. We live with phantasies about friendship as we do about human love, and the reality concerns more what we do not receive than how we understand or comprehend, how our mind goes out and returns. It is that subtle reciprocity of emotion that ultimately counts and gives gravity or impetus to companionship, regardless of other experience or the more rational or historically received values; it is the mutually unspoken that really binds and the acceptance of those silent distinctions.

Another of our autochthonous friends during those years was a physician who lived with his brother and the brother's wife on the edge of Mandvi, just across the river: this was Dr. Pulin Vasa. His was an honest and mild soul, impish with the lightness of mirth. Prashant, his brother, also possessed a similarly quizzical humor, and whenever we used to visit their household, it was always to laugh. We had been introduced to Pulin some years before, one day after we had been inspecting the wreckage and ruins of an overgrown and vandalized British cemetery that had existed from the time of MacMurdo, two hundred years earlier; it was located among some fields near to the town. Our guide, a young schoolteacher, had told us to contact Dr. Pulin, an antiquarian who knew much more about the old and rather baroque-looking mortuary sculpture.

Pulin had been trained as a physician in Mumbai, but Kacch was his great passion, being the place where he had grown up as a boy. He remembered those days before electricity came to the land, when bullock carts were the means of transport and there were only narrow sandy tracks and no roads. He had one son who lived in Manhattan, whom he would travel to see each year, cramming the time with visits to museums, for he loved natural science. He was also a poet and an amateur archaeologist and had been—at the weekends—excavating the site of an ancient port for twenty years: a place called Nani Rayan, a mile or so inland from where the harbor of Mandvi now stood. Pulin had a *cabinet*, two small rooms without windows built upon the flat roof atop his house, which was a private museum where his finds were displayed on glass-fronted shelves. There he kept paleolithic tools, fossils of dinosaur eggs and long vanished marine creatures, and Indus Valley artifacts and many ceramic objects. His recent find, which a farmer had unearthed and brought to him—the farmer was one of his patients—had been a large Roman pot filled with beads made of precious stone and shell. This amazing hoard was one day destined for the museum in Bhuj. When our daughter had been born, he had given her an exquisite silver five-*kori* coin from the previous century, which a jeweler mounted for us and hung on a chain; the piece weighed four and a half grams, and it was so fine that it was like a platonic type in its ideal of money.

We often used to visit him whenever we were in Mandvi alone, for his surgery was up behind the old vegetable market; he would always be welcoming and take time off from his patients to talk with us, and I learned much about the current pathologies and medical conditions of Kacch during those meetings. Sometimes at the weekends, he would take us to one of his archaeological sites or old burial grounds, and we would wander awhile looking for finds. He was very wise about the human condition and human suffering, and he was also extremely well read in natural history and could always answer my questions about birds and shells and fossils. Pulin was a profoundly humane and careful pursuer of scientific information, and I admired his intentive and consilient truthfulness; this was a quality that had not been achieved without personal ordeal.

Pulin was also an excellent poet who composed both in English and Gujarati, and much of our conversation concerned poetry and the value of poetic life. There was something rare about this man, about his endeavors, his complexity and kindness, and his attempt to reach something via art which was not available elsewhere in life. Poetry for him was very much a medium and a means, a philosophical practice, and his work was infused and informed by his love of knowledge and scrutiny of the natural world; he too was a great humanist in the old tradition. He was also a pedestrian, and each night after a long day at the clinic, he would always drive to the shore and walk the coast towards the Jakh temple at Ravalpir, lone and monadic in the dark, loving the sea and heavens. I think that was where he composed much of his verse, patrolling for singular hours in the moonlight along the open shore, listening to the breaking and retrieving ocean. His most recent collection of poetry was entitled *Oceans of the Heart*.

We once spent a midsummer's eve with Pulin at the beach beside the village of Moti Layja, to the west of Mandvi. It was a village with an important temple to Ashapura Ma, whom the Kharve, the seafaring community to which Jagdish belonged, patronized. We left the car and walked down through the dunes to the shoreline and strolled in the pink dusk. A solitary flamingo passed us, winging along the coast, and out at sea, the first of the dhows were returning towards Mandvi, from Basra or Mogadishu or Dubhai, for this day marked the opening of the season of homecoming for the fleets. Visible in the sea was a long, thin, treacherous reef, running perpendicular from the coast into the waters; once they had passed the spire of the temple to Ashapura Ma, the captains and pilots knew that they could turn in towards harbor and were clear of those bitter rocks.

Pulin was speaking about his new book and had with him a fine Neolithic hand-axe which he had discovered only the day before, at his site inland from Mandvi. Maxim was fascinated by this tool and had insisted on carrying it when we had left the house. Pulin had also shown him a flint core that he had also just unearthed, which had similarly captivated Max. Manki was on my shoulders, sleeping, and Leanna had walked ahead to be barefoot in the tidal pools and was searching for unusual shells. Pulin spoke about how there was no *either-or* in life, how it was all the same, the happiness or the ordeal, for ultimately there was only experience and events only proceeded in one direction.

"We have to draw from time its truth and forcefulness, that particular substance which manifests itself as time on earth," he said. "Great souls do not actually suffer, for they know how to wait. They have learned how to receive everything without identifying or weighing it."

Later, as we drove homeward, we paused to look at a field where a solitary man was leisurely walking up and down his land, casting either seed or fertilizer upon the furrows. The rains had still not come and the earth remained dry. Pulin slowed down the vehicle, and we watched the fellow for some minutes as he paced solo in the twilight.

"Sometimes I feel like that," observed Pulin. "I am always optimistic about the rain and promiscuous in my hope."

Jagdish in his quirkish and serious way became virtually one of the family. He dressed in a mildly eccentric fashion, in striped trousers and uncommon shirts, and was always keen on meals; we had to make sure always to stop at good places for him to dine. There was nothing suppressed about Jagdish in his appetite or gusto for life. He was of a community who were mariners but claimed to be *kshatriyas*; his father, who was now in his nineties, had been a captain who had once traded his dhow along the East African coast. In those days he had sailed merely by dead reckoning and used neither a sextant nor navigational tables, nor had he any motor in the vessel; such was the dexterity and aptitude of his sea-manship. Jagdish himself as a youth had also been to sea on a freighter out of Mumbai and had then, like so many Kacchi men, worked in the Gulf at Dubhai in order to save cash to purchase an automobile, his beloved *Indica*. He and his family lived near the Daryalal temple, the sea-farer's temple in Mandvi. I was amazed when Jagdish told me one day that there were so many Indian migrants permanently in the Gulf that there were many *mandir*, Hindu temples in the towns there. Jagdish's son, Karan, was going to go and work in Emirates as soon as he had concluded his advanced education at Gandhidam University, where he was taking a degree in business studies; this was the most popular course of study for young people nowadays. Everyone wanted the MBA.

Whenever we were with Jagdish, he always gave us our news, as we had no wireless and rarely purchased a newspaper any more: all the latest on Pakistan or terrorism, as well as the shipping news, came from him. When Mandvi ships sailing in convoy and carrying coal towards Somalia caught fire and sank—and this was quite common due to the auto-combustible nature of coal—Jagdish was the first to inform us. Whenever a scandal in the Bollywood world was happening, Leanna and Jagdish would discuss the details for hours, with much exclamation and incredulity.

Jagdish detested the Wagar *kshatriyas* of Sodhas, Jadejas, and Kolis, and whenever we were in that *taluka*, he always decried the men there for violence and fighting, for their drinking and use of opium and *bhang* or hemp tea. "They are all bad," he used to say. Men would often become angry concerning land or women or dignity, and the *talvars*, the curved swords, would appear and the offence would be decided by bloodshed. The police, as they were also *kshatriyas*, rarely became involved in these issues of honour. Jagdish could not tolerate such behavior and would always criticize those involved when he read of such reports in *Kacch Mitra*, the Bhuj daily.

Once he drove Max and me out to the village of Katarya, where a temple was being inaugurated; it was one of the events that the Maharao had suggested that we attend. The older temple had been razed by the earthquake, and a new structure had been erected at last with money from villagers who lived in Mumbai and abroad. On that day when we visited—for the festivities went on for several days—the *murtis* or images were being installed in the new shrine. It was the height of the hot season, and we arrived having driven for five hours along crude dusty tracks. We parked outside town and joined in a procession that was circumambulating the bounds; the *murtis* were being taken about the boundaries of the village and were mounted on decorated carts drawn by tractors and small trucks. The procession was preceded by drummers and *shehnai*, clarinet players, and the air was raucous with the repetitive short rhythms and refrains. A group of young men were dancing—almost possessed—and leading the way; their clothing, in the extreme heat and clouds of dust, was soaked and dark with sweat. Behind the statues came tractors that drew wagons crowded with youthful women who were singing praises to the goddess in high-pitched and shrill melodies. The procession moved very slowly, and the combination of superheated shadowless sandy air and the blaring noise of drums and din of the pipes, along with our thirst, was unhinging; many of the dancing youths were obviously intoxicated.

Maxim loved the scene and kept on asking me to raise him up or lift him onto a wall so that he could watch the gaudy and frenetic celebration. Whenever people would throw money for the musicians, and the band was wearing a uniform of red peaked hats and bright blue jackets and trousers, Max often tried to dash in among the feet and legs to seize a note or a few coins, and men would try to restrain him. Now and then the long parade would halt in the narrow and confined lanes and the drummers and pipers would rev up the frenzy and the weapons would appear. One man at a time would go through the evolutions of swordplay, faster and faster until he and the blade became dangerous and on the verge of being out of control, as the *talvar* whirled round, swifter and swifter. It was beautiful to watch, for there was something formal about the moments and yet it was ecstatic and potentially extremely violent. Max loved these scenes and scrambled to find a high vantage point in order to stare, completely agog at the flashing swords and the expressions of the encircling emotionally supercharged men. Companions would always halt the swordsman at a point when he might not be able to hold the blade any longer and someone could be wounded. For me the scene was fascinating, for this was exactly what heroes would do during battle in the epic *Mahabharata*, bewildering their opponents with ever-faster demonstrations of swordsmanship and then striking when the enemy was fully confounded; the real adepts would play with two weapons simultaneously, one in each hand.

Kshatriya women were traditionally secluded, but the maidens on the cart behind the tractor who were singing to accompany the statues as they processed about the village were thoroughly public. All the other and mature women whom we saw that day were standing in doorways, veiled and severe, and the look on their faces was stern and unmoving. Such was their culture. Often the older ladies would be offering cups of water to the crowds of men in the procession, for the meridian heat, the dust, noise, and the mood of the day were overwhelming.

Later in the evening, on the way homeward, Jagdish was nothing but cynical and fulminated against the bad practices and rites that we had been so keen and enthusiastic to watch. For me, it had been one more crack through which to glance at the old lingering world of epic poetry and its customs.

Another of our company during those years was Krutarthsinh Jadeja, a scion of an old *thakur* family who, like Harshraj, had put his antiquated and fortified house, the *darbargadh*, to use as a school. Krutarth was thoroughly permeated by his *kshatriya* heritage and loved Kacch and its culture and history. His ancestors had been associated with the Maharao's family for centuries and also with the clan who had ruled from Rohar: there was a large portrait of that chief in Krutarth's office at the school. Not long before we met him, he had married, and his bride had come, appropriately, from Jhalawar.

Whenever I needed to know something about Kacch or was in doubt concerning a tradition or festival, I would turn to Krutarth, who would always have a detailed and exact reply, given in polished and precise words or prose. He and his family struggled—with the school—to sustain the old and dignified *kshatriya* ethos in a new millennium, trying to transform it so that those ideas might once again become more legible in time. At one point they even had a young Rabari boy as a pupil. We frequently used to visit him at Devpur and sometimes went on happy car trips together to visit the old sites. Krutarth always wanted us to send Maxim to his academy, but it was just too far from Bidhada. Like Harshraj and his wife, Krutarth had realised in a very practical sense that only through education would the future be able to retain its traditional dignity and any right measure of humanistic valence. As the Maharao grew older, Krutarth would often stand in his place as a royal proxy during the great social *pujas*.

One summer, Krutarth and his wife went on a pilgrimage, a *yatra*, to Mount Kailash in western Tibet and circumambulated that sacred peak. In Hindu cosmology, Kailash stands at the centre of the cosmos, and it has been a place of great sanctity for ages. Krutarth had gone in the company of his *guru*, someone who ran a well-famed school far to the north of Kacch and who adhered to the pedagogic principles of Krishnamurti, a twentieth-century visionary and teacher. It is common in Gujarat to have a *guru*, someone to whom one is spiritually devoted and whose wisdom and moral learning is respected and attended; in early autumn, *gurus* all receive honour and visits from their devotees. This is an aspect of religion that does not obtain in the West, perhaps due to the more centrally organized nature of the churches; even in their homes, Kacchis will not simply worship family and clan deities, but they will also have a place for their teacher, who is the object of *puja*, just as much as deities and heroes are. For them, devotion itself can be as transcending as ritual or knowledge, and the beloved need not be an immortal. It was not so much the possibility of vision that attachment to a *guru* enabled but the metonymy, the actual emotional connection with someone who was illuminated, that counted. There was no transmission of view but a correlation that existed by virtue of the bond.

Jehan and Krutarth became quite close companions, having met at a seminar on climate change in Bhuj one evening; all the Bhuj elite were there, and it was quite a showy but learned and sincere affair. Leanna slipped outside with the children in order to go and spend time in the playground across the road, and I sat behind Jehan and Krutarth. How similar they were, I thought to myself, in their quiet and gentle modernity. Like Mr. Shah, I think that neither of them had ever imbibed alcohol and were not tainted by that kind of use; they both possessed a similar tenderness towards the world, which I admired as it was so unlike my own immoderate Western inheritance.

Also among our social community in those days were the Bhatt family, who ran the guest-house at Mandvi where we had once lived for several months. Their twin daughters became good friends with our son, and we often used to leave him there to spend evenings with the girls. The Bhatts were always liberal and caring to us, even though they could never quite understand what we were doing in the Kacch. Mr. Bhatt's brother was a cardiologist, and the guest-house had once been his hospital; he had migrated to America, to Louisiana, and had become highly successful in his practice. Mr. Bhatt never quite comprehended why Leanna and I had put that Western world behind us in favor of Kacchi living.

In time the twin girls left their parents and went to stay in Louisiana for the sake of learning, which was sad for our son, as they had been his best chums. This also left the Bhatt household somewhat bereft and silent, but the parents spoke with the girls every day by telephone and were keen for them to receive a good education. I suppose that one day soon they too will migrate towards Louisiana and rejoin the family, and I wrote several letters for Mr. Bhatt to assist him in visa applications. In Kacch, schooling is perhaps the only means to break through and away from old hierarchies, and unfortunately that usually means leaving the country. To us, this always seemed a sad if not desperate choice, but realistic; we had witnessed the same phenomenon in Greece, when families sent off their best children to foreign universities.

The children of course never returned, for experientially they could not, but one day they would send back money and also airplane tickets. Later, the aged parents would join their offspring—by then with children of their own—in the new land; this was how the New World had become populated, and this was very much a paradigm of contemporary Kacchi living. Whenever we were at the airport in Bhuj, I always noted these third-generation young people who had come, somewhat uncomfortably, in order to visit their distant kinfolk in the villages and hastily return towards London or Seattle.

There was also a young Jain bookseller in Bhuj named Kamlesh Shah who became our friend, even inviting us to his wedding. He charmed Leanna and kept her supplied with reading material, a crucial component for her emotional well-being at Bidhada. Kamlesh was always benevolent to us and the children, giving them little books whenever we visited his emporium on Station Road and ordering me titles from Delhi. His father had been a publisher and his grandfather had founded one of the first Kacchi newspapers, and Kamlesh possessed that particular quality of precision that bibliophiles often display, having grown up in a bookish and literary family. He loved Nehru's book, *The Discovery of India*, and sold me my copy, and at his house there ware framed photographs of his father together with Indira Gandhi. He was very proud of his learned heritage and displayed pictures and prints of his family at the little shop. When we had first met him, he was still youthful and playful, and as the years passed, he gracefully and visibly moved through time, becoming more established and studious, more considerate and beneficent, and more quiet. I had always envisaged the old John Murray of Albemarle Street in London to have been such a character: deeply imbued with literacy and yet minutely gracious and always particular in his knowledge.

So these were our friends and their places, all that we loved, what in modern Greek would be called *paréa*: one's community of speech and shared time. These were the persons who surrounded us, not always immediately, but emotionally. They were our landmarks in the Kacch, our points of reference and pendance that encompassed our family and our minor and habitually diurnal ways; these were our autochthonous company, men and women who led us into their homes and exchanged kindness with us, particularly with our children, and who made our lives in India not only sustainable but affectively rich.

We did not return to Dhrangadhra for some years; either the monsoon was too heavy and the roads were difficult, or Harshraj was busy in Delhi or on business in the Gulf. One of his brothers had acquired land in Goa and was building a house, and that project inspired him to think more about refurbishing Halvad. Then, when Manki joined us, we did not move about so much with the babe, but we would correspond by letter and exchange family news. We did make the effort early in the autumn of one year, however, taking the train across country, a journey of half a day; Indian trains have a subculture of their own, and we always enjoyed our travels in that mode. Maxim especially enjoyed the sleeping carriages and used to secure the upper berth, where he would set up a boyish camp. We could always relax on a train, for everything was controlled and ordered, and I used to love to sit and drink tea and watch the landscape as it rattled past the window. It felt luxurious to be merely a spectator and to do nothing but view the world as it moved along and passed away in another direction, just like time itself. The textures and odors and sounds of those trains were so specific, and the men who worked on them were professional and curt; such travel always felt contained and secure and satisfyingly unmodified by the present. Even the sound of the carriage wheels moving along the iron rails possessed a particularly familiar and repetitive charm.

We arrived at Dhrangadhra and walked towards the *darbargadh*; strangely, after all the years, I could still remember the arrangement of streets and roads. The town was almost a city by then, thriving, busy, and apparently prosperous with new and flashily designed buildings. After Kacch and Bhuj, the organization of the place appeared formal and rational, with many of the roads laid out on a grid pattern, a scheme that Harshraj's grandfather had determined. It is always odd to return to a place where one has been deeply engaged—to appreciate that it possesses a life apart from ourselves and has changed and that the passion that we felt before no longer exists and is, in fact, now quite irrelevant. It leaves an uncomfortable feeling to realize that such a love has become useless and completely unmemorable, that such love had become merely nominal and was no longer a verbal state. I suppose that this is really an indication of vitality on both sides, and for nostalgia to have arisen would have been to signal a certain desuetude on one part. We are never really aware of time unless we step away from it and return, and then its passage is glaringly apparent.

At the palace, the old *zenana* appeared smaller and a little more dusty, but actually more beautiful and reserved and more apart from the racket and bustle of grinding urban Dhrangadhra. It was pleasing to see Harshraj and his family—his daughters were also staying then—and to realize how we had all aged in the recent years. Often we do not notice how the years are gently carving us like a piece of stone, slowly cutting and chiseling away at our form and energy as they intervene, until suddenly, *presto*, some counterpoint arises and our sense of self is thrown into contrast with an earlier light. For our bodies move intrinsically with the speed of blood and possess, like the sun itself, an inherent tempo of their own, apart from everything else, and we actually carry time within ourselves; it is not located elsewhere. In that sense, we are fully encoded with our own destinies, each utterly separate from anything else despite our illusions and our intrinsic desires. That is perhaps the secrecy of time and how immortality finds a place, how it is that truth adheres and is transmitted between souls. We are unaware of the freight we bear, its indifference and monotony, and do not know what we convey of universal privacy; only the unison of love is prescient with outward sunlight.

As in previous years, we used to go walking of an evening out towards the west where the terrain was open, uncultivated and *sauvage*, taking the dogs with us, who used to race off in pursuit of any animal they could track: rabbit, deer, wild ass, jackal, and now and then a wolf. Then we would eat together later in the small and enclosed dining room deep within the heavy *zenana* walls, the table surrounded by silver-mounted photographs and portraits of family members and ancestors. They were moments and hours of civility and stability, removed from the tension and compression of what was an exterior world of business, agriculture, and relentless traffic. Both daughters worked in the theater—in London and in Delhi—and when they were present the conversation around the table was always mirthful and dramatic, performative and tense with good humor.

I so respected what Harshraj and his wife had accomplished in their lives, their marriage and love, the liveliness, vigor, and animation of their household, the beauty of that great courtyard with its old sculptures and many small birds, including a pair of curious and nesting owls, and the coming and going of children, dogs, servants, and guests; the general busy-ness of the situation, which they had cautiously formulated and arranged over the years. It was a real provincial establishment, one to be envied for its largeness and genial humanity and affection. The building had been a wreck when they first moved there, a ruin of sorts, and they had carefully built it back into something wonderful and it had been vigilantly developed during many years.

I held great esteem for Harshraj and the fact that he had grown up mostly at Dhrangadhra and had not departed for long, although he moved about the world: he had kept to his home and made it more beautiful as well as simultaneously helping his people. I was always fascinated by those who lived where they had grown up and who loved their native *environs*, feeling no impulsion to ramble the globe and recreate other, newer lives. To me that was an enviable situation and always mysterious because I had not experienced it myself, nor had Leanna; we had both spent most of our lives trying to apprehend our alien surroundings and culture and the society where we lived and where we did not actually belong. This was not something received but only to be struggled for if we were to comprehend a world.

The old Maharaja was not in good health then and had withdrawn to the *mardana*. He had apparently been recently pleased because the townspeople had erected a statue of him in honour of his great age and dignity; dams had also been given his name. Not since the days when he used to represent the state in Parliament had the old Raja been so popular, and this delighted him.

A year or so later, Krutarth sent us a message to say that the library at Dhrangadhra had burned: some of the upstairs rooms in the *mardana* had caught fire, and all the books, papers, and archives of His Highness had been reduced to ash in less than an hour. For a scholar to lose the documentation of his life like that was awful, and I felt sad for him, having to forsake such a treasury of works, a collection which must have taken many decades to assemble. For those of us who live and dwell in literature, the sudden eradication of a livelihood by flames is tantamount to an annihilation of identity and personal situation. If my own library and the trunks of manuscripts and notebooks that I had gathered over the years were to vanish in conflagration, I would feel destitute; for in a way, that was my essential property and intellectual estate, and to lose such would be to become a refugee without material location or station. It was a kind of deletion that I always dreaded, and I contacted Harshraj, expressing condolence for the destruction. A year later, the old monarch passed away; more than two hundred thousand mourners—from the clan and the town—attended at his pyre, and the formal *kshatriya* obsequies continued for weeks thereafter. Something of the old century expired with him, that association of the political, intellectual, the social, and even the sporting vanished; an accomplishment of sorts that does not obtain any more.

Harshraj we did not see for a long time, although I used to write to him now and then. He was suddenly spending more and more of his days in America, as his two daughters had become successfully engaged with work in that country and married. I know that in his heart he still dreamed of a resurrected Halvad, and wondered what became of those plans. His Buddhist wife had grown up in the hill tracts between Myanmar and Bangladesh, close to where Pragmulji's wife had been born, and because of all the armed conflict in that area, she did not want to return to her homeland; in fact her brother had ended up serving as an ambassador for the state of Pakistan, and the old family house—a beautiful wooden structure of great age—had disappeared beneath the rising waters of a lately constructed dam. Thus her life had in a way also gravitated more towards America, having lost its original situation and kinship and all those associations and messages; plus, she had became a grandmother.

I always feel a sense of loss when people whom we had walked with and shared time with vanished from companionship, just as when a place itself no longer held any weight in one's life. It was akin to returning to a site that we had formerly loved only to find it developed and no longer like what was recalled but changed beyond recognition. This was a kind of loss, different from death and bereavement, that opened up a great and strange cavity both inexplicable and bare, and I always felt an ineradicable sadness at the disappearance of friends or the recession of a place that had once been beloved. As we grow older in time and more burdened with years, such small and irrelevant deficits do leave a stain of poignant melancholy, a mild cheerless gleam that cannot be assuaged, as if certain sharp edges of definition are smoothed and worn away and the form that we once possessed of our own image becomes less clear and less distinctly overt.

Momin was in this category, for he completely disappeared from our life, although I think that we spotted him once in Mumbai when we were visiting Colaba for a few days. If it was him, he ignored us. According to the Maharao, he had become involved in some shady financial business at the school and had begun to cut all his former connections. His family

had arranged for his marriage and there had been some changes at the
school, whereby it became no more an institute for English medium education but had become solely Islamic and religious in focus. We did visit
him once at the *dargha*, but he was obviously uncomfortable with our
presence and we never returned. I was distressed to lose his association
in our life, for we had sincerely liked him. Leanna said that he was uneasy
with us as we were perhaps the only ones to whom he had revealed his
affair with the brahmin woman: perhaps someone else had learned of this,
and because of his position as a hereditary saint and because of his following, he had been forced to cover his tracks and deny the alliance. I was
unhappy to lose his company, however, and never liked it when close
friends disappeared like that and spurned a past amity. I always felt that
there had been terrible error on my part and carried that guilt with me
as if I myself were a betrayer.

There was one other person whose being informed not so much
Leanna but me during those years; that was James MacMurdo, a young
Scot who had been one of the first Europeans to visit Kacch. There was
an uncommon element or thread in his sparse writings that had captured
my imagination, much as the descriptive prose of William Leake—a young
traveler in the southern Peloponnese of Greece who was contemporary
of MacMurdo—had done for me when I had lived in that country. Even
though he was long dead, I often used to think about him and wonder
what it was that he had seen of Kacch and Kacchi life two hundred years
ago, for in his writing he obviously loved what was then a kingdom and
its people, and one had the sense that his colleagues and peers also loved
him. He was a charismatic figure from the past who strangely lingered in
my thought; I had even dreamed about him in my sleep.

For years I had been curious to locate the site of MacMurdo's tomb;
he had perished in 1820 of cholera in the Wagar region, and his body had
been interred there. It was one of those projects towards which I had never
quite trained my mind until recently, when I had gone alone to visit the
temple of Momaya Ma on the occasion of an annual *mela*. The Maharao
had called to inform me that it would be an event worthy of viewing, as
all the Jadeja *kshatriyas* would be present; he could not go himself and
wanted me to be there as an emissary.

It was cruelly hot then, with the sunlight almost at ignition point,
and Leanna and Manki did not want to leave Jalaram Bag; Leanna, I think,
also wanted Maxim to be at home with her for company, so I went alone
with Jagdish towards the temple, which was situated apart and isolated in

the landscape. I knew that MacMurdo's *chattri* was in that area, but no one whom I asked had ever heard of the spot; I thought that once we were thereabouts, Jagdish's remarkable navigational competence might be able to locate the place, and I was right.

I do not think that I have ever experienced such an anvil of heat as on that day, for the air was like a flame and I felt that if I held a sheet of paper out in the sunlight, it would catch fire. Jagdish informed me as we were sitting at the temple of Momaya Ma taking our lunch that it was 48.5 degrees. Thereafter, it did not take long for Jagdish to locate the *chattri* that was near the edge of the Rann and beside a small walled temple of Mahadeo. We first went into the cool banyan-shaded precinct to make obeisance to Lord Siva, and an old *saddhu* with thick unwashed hair down to the ground offered us refreshment and we took a dish of tea with him. I examined some old hero stones that were next to the shrine, which had some untypical carvings on them; I felt excited to have finally arrived at the site and wanted to delay an inspection of the tomb until I had recovered from the heat of the morning.

The *chattri* was situated on a small rise above a tank and beside the temple walls. It was of dull crimson sandstone with some decorative markings of chain-link design and had only been marginally damaged by seismic forces. It was somewhat Tughluk in style and had once been plastered. The four arched sides were open to the air, and the elevated grave within was intact. Inserted into the stones was a slate plaque with an inscription naming the deceased and giving the date and cause of demise; it had been placed there by his admiring friends and young fellow-officers. I carefully examined the structure and its formation and looked about at the surrounding terrain; two thin boys were peeping in at me whenever they could, curious as to what I was doing, and a small weak-looking dog was obviously displaced from the shade by my incursion. The building reeked of bat droppings.

There was a feeling of transcendental beauty to that spot, stainless, immutable, and infinitely kind; a sense that someone had fallen irreversibly in love with the place and had been accepted by its light-filled patron spirits as one of them, involved in their printless hours apart from impermanence. I had the sense of *une belle mort*, a good death; there was nothing grisly nor morbid about the tomb. Rather, a sensibility of great dignity and tranquility inhabited beneath that dome. There was an air of vast serenity, looking out upon the colorless fire and numinous heat of the uncreative desert and its thirsty flocks, where a single Rabari shep-

herd sat beneath a thorn tree and the distant Rann shimmered a deliques-
cent diamond-blue. Love of place had ultimately been hallowed by place
itself.

I do believe that we receive an inner vision whenever we accept love,
and the efficacy of true loving and spirit is then caused to reveal itself; for
me, love of place had always been as significant as love of person in its
transport and incorrigible truthfulness. There remained a few grains of
genius and love within that *chattri*, indicative of how much MacMurdo
had been inspired and simultaneously of how much he had inspired the
friendship of his companions: he had been their pioneer. For me that was
a truly unique spot, and it was a credit to Jagdish's sensitivity that he realized my emotion and later inquired about MacMurdo, curious as to my
respect. In time, my recollection of that site worked as a key metonym or
emblem for all of Kacch, and recalling that situation would always elicit
my great love of place for the region and its elusive people.

We never went back to Delhi, although we often spoke about revis-
iting the book-sellers at Connaught Circle, Kamlesh removed that necessity. Mumbai was so much easier to reach and more human in its scale,
and Delhi was far away, vast and imperial with its conurbation of twenty
million souls. Mumbai, despite its wretched impoverishment and social
darkness, had a charm about it come from an old and slightly bourgeois
world that here and there remained, as at Colaba. It was also more of a
pedestrian city and the air was not as unhealthy as that of Delhi, especially
during the winter months when heating fires burned and clouded the
Delhi atmosphere. Leanna's great-grandfather had once been in charge of
the main hospital in Bombay, more than a century ago, and she felt an
attachment to the place and a fondness as if it were her heritage.

We would visit the city and stay near to the Gateway, taking rooms
that faced onto the bay and islands. I loved that spot, its outlook upon the
sky and ocean and ships and the small moored yachts, and I spent many
an hour sitting at our hotel window where there was a desk, just watching
the marine and mercantile life out there upon the water, whilst Leanna
and the children would visit the Taj Hotel and cruise the shops. Now and
again I was reminded of the Piraeus in Greece with all its dark ships on
anchor, so Homeric an image. Often we would go up to the Hanging Gardens of an afternoon and wander the grounds whilst the children sported
on the swings and lawns, the eastern bay of Mumbai below us and the
concentrated urbanization of that peninsula like some giant mineral crys-
tal in the distance or future. I used to love the neighbourhood about the

Bhanganga tank, for it was quietly unurban and without the *angst* that touched so much of Mumbai.

When the Taj was attacked in the winter of 2008, I grieved for days afterwards, remembering all our happy and easy times within those walls and the many hours spent at the luxurious foreign bookshop. I wondered who among those we had encountered there were still living: the old Parsi in the jewelery shop, the sage brahmins in the bookshop, men whom I knew by face and greeting if not by person. Thereafter Colaba always seemed to possess a moderately uneasy or uncanny mood because of those executions; it lost its former lightness. We once met a young rabbi who had been sent from Moscow to Mumbai in order to reconstruct and revive the synagogue and congregation after those November attacks and murders. Avraham was clever and confident and self-possessed, but I wondered how long he would last given the climate of the times. I wrote to him once, hoping to enter into a correspondence, for I admired his bravery, but he never replied.

We always liked Mumbai for its strange homeliness and its seeming sophistication after rural Kacch, but it was always a great relief to put it behind us and return to our house and gardens. The disorder and accumulated filth of Mumbai, the private opulence that coexisted beside public squalor, the refuse and architectural wreckage that existed immediately alongside the elegant and polished world of wealth all ironically seemed profoundly realistic, for I think that the cleanliness of the West, its civic order and tidiness and the complete regulation of human movement and activity, is actually unnatural and not something that can be sustained for long. The ordinary or innate condition of humanity is not so orderly in arrangement, and civil life is normally messy, chaotic, and dangerously muddled; what we practiced and knew in the West would not last long before one day reverting to disarray and commonplace confusion once again, just like Mumbai.

Regardless of all the tawdry and invidious modernity that was beginning to creep upon and into Kacch, we always made our daily ventures out into the countryside in search of new landscapes to explore and to walk alone together. A most special place that we favored during those days at Bidhada lay among the gentle hills behind the village of Pundi, surrounded on all sides by the flat expanse of Kacch. We would take the Bhuj road and then branch off towards the east at the dark old stronghold that stood above Pundi, then park our motorcycle or later, our small automobile, beneath a row of saru trees next to a stream bed and walk uphill towards the ridge. There would be pipits and buntings fleeting about; perhaps a nightjar would shoot away at our approach; kestrels would be hovering in the air and hares would often bolt from behind bushes. The topography was softly undulating, with hollows and—during monsoon times—small brooks of water; it was a rustic and harmonious corner of the world, sylvan and naively beautiful.

At the highest point, the panorama stretched for tens of miles in every direction, and below us there would be—at times—quietly moving flocks of goats. There would always be the cry of lapwings upon the vast expanse of open space, and occasionally comb-duck would skim past. A group of *nilgai* who lived in those hills would now and then appear and scatter away and run downwind of us, halting to turn around and stare suspiciously at our invasive presence. There were young shepherds up there with their few scraggy sheep, and during the chilly part of the year we often came across small burnt-out hearths where they had crouched to warm themselves in the icy mornings and smoke a cigarette. Maxim adored those shepherds for their wild *mystique* and desperately wanted to join them and to become one of their kind. He used to emulate them, going off alone with his cane, wandering the dips and rises. Being of darker complexion than either Leanna or me, he was always more accepted by people; we were pale-looking, whereas Aryan Max could easily blur and vanish into a crowd.

The vista from that point was greater than anywhere else that I knew of in the region and far more so than at Kalo Dungar. The ground of those hills was littered with the delicate fossils of seashells, and small conical hills rose here and there in almost musical perfection. If the monsoon had just passed, the land would be clothed in a startlingly bright jade, and here and there distant bodies of water gleamed metallic in a strong vertical sunlight. I found much gladness among those slopes above Pundi, for there was a serenity about the spot that was entirely unconstrained and without the severe absolute quality which existed elsewhere due to immanent desert. There was a lyrical charm to the location with its gentle declivities and small animals and birds and the shepherds, who would suddenly appear from over a hill with a shocked expression on their faces, seeing us walking towards them. It was truly a place of idyll, and being surrounded by so much clear space and land only emphasized its benignity. Near the summit was a small shrine to Devi, the goddess, with an orange pennant shivering in the breeze and the remains of offerings lying about the earth. Leanna and baby Manki frequently took themselves to that spot for small private and womanly rituals. There were larks in the sky in those Pundi hills, singing as they rose into blankness and invisibility, and I used to love to lie on the earth and watch them as they vanished, listening to their fragile songs. There were owls and hawks that cruised the breeze and caused all the other birds to scatter in panic.

I always felt transported up there and removed from whatever my anxieties and preoccupations had thrust upon me earlier in the day; such conditions were less material and pressing in those hills. Sometimes if the rains had been full, I used to walk up there alone and then there would be thick grass that remained wet long into the post-meridian. Birds, bees, and butterflies populated the light air, and the ponds and tanks in the distance reflected back a blue of the sky. For me that spot captured all of the Kacch, and Kacch was, for me, my India. Often during colder times I went up there alone and would sit on the topmost ridge, reclining upon the stones, and look out at the world. In winter there was often misty fog visible along the coast, and in the hot summer afternoons the land below oscillated and vibrated with fluid dusty heat. I found great peace and stability there, and the hours would slip by and vanish whilst I simply gazed and thought about life and my work. Sometimes I even fell asleep on that summit, such were my reveries, and once I awoke to see a young chinkara fawn playfully sporting with its mother whilst the male wandered nearby. Such was the rare bucolic vivacity of the hillside.

On another occasion during that same year, we drove up towards the north and the old volcano site of Dhinodar. Beyond the low walls of the *ashram* with its laburnum trees and shady eucalyptus, a hot glare from the sun struck down onto the many miles of Kacch, which were level below us. A flock of pigeons launched themselves into space, only to be driven back by the wind of that altitude, and Maxim and Manki played about with a bucket of water and tried to ring the bells whilst Leanna and I visited the cool gloomy interior of shrines and lit some incense.

The terrain beneath us was just as it had been for millennia, with its dry, waterless, and maroon-colored sandstone earth. It was a place for migrants, for those who walked with herds and flocks and who camped about small thornwood fires at night; like us, those people must sometimes have paused, wondering at the unsullied and vacant silence of the region. They would send on the young men and animals ahead whilst the women followed later with chattels and children and newborn creatures all bound up together on the backs of camels. In my mind's eye, I could picture and hear those people and hear their rough voices, the sound of their feet and the random noises of tired and thirsty animals, an occasional loose tinkle of metal.

That day Leanna was in a withdrawn mood, and we spoke about love and vicissitude, about the sadness in the fact that nothing ever remained of human life apart from the few broken items of mineral or pottery.

"If there is neither attachment nor meaning in life," Leanna asked me as we stood by the wall overlooking the dry, infertile expanse, "this can only lead to sorrow. Is that not so, Kevin? Where is the belief that you always spoke about, or the great joy of love? Is there nothing that we can keep with us? I have lost my belief since we came here; I have lost my power," she said.

Below us the land extended, lost in haze and unspoken years. It was as if the terrain was iridescent and quivering in a lucid molten light. There was an old silence about that place, with only the passage of breezy air to mark the quiet.

"There is amity and companionship," I said. "A sharing of days as we walk and pause and sometimes a sharing of loving bodies. Illuminated and not dispossessed, we are freed of the illusions that wreck love; that is our achievement. So let us not lose ourselves but stay true to our one good fortune. We are here and we are together and we have these wonderful children; let us not cause our brief time to founder with anxiety. Immediacy is a great gift if one is aware, for there is nothing else to say."

V. Lakhpat:
Modernizing a Tradition

T here is so much to do, and so little time is left, it seems, before the remnants of traditional Kacchi life disappear. A society that has existed in form for centuries if not millennia is suddenly being forced to contract and to modernize. How does this actually occur, and what are the transitions and conversions? I have attempted to capture in words some of the scenes and images, but the truth of all this is elusive and friable and so much more complex than my naïve level of apprehension admits that I feel that I have only scarcely delineated a few sparse lines of its pattern. Can we truly identify and track such moments, or are they random and unpredictable?

Perhaps all of human society is founded upon two fundamental and hypothetical events or activities: firstly, there is always an act of prohibition, something that delimits or defines a margin or periphery and supplies definition, like incest, phallic circumcision, veiling, marital exogamy, or the place of land itself. The prohibition can be not so much an interdiction but simply a mental exclusion, a delineation beyond which no categories are sustained. Secondly, all of human engagement is based upon exchange, and implicit to these transmissions is a mutual understanding of value, values that are generated socially because they are not naturally extant; to exchange is to substitute. The fundamental moments of exchange occur during the creation of kinship structures, and it is there that value is most profoundly implicit. In a nutshell, these two axes can be expressed by the metaphors of death and sex.

If all of human social life is founded upon these two abstract moments of inhibition and exchange, this is where we must begin to isolate and observe how change and timeliness enters into cultural life. I would propose that the first action of these two instants is necessarily terrestrial, that landscape supplies the primary terms for human life: such is one of the grounding axioms or projects of this book.

Throughout these pages I have been attempting to illuminate some of these marks, definitions, and the interactions that occur across such boundaries. What are the edges, and how did those borders arise, and what is the nature of mutual life when two or more such rims coincide? In other words, what are the phenomena of the human soul in time, and how do they proceed? Where do the points of negation lie, or where are they socially located, and where do exchanges occur, particularly in terms of gifts or kinship, and finally, what are the bases for any judgement of value at those points? I suppose that for Kacch the greatest moment of inhibition came with the *bhokam*, the earthquake, which newly delimited all of life in the district, for it is always the terrestrial that supplies the fundamental ground for social life and exchange, and in this I would include climate change, earth being the warp for air's movement or weaving.

A primary aspect of human culture—and perhaps of certain animal cultures—is that it only exists by virtue of reduplication and the necessary transmission of that repeated effort. Cosmopolitanism—and the Kacch is intrinsically, traditionally, and increasingly cosmopolitan due to immigration and emigration—only goes to increase the work and valence of culture by augmenting in a marginal fashion the possibilities for repetition. This is particularly the case where intercultural liaisons of the heart occur or when human passion profoundly effects the force of reiteration or translation.

At the heart of the animal and human psyche exists an initial and immediate eidetic impulse: in, say, how fish swim in schools or birds flock together. Humanity at its most original will always simply reduplicate: this formula lies at the soul of culture. For instance, I have noticed how crucial in the life of memory the role of photographs or portraits is, for so much of recollection is organized according to how images function as iconic metonyms, formulating personal narrative. There is no recollection without the key of pictures and, of course, no emotion without the act of recall.

To put this more experientially or allegorically, I was once sitting on the steps of the tennis pavilion at Vijay Vilas palace; we always used to go there when we went to see Pragmulji, just to attune ourselves and rest a little before the interview. It is a fine, classically Indian building, but is closed and in ruins and overgrown; the metal sheeting of what had formerly been a scoreboard clatters in any gust. On that particular occasion I had taken out my monocular and was observing two hawk-eagles who had perched on a nearby tree; the male was periodically whistling, making a short mewing cry, *pheeoo pheeoo*. That is all there is in life, I thought to myself. The voice of that bird said everything: he was crying to announce his territory and also to proclaim his relation with a mate. There was actually nothing else in the world apart from those two momentary statements; all else was secondary. That voice was the source of every successive metaphor on earth: there was terrain and there was reproduction, territory and sexuality, and that was it. There is a third component, I suppose, and that is a movement—a planetary motion—which we often simply call *change*, the migration of time itself, for the tennis court is now a melancholy place.

I had witnessed the progress of modernization during my youthful years in Greece, where a predominantly rural and old-fashioned agricultural society with many ancient and wonderful traditions and manners was actually a system of great manual hardship and uneducated credulity. Yet it was beautiful, and its presence within the landscape was harmonious. All that vanished with the European Community and the advent of massive consumer tourism; cisterns were padlocked and chapels secured. Now there are no barefoot children in the Greek villages and life is no longer mean or at times bitter or close to famine: the loveliness has gone, but the children can read. Tractors and diesel pumps have replaced working animals, and the social life that centred around wells and springs has dissolved. One cannot be overly romantic about the beauties of dearth, duress, and human perseverance for survival, but I do lament the loss of centuries of acquired knowledge and patterns of habit. Human creativity grows and exfoliates slowly and, once expunged, cannot be simply superimposed again or restored; what is frequently described as spiritual empathy is often in fact a very real cultural sensibility developed from centuries of natural attunement to place and season. Kacch is not a secular society in any way, although—as with mainland India—there exists an undercurrent of slight change. However, there is an increasing disjunction between a shifting material life and relatively fixed cultural life. As the former adjusts towards post-modernity, the latter often continues to remain in its pre-modern mode and so crisis ensues, particularly in the form of official amorality, as the old balance of physical wealth bubbles over, lacking new courses where earlier paths have disappeared. Kacchi society is one that is thoroughly based upon hierarchy, in which communal loyalties are near-inflexible, and marital arrangements are typically endogamous or repetitive.

The word *religion* is not a expression that is used in India, being a
term that is essentially Western or monotheistic in reference; in India
today Hindus speak of *dharma*, a conceptual order that is presumed eternal and individually fitting and whose icon is the wheel, in or on which
human beings have a revolving place. There exists no central nor unitary
doctrine nor institution to integrate belief, and what is referred to as Hinduism in fact represents no geographically organized system—except for
the powerful Swaminarayana sect—and certainly no dogma. What is com-
monly identifiable is a uniformity of metaphor and a paradigm of hierarchy. Also, it is often the case that both Hindu and Moslem shrines adjoin
at one site and devotees do not worship exclusively; *dharma* is not necessarily discrete. The hard political distinction between Hindu and
Moslem originated with the British imposition of a census and their need
for categories of enumeration. The word *Hinduism* today is a noun that
is spoken more by right-wing politicians than by anyone else, and often
at the shrines of Moslem saints, Hindus will offer devotion; similarly, at
Hindu sites, Moslems will frequently pay their spiritual respects. At times
two distinct places of worship will actually physically abut each other. At
the great Jain temple at Koday near Bidhada, one evening Leanna and I
were attending an evening recital of *bhajans*, songs of love for a deity.
After the session had closed I went to speak with the performer, who,
along with two drummers, had led the singing accompanied by an harmonium. He was Moslem, as were his percussionists, and indeed, his
father and grandfather had performed similarly in Jain temples. Such is
not atypical.

Manners and thought in Kacch are utterly different from the ways
by which people proceed and think in the West, and at first any real social
intimacy was difficult for us simply because the parameters were so dis-
parate. Human identity partakes of so little that is unanimous that to
understand how life progressed about us was initially obscure. Love for
children, and obversely, human cruelty or grief, are perhaps the only universal traits; the rest of the human psyche is very much a matter of *locale*,
of language and cultural arrangement and physical environment. Attempting to understand that small world presented great problems for us during
the early days, for how is one kind of cultural being going to comprehend
and communicate with a person of another culture when the ideas and
forms of thought exhibit neither congruence nor coincidence? This is not
a linguistic *impasse* but a cultural and mental affair, and this was the problem that the Kacch presented to us and the question that underlay much

of our early days in that province. Even now, in retrospect, this *aporia* still confounds me at times and yet strangely intoxicates me with its implicit and adjacent beauty and terrestrial sublimity: for a sense of possible liberty is generated when one realizes what one is not and what others are. Usually the latter frame is unavailable due to an intellectual space or hiatus that cannot be traversed but only witnessed, and as this is ineffable, it creates a feeling of irresponsibility or impunity.

Many years ago we had occasionally traveled among the West Indies, particularly among the Grenadine Windward Isles, and had frequently sojourned upon the tiny island of Carriacou. Curiously, a lot of the plants of that archipelago had been introduced by the British from East Indian stock during the eighteenth century and had successfully taken root in those more occidental Indies. I was always struck by how on Carriacou—because so many of the men had been forced to leave the isle in order to work on ships, and then in more recent years, to migrate towards North America and England to secure incomes—marriages were rare and men would beget children upon a series of women, whom they would then sometimes support. I recall a driver once proudly telling me about his eight children and their seven mothers. The elements of such kinship were primarily organized about feminine groups, as women would have children and remain close to their own mothers and to their brothers and uncles. Carriacou kinship and the subsequent necessary social identity was thus so different—almost the polar opposite—to what obtained in the Kacch, where it was the women who were the mobile agents. It is not simply a question of lineage that was at stake, but of how an affective world comes into existence and where that scale of emotion in its generation lies.

One could argue that in terms of kinship, syntax was everything in the Kacch, whereas in the Windward Isles, it was the grammar of the particularly inflected familial relations that bore greater ontological weight. In the latter case, it is the sanguinity of the mother, siblings, maternal grandparents, and the uncles and aunts—the uterine kin group—that is significant, whereas in the Kacchi case, it was the affinity of fathers and nephews and cousins that rendered meaning to notions of self. The emotional spectrum, valence, and scale of feelings are consequently very different in these two models: love and affection being so colored in fashions that are in no way similar. What is actually locative in terms of human immediacy and the axes of desire is not universal, and for outsiders like Leanna and me to enter a system in which we were not familiars was to be placed in an uneasy situation where the determining knowledge was not common. Matters of land tenure and inheritance procedures only complicate these systems further. On Carriacou it is the menfolk who function as fungible units, who move between domiciles, whereas in the Kacch, it is young women who perform this exchange, an event that hypothetically, in its origins, generates all other values, as the initial substitution creating worth.

As a rider to the above, in more archaic and ancient systems of marriage and affinity—which are usually referred to as Dravidian or non Indo-Aryan and typically found in South India—conjugal union is *always* between cross-cousins. Also, in those formations of kinship, the terms for brother and sister are much more extensive and not simply governed by immediate parentage; they are structural rather than historical, as too are the terms for varying kinds of father or kinds of sister. How human affection is organized and patterned in those societies partakes of an invariant form, making the orders of love and intimacy strong in their durability, if not complex nor profound. There, emotional life, because of these fundamental templates of repetition, puts love almost on similar terms as commensality, making it constant and unwavering, for there is nothing ventured or at stake and the joyful is not particular. The semantics of love are not only social and non-individual but also atemporal, and marriage is often considered as a gift that bears unseen fruit, but in another life rather than presently.

Such complication of human kinship patterns, the nature of a very different calendrical arrangement of time, and the presence and significance of the *object* and what constituted the *object*: all these masked any immediate comprehension that we might have enjoyed that was pertinent to how the Kacchi people thought and reflected. This was apart from the fact that the communities in those towns were composed of many diverse social elements and were probably the most culturally multiform folk that we had ever known. We were not inhabiting a unified society with a single pattern of values and practices, and yet simultaneously, it was profoundly consensual: this was thoroughly frustrating for us at first, especially for Leanna, who was much more social than I. It was as if we were merely floating and superficial, not involved, and yet we desired to be part of that world so much because we loved it. Being an Indologist and Sanskritist helped, for that supplied me with some station in the fixed scale of lives, but this was cursory.

It was this complete preliminary disjunction between Kacchis and us and the corollary of indifference that made life intricate and not easy; yet coincidentally it was this factor which made our time in the region exciting and intellectually satisfying. The fact that I was a specialist in the *Mahabharata* and had written books about the heroes and women of that epic gave me a certain *cachet* and an unusual—for me—status, because that epic is now essentially a religious text and has become a sacred document. Thus we did have some pale introduction into Kacchi life, and frequently over the years I was asked to recite ritually appropriate *mantras* when we become involved in the reforestation projects of Mr. Shah and had to officiate at the planting of trees. Yet we always remained classed as foreign.

One springtime the Maharao introduced us to someone called Judy Frater, a woman who had long ago come to the Kacch in order to do research for a study of textiles; Leanna immediately befriended her. Judy had lived in the Kacch for many decades, knew more about the region than most Kacchis, and had written a renowned and scholarly text on local embroidery—*Threads of Identity*—which was the focus of her expertise. She had traced, via her extensive knowledge of women's art of textile design, how embroidery patterns were bound up with the semiotics of kinship structure and how they codified personal identity and recorded the lineage systems of migration; I was fascinated as to such continuities of design and how exactly innovation occurred, if it did at all. All this she did working alone in the Kacch, publishing her work in Ahmedabad. Judy had that very American forthright and direct manner that Leanna found refreshing after the *politesse* and equivocation that we usually came across in the villages, Kacchis never spoke explicitly but always politely and with delicacy; they were naturally enigmatic.

We knew about Judy long before we had met her because of her excellent book. She was a little older than I and originally came from Germantown in Philadelphia and had given her life to the Kacchi people, founding and establishing a notable textile museum and school where women and sometimes men—mainly Rabari but many other communities were also involved, especially Moslem weavers and dyers—used to come and learn how to translate traditional design and technique into something that was economically viable in a modern setting: work that was more attuned to a market rather than simply being accumulated as dowry or as kinship items of exchange.

She had built her school near the coast to the south of Bidhada, and we often used to visit her and take lunch with her and talk in the afternoon shadow. Sometimes she would join us and Mr. Shah at Jalaram Bag, for she had known him from many years before in Mumbai. Judy was thoroughly Indian, wore lovely *saris* and jewelery, and spoke flawless Gujarati. She was a trained intellectual and knew the world conceptually, not simply as experience. People respected her, just as they esteemed Mr. Shah, our host, for having given so much of her life to others and for her unalloyed love of Kacch; they were both admired for their rare goodness.

Judy and Leanna shared an affinity with each other through feminism and their concern for the position of women in contemporary society. My wife often remarked how few women owned cell phones, for this was typically a male prerogative, and she often commented on how her presence was sometimes considered a *minus* and only politely tolerated by some men because she was Western. Even Harshraj's wife had talked about how Rajput men, unless they were staff, always ignored her as if she did not exist. Certainly, illiteracy was a phenomenon that was much higher for women than for males, and it was not uncommon for families *not* to send their daughters to a new village school simply because the girls were required to be at home and to be working. Men and women are asymmetrical in rural India; the parity is not of two differing elements but of unlike yet complementary systems, yet this is changing rapidly with the advent of satellite television and the internet. A Kacchi man is traditionally closer to his mother than to his wife, and a woman is closer to her brother than her husband: these are the irregular kinds of axes at work. An elder brother often acts as if paternal. Women, of course, do not hold or inherit property—that is, land.

Even today, daughters are not always welcome at birth and there are what social scientists—like Amartya Sen—refer to as *missing women*: the female deficit in population caused by varieties of abortion of potential girl infants, now possible due to sonograms. Early nineteenth-century accounts of Kacch all speak about the pervasive practice of girl infanticide and how the British legislated for its abolition as well as for the elimination of slavery and of *sati*, immolation of a widow upon a husband's pyre. One exaggerated figure of census from the 1850s describes the male Jadeja population being approximately twelve thousand whilst the female numbers amounted to a mere five hundred, but more likely it was about one to four. There must have been a tremendous influx of young Sindhi or Saurashtrian brides in those days. Nowadays, girls are also often seen as a liability because, in order to marry them off—and most country girls in India, not only the Kacch, are married in their mid- to late teens—they require a dowry, typically in the form of moveable wealth; this is even though the Delhi government has legislated against dowry transactions. The lot of a daughter-in-law in contemporary society is traditionally portrayed as one of dejection and exploitation, a trope that appears again and again in twenty-first-century Indian novels. Yet conversely, among the Moslem communities, seclusion and the veiling of women is more of a statement of affluence, of social distinction and disdain, than an expression of feminine obscurity and erasure.

Once, invited by Judy, we attended an annual celebration of the Rabari who lived at Tunda Vandh, a small hamlet of about a dozen agnatic families on the coast near to Bidhada. People from the village gathered beside an estuary of sand flats—what had in fact been mangrove until recently—to celebrate a founding sponsor of their community, a Moslem *pir*. This took place at his *dargha* across the empty bay. The tide was out and the sands were gleaming gray-brown and bare, and a moving silhouette of dark figures was visible as devotees crossed the flats. The dark cloaks of women were streaming in the air like victorious wings as people began to converge on the small whitewashed building.

We arrived with Judy in her vehicle, having abandoned our small car and Jagdish due to the holes in the track and the roughness of the way. There was a great air of excitement and festivity about the place as women and children and men gathered. All of them were in their Rabari outfits, splendid if not spectacular, tattooed and with heavy silver jewelery and thick gold ear and nose rings, their clothing richly embroidered with strongly colored thread. It was an extraordinary gathering, small and busy with vitality and yet unassuming. The men, moustachioed and turbaned, were sitting to one side of the *dargha* and eating a sweetened milk dish or just smoking and talking; a group of them were singing. I wished that I knew what the lyrics described—but I could not detect the words of dialect and accent—for there would have been a special and unique truth therein. Women and children were sitting before the door of the building, and there was an atmosphere of pleasure and fun, of happiness at this isolated and remote spot next to the sea. We felt most privileged to have been invited, and everyone was fascinated with our baby, who then was not even a year old: I was carrying her in a small rucksack on my back.

Men and women were entering the little *dargha* in order to do *puja*, and outside, certain men and one or two women were entering into states of mantic possession, quivering and shaking their arms and hands as they gesticulated with their upper bodies. People would come up and touch them hoping to receive benison from that enthusiastic state. These seers were the *bhuvas* and *bhuvis*, who behaved as intermediaries between the divine or supernatural world and the community; the men were poets and by virtue of this supra-human ability were treated as healers and prophets. Our son Maxim was fascinated by the sight, thinking that demons were at work. In fact, the possession was more of a formalized approach by the *bhuvas* towards a sacral station, a carefully inspired impersonation of the spirit of that *pir* which was now localized in the shrine and which they, by virtue of their poetic ability, could absorb and represent, incorporating his psyche into their beings. That morning was for me one of our most exceptional and wonderful occasions in the Kacch, emotionally pure and unclouded and aloof from all conditions of encroaching modernity, even though the towers of Asia's biggest coal-powered electricity generating plant were visible in the near distance. That corporation had just ripped out all the mangroves in the bay in order to prepare to build a port for the shipping, which would soon be delivering coal for fuel. Yet for once we were apart from the contracting and quantifiable world as quietly and pleasurably something occurred that was unfitted to the present century and in its way atemporal. Yet there was nothing artificial or staged about the gathering; it was spontaneous and pleasing, unconcerned with anything but its own dignified tradition and the potent fellowship of Rabari communal life. We had even met someone whom we had known from before, a young man who had been pasturing his herd of a hundred camels in and about the fields of Bidhada. He was surprised to see us and made us consume some of the milk dish and introduced me to his male kin.

A cool breezy vernal air was about us—it had been raining—and soon everyone was departing, noisily and happily. Leanna and Judy were taking photographs; then we were in the vehicle, and Judy's driver—a slim and obliquely swaggering young man who appeared like a youthful *roué* or cinema character—was handling the spinning and slithering jeep along the narrow muddy causeway. I had wanted the event to go on for hours; it had in fact been too brief, and I wanted that amazing intensity and quality of the moments to extend further so that we could comprehend them more: they were so uncommon and yet coherent in their performance. Yet nothing prolongs time, and it was soon gone and we were left struggling with thoughts and images, trying to construct what would become memorable before everything vanished. Then I envied Judy the life that she had made for herself over the decades and how she had managed to turn away from the West and devote her years to living among these wonderful people. It was a rare and generous accomplishment, more than altruistic and unusually selfless, and I deeply admired her vision and its detachment.

There are many pastoral *maldhari* communities in the Kacch apart from the famed Rabari, and their economy has always been primarily a moral economy rather than a market economy, one founded upon an interdependence between the divine, animal, human, and nature itself. There are the Jath, who migrated from Sindh in the west, and before that from Halaf in the marches of Iran-Iraq; there are Ahir, Meghwal, Bharvad, and the Caran—the latter were once a poet-caste—and many others, evidenced by the nine hundred-plus villages that dot the Kacchi landscape and are distributed among ten *talukas*. Certain Meghwal groups only migrated into the Banni in 1971, coming across the Rann from Sindh. Nowadays many of these communities lack the access of metalled roads, and camel, water buffalo, goats, sheep, and cows make up their free-roaming herds. Each of these clans is visually distinct from the others by virtue of specific attire, the cultural diacritics of dress: the color of *paghdi* or turbans for the men or the color and design of the blouses and skirts of women, or the patterning and type of their embroidery. For women, the shape and design of nose-rings is frequently a crucial indicator of communal identity, as are the designs and positioning of earrings or tattoos.

Even among the Jaths there are three sub-clans: the Phakirani, the Garasia, and the Dhanatiya, who all maintain specific distinctions of personal attire. Clothing is a special index of kinship, and often the form and imagery of these decorations date back centuries in time, providing a community not only with personal reference but also with topical, physical, or historical indications. All these communities are strictly endogamous. Many of the Rabari, for instance, only celebrate their marriages communally on one day of the year, just after the monsoon in August, when villagers will gather in a private and outlying locale. Rabari lineages, the *sakh*, of which there are over a hundred, are common knowledge among these communities, as are the complex extended family paradigms of unit, the *atak*, and marriage always sustains and augments these structures. The *sakh* descends and concerns male progeny; the *atak* extends through horizontal kinship.

Modernity first began to intrude upon this community beginning in the nineteenth century with the advent of a railway; then, towards the second half of the next century came the roads, foreclosing the traditional Rabari monopoly of camel conveyance. Yet the camel remains the sacred icon of their livelihood, and even nowadays, when flocks are made up of sheep or goats or herds of water buffalo, they will traditionally keep a single camel for ritual purposes. Camels, once *the* vehicles of the Kacch, are now bred for sale as either traction or draught animals, although they do produce milk and wool. Formerly, milk was something never to be exchanged and only to be given, and the sale of milk was actually taboo, was viewed as if it were the sale of blood. But now Rabari drovers are often the community milkmen and ride bicycles or Enfield motorcycles. In this century, it is not unheard-of for big dairy corporations like Amul to actually pay and assist a pastoral community to cease wandering and to settle in a particular spot, in order to supply a market with milk and milk products. The Bharvad *maldhari* are more successful in making this transition in becoming urban milkmen, for their herds are smaller and their ethos is more innovative.

Graziers will often nowadays sell sheep and goats for meat, and these animals end up in a market in the Gulf. Most pastoralists now actually own small parcels of land and have been making purchases in the recent years, especially since the advent of piped water from the Narmada dam in Gujarat, and this is particularly the case among Dhebaria Rabari. The acquisition of land is often a corollary to the shift from sheep and goats to buffalo herding, a move that the government approves, and herders receive loans for such purchases, insurance assistance, and government aid in times of drought. Such animals of course favor a sedentary way of life. Thus the old pastoral ethos is slowly being diminished by the forces of market economy, and this is often profoundly demoralizing for those who participate in such an ancient tradition.

Now it is the increasing shortage of groundwater in the Kacch that presses upon *maldhari* livelihood; if the monsoon does not arrive, animals can perish for lack of grazing, and this itself leads to curbs on land use and famine can ensue. Rabari pastoralists are frequently driven—for lack of water and fodder species—to migrate towards Saurashtra on the mainland in search of grass; if the rains have not come, many animals can die during these movements. These travels—with the flocks down into Saurashtra when water supplies are short—are also being impinged and trespassed upon, for nowadays they cannot always keep to open land and are often to be seen on the highways, guiding their stock forward as trucks and automobiles race past. It is only a strict sense of domestic propriety that sustains the Rabari today, along with their practice of endogamous marital union, and the various groups—according to *locale*—continue to be rigorously organized according to genealogy and family deity: typically a patron goddess in her numerous names, aspects, and manifestations. Nowadays more and more Rabari take to a sedentary life and have settled in small villages. Yet sometimes they still leave their *bhungas* and return to the wilderness to construct a *vandh*, a camp, and shelter beneath a temporary roof of branches and cloth whilst the flocks graze.

After the earthquake some years ago, various groups moved to live in new villages on the edge of Bhuj, where—drawing upon their highly developed and sophisticated embroidery techniques—there is presently a burgeoning craft industry that produces materials for export to the rest of India, to the tasteful *bourgeois* boutiques of Delhi and Mumbai. Strangely, it is the women of such villages who now produce much of the wealth, diluting a former dependence upon flocks and male labor. Those traditional round mud-walled and thatched dwellings will soon be an aspect of the past, merely because it is so much easier and more substantial to construct a rectangular home of concrete blocks with a tile or tin roof.

A sub-group of the Jaths, the Phakirani, are deeply engrained pastoralists who herd camel and buffalo and who soundly eschew all accumulation of property; in fact, in times of surplus, families will traditionally pass on the excess milk to the head-man so that he might redistribute it. They are poor but rigorous in their frugal sense of life and live in reed houses in the area south of the ruined city of Lakhpat, migrating up to the Banni during the months when grass and water obtain in that area. Their livelihood is essentially pre-monetary in terms of how value is produced and transmitted, and they practice a moral injunction—originally inspired by a wandering life—not to acquire burdensome wealth: in this they are probably the most true in their adherence to a nomadic *élan*, the free spirit possessed by a walking people, although this too is changing. Their life of *hakumata*, which is almost a form of communal renunciation, seeks to remove itself from the necessity that property obliges. Hardship for them in fact is merely a simplification of life in order to maintain a finer sensibility for what experience over time has revealed to them as truth. For these Jaths, the *hikamata* of the earth, its beneficent and moral energy, is to be respected and engaged by maintaining a peripatetic life, by never exploiting the earth, as with cultivation, and for them, the ideal of roaming possesses a moral valence or essence.

To meet with these people is to look into the eyes of something strange and almost preternatural, for their conscious is distant and unconfounded by material things. I have sat with some of them at times during our sojourns, and their silence and dignity is uncanny, as if they were not actually present, and yet great warmth of feeling and kindness emanates from their company. It is perhaps the Phakirani who sustain the most truthful ideal of the solely migrant and pedestrian, who are attuned only to terrain and not to the accumulation of *realia*, moveable or immoveable. Their world is a phenomenal world but it is a world, that is also being impinged upon conceptually and physically.

The Kacch is thus experiencing that not-uncommon historical movement present in so much humanity today: a shift from the traditional to the modern, with all the subsequent imprudent dislocation that this presents. The region is now in crisis as the new century gathers force and a system of livelihood that has continued for millennia becomes no longer practicable. Due to a swelling population, the former stability of life no longer obtains, and this puts stress upon the equation between humankind and the natural world, to the detriment of both. Ancient patterns of mobility and of cultivation are no longer viable and cannot support communities, and the versatility of human and animal existence is thus inhibited and constrained. Dearth and immiseration are not uncommon in the countryside, and civic lawlessness is conducive to exploitation. However, gone are the ancient days of famine, and certainly, despite an increasing paucity of groundwater, Kacch in many parts is becoming greener, perhaps due solely to drip-irrigation techniques.

Land in Kacch is held in a fourfold system. Firstly there exists government land, and this—supposedly—includes areas for public grazing. Secondly there are those terrains that come beneath the jurisdiction of the Forestry Commission, a body that is famed for its inutility and mendacity. There are, thirdly, those parts of the landscape that remain in private ownership, and lastly, there is the *jangli*, the wilderness. Banni, for instance, is thought to belong to this latter category, but no one is quite sure, and this is being contested by those in the pay or benefit of industrialists and entrepreneurs. All these four relations are constantly disputed, depending on interests, and the old margins are thoroughly labile.

What was once a mutually beneficial relation between pastoralists and agriculturalists—where migrant herders would pen their flock in order to dung fields in return for grain and other items, sometimes selling wool or *ghee* to the landowners—has collapsed in the face of modern farming techniques, which utilize fertilizers and mechanical equipment and a tendency towards the enclosing of fields and of commons with fences, so that former grazing areas become new and exclusive farmland. At times these innovative farmers have even obstructed the pastoralists' access to water supplies. Government policies, of course, presently always favor the agriculturalist—especially the Patels, a dynamic upper-caste group—to the detriment of the pastoralist. What was once mutually agreeable—manure being exchanged for a small fee or cereals—has now become a competitive cash transaction wherein different migrant groups, *dhangs*, will actually bid for access to pasture. Thus, agriculturalists, pastoralists, and the Forestry Commission are often nowadays in a state of acute contention, as all former social and economic equivalence has gone and skullduggery becomes rife.

Often will erstwhile nomads settle on the edges of towns, and some have even become owners of transport vehicles. They sometimes carry the flocks of their kinfolk who continue to pursue old paths of seasonal migration, especially in times of lean, unconsummated monsoon, yet in their poetry, songs, and stories they still long for the Banni or Sindhi homeland, the *mulk*. Nowadays, the migrations southward in search of grazing and fodder can last for long periods, a year or more, until good rains come and they might return homeward. The word for migration, *hijrat*, for a Moslem possesses a moral association of spiritual movement akin to pilgrimage; that is, there exists a moral efficacy in pedestrian mobility. Movement is considered as being salutary and purifying for the soul, and those who pursue such lives are worthy of great respect. "Those people are very close to god," Mr. Shah once remarked to me, concerning a small group of Rabari who were camped on the edge of Bidhada for the night, as they moved northward back towards their landholdings after the monsoon had arrived.

Observing the Rabari over the years and visiting the villages of other pastoral groups taught me something simple and yet ineradicable about human existence. For so much of human occurrence, almost all of it in fact—as Leanna would always remind me when I became tense from spending too long at my desk and typewriter—is instantly subject to dissolution, as we recollect so little of our lives apart from a few rare instants; consciousness merely floats upon an opaque past as if with gravity, a small boat upon a large and anomic ocean. I have often wondered what trace remains of human experience, not over time but simply within a single life, as the totality of events is soon beyond recall and remains lost from memory. Perhaps we are imbued and stained by the incidence of life, and it is only our emotions that are colored and dyed by particular events, which soon vanish from recollection. In that case all emotion is but memory and the world of emotion is one of non-specific remembrance; emotions are the only reminiscence that remain to us, and in that retrospect it is place and not only person which retains the metonymic charge. The migrant or nomadic psyche in particular is one that is organized simply by the close influence of kinship and by the necessary immediacy of landscape.

We are all actually migrants both in time and space and rest only briefly and move with virtually no recall of how it was that we ever paused. Neither union nor separation are permanent states, and our true substance concerns the emotional world of amity and the mineral world of topography; some might aver that there exists a tensile fusion of real and unreal only in the language and diction of poetry or song and nowhere else. For us, it was in that little circular house at Bidhada that we truly began to comprehend the Kacch and its genetic heritage and were able to interiorize it, to hold onto it as something familiar and internal and recognizable, and only then did the landscape cease to be boundless but became a situation of almost ethical suasion in which we could participate as members.

Since the earthquake shattered social life in the Kacch district of Gujarat that January morning, life in the region has shifted radically and relentlessly. In response to the crisis caused by seismic devastation, tax benefits granted to industries investing in the province caused a sudden and massive economic promotion that brought with it extensive environmental depredation and social instability. Certainly the benefits following the disaster were necessary, but the costs in terms of traditional life have been exorbitant. When I had begun research on local traditions of the region in the 1980s, old Bhuj was a small and gentle town; new Bhuj is now a grinding, slouching city in the middle of the desert. Industries have come to Kacch, principally in the south along the coast, in the northern Banni vicinity, and in the west towards the border with Pakistan, and the consequences are devastating: mineral extraction of bentonite, bromine, bauxite, and lignite ruining the landscape, aerial pollution tainting the air, and a plunging water table due to over-use of groundwater assets. There are now also many thousands of motor transport vehicles cramming once rustic byways and discharging foul waste.

Cheap subsidized electricity for agrarian use—like pumps—has led to a widespread exploitation of hydraulic resources; indiscretion in the consumption of water is gross as well as causative of hollows forming in the tectonic crust, a phenomenon conducive to further *seismos*. Recent practices of cash-crop cultivation—such as ground-nuts or cotton—are also water-intensive, unlike more traditional forms of agriculture that depend simply on the monsoon. Villages that once survived adequately on shallow wells and tanks that collected rain have become starved of water. A hundred years ago India consisted of almost forty percent forest land; now, that figure stands at six percent and continues to steadily diminish, and in the Kacch conditions of ecological harm are approaching the irreversible. Nowadays the equation between nature and humanity is such that former levels of consumption have been so far exceeded that little of the old life can be saved or retrieved: the ample and adequate proportions of life have gone awry. Without the water that is pumped through huge pipes drawing upon the great store of the Narmada Dam—far to the east of mainland Gujarat—life would presently be almost untenable. Yet the construction of that dam wrecked the lives and livelihood of tens of thousands of small farmers in the Narmada region, and the fluid came with an awful social price.

Adjunct to this, almost seventy percent of rainfall is lost due to poor or non-existent harvesting techniques: the monsoon, which usually arrives in July–August, brings on average a deluge of twelve centimeters, augmented by further showers that leave an overall deposit of thirty to forty centimeters of water. Occasionally the monsoon is double in quantity, and in those years, the extra supply is simply lost due to a lack of organization in the gathering and distribution of rain-water. I recall being at the Vijay Sagar dam once with Leanna and Pulin, our Mandvi physician friend: that year the rains were prolific and copious, but millions of tons of water were lost because there was no means for its collection. At the dam, the overflow was gigantic: it was very beautiful and we took photographs, but all of the water went to waste, running off into the sea.

Conversely, sometimes the rains do not come at all, and supplies have to be brought in by tanker. Regarding this import of water, there are in many villages abusive caste politics that stigmatize those who are in possession of little or no land and hence with little or no access to wells and tanks. There, water that is shipped in by road often never reaches its destination. Similarly, political allegiances that cluster about the water that is piped in from the Narmada Dam conduce to chicanery and inequitable distribution. There is an imminent calamity facing Kacch today, and I feel that the society Leanna and I had chosen to become part of is soon to face critical times, during which many of the older ways of life will be shed forever, unless tourism here and there encapsulates a few traditions within quaint and artificial bubbles. Certainly, increasing wealth should mean an increase in literacy and child health and a presumed decrease in penury and malnutrition, but such transitions do not always occur.

Perhaps the single major problem for today's Kacch—apart from the increasing industrialization that is occurring to the east—is caused by modernity's ability to sink deep artesian wells, so that in time, due to an over-liberal irrigation and excessive extraction, the water table has consistently sunk—at a rate of one meter a year—from thirty or forty feet to what is now several hundred feet below the surface of the ground. Traditional methods of harvesting rain can thus no longer function as aquifers become exhausted and sometimes also radically contaminated by intemperate use of pesticides and fertilizers. Even at Dholavira, the huge systems of catchment and storage of water indicate the longevity and efficiency of such practices. There are attempts nowadays to renew and restore such habits of retrieval—and I myself, along with Mr. Shah, attempted to develop a cistern construction scheme—but due to the indigence of so many villages and inherent conservatism of the villagers, there was not much success. In the part of Greece where we once lived, there were often no wells, and water supplies came from cisterns into which the winter rainfall had been directed, having been collected from the rooves of houses. This could work in the Kacch, except that a certain amount of funding would be required to construct so many concrete tanks, and that funding is as absent as is the direction.

Today, out in the desert, one comes across new walled-in farms of up to sixty acres in size. Surrounded by dry and rocky environs, these small holdings—because they have sunk deep bores into the earth and can pump up water and irrigate the soil—produce all manner of fruit trees: dates, mangoes, even bananas. Such modern wells drain the older village sources, however, and in general the water table continues to subside. Parallel to this process—and this is common throughout the subcontinent—deforestation, soil erosion, and desiccation are caused by an increasing population that requires fuel for cooking and fodder for its animals. Hence the ancient symmetries fail as the ratio of life destabilizes between fauna, humanity, and geography. Added to this disordering is a complete lack of waste disposal practices, particularly in the built-up areas, so that the accumulation of filth and disjected plastic makes for even greater unsightliness; also, thirty years ago, there was no plastic. Oddly enough, there is no civic sensibility either in the villages or the towns to organize this dispersal of refuse, and only if an important political personage is about to visit is the rubbish removed. Consequently, the amount of detritus—particularly used plastic bags—that lies about the ground and sticks to vegetation is prodigious. Clear fresh water, either running or standing in tanks, is virtually nonexistent, due to being polluted by the feces of humans and bovines, and after the monsoon there are always minor epidemics of dysenteric diseases and malaria.

Not so many years ago there used to be vultures and kites constantly visible in the sky. Now, because of certain medical treatments that have been given to cattle, these birds, especially the former, no longer exist: they have been poisoned by the dead cattle, the food of such birds. As a consequence there was an increase in the population of feral dogs, who presently perform the scavenging. Similarly, the feral pigs who once used to keep the towns and village clean of waste and fecal matter have suddenly vanished, for reasons that I have been unable to fathom. According to the Maharao, during the reconstruction of Bhuj, the pigs were exterminated, a bounty being placed upon each individual snout. According to another story, they were all rounded up and taken away and made into sausages by urban entrepreneurs. Thus the canine population suddenly rose even further.

When MacMurdo described the seismic disaster that struck Bhuj in June of 1819 he wrote, "It certainly was terrific to behold hills, towers, and houses, the stability of which we had been in the habit of considering as proof against every power, and against the lapse of centuries, rocking to and fro, or rising and sinking." In January of the year 2001, the terrible tremor that shook the Kacch destroyed many tens of thousands of lives and whole villages and towns; the main hospital at Bachau was completely levelled. At Anjar, two hundred children instantly died as their school fell upon them. The subsequent aid brought a plethora of funds to the region, most of which never reached its intended goals, being slipped into fraudulent or tendentious pockets. Bhuj, the capital, was devastated, and its rebuilding since then has completely changed the complexion of Kacchi life as the new city lounges across the plain and makes demands upon the region for support in terms of food, water, fuels, and labor.

Throughout the area, fifty thousand domestic dwellings needed to be immediately rebuilt. The event was a major social trauma, and the subsequent disorder caused by human greed and turpitude—in the long run— as groups competed for aid was possibly more harrowing than the grief of bereavement. For those seeking help and support, affiliation with the religiously conservative and ruling Bharatiya Janata Party, the BJP, gave priority of claim: need was irrelevant and disregarded in favor of political or communal allegiance.

Ironically, however, the calamity led to immense amounts of money being directed towards the Kacch, and affluence is now increasing rapidly. Factories and mines have appeared everywhere, and two mammoth electricity generating plants are being built on the south coast. This has meant that a rising number of salaried positions—employment, in other words—has benefited society in many ways by introducing cash into the economy. Yet the increase in the number of outside workers who are newly resident in the district is having adverse effects on the poise and steadiness of society, as these mainland laborers, living in bachelor households, do not always respect cultural norms concerning alcohol consumption, for instance—Gujarat is a dry state—or even prostitution. There are more than two thousand Chinese engineers working on the Adani power station near Judy's institute who have altered the complection of village life in that area.

As many of the staff for these burgeoning enterprises are not Kacchis but men who have been drawn from other states, the wages earned do not always enter the Kacchi economy, and despite the enormous and rapid increase of industrialization in the district, few Kacchis actually work in these new factories and mines; non-skilled labor has to be drawn into the area from other parts of India. Thus once again, the resident population receives little employment benefit from the new economy; in fact, the shifting demographic pattern indicates only further crisis for rural Kacchis. Former pastoralists who had never purchased but only exchanged will now often work in a factory and take home money to their families, yet to put a nomad on a production line does not conduce to his or her happiness. The moral integrity of pastoralists is proverbial, and such men often find employment as night watchmen in places like petrol stations or as security guards where cash transactions occur, but this is deeply alienating of their livelihood, thought, and the old morals of well-being.

Obversely, an educated Kacchi will nowadays typically migrate away to other parts of India or the world; in fact, significant higher education only occurs beyond the frontiers of Kacch. Migration out of the district began to gain in force during the nineteenth century after a series of natural disasters and calamities: seismic tremors, excessive monsoons, cholera epidemics, all conduced to periodic famine and hence a drifting population. At the beginning of the twentieth century, there were five years of frightful famine, the *chapaniya*, due to the rains not coming, and this in particular impelled many thousands to leave the region; a fifth of the population actually perished then, as did a vast number of animals. The typical practice today is for young men—and increasingly, young women—to migrate as soon as they can, and there are thus more Kacchis living outside the region and also outside India than actually inhabiting the district itself; rural Kacch is thus seriously deracinated. As Bombay rose to become a great harbor and city, so the mercantile and maritime life of the Kacchi ports diminished: hence the migrations, particularly by the Jain populace, who were instrumental in the building up of Bombay as a commercial *entrepot*. Only a few centuries before, the Jains had for similar reasons of natural crisis, transferred into the Kacch from further north. Today, the Kacchi economy is fueled by remittances from outside its boundaries, not only from Mumbai but from further afield, from England, East Africa, and North America. The population of Kacch presently stands at about one and a half million, yet more than twice that figure compose the Kacchi diaspora, as young men continue to leave their homes and migrate towards Mumbai or the West. Sadly their cash remissions often find a way towards temple construction and non-secular activities rather than into the establishment of clinics or schools, and the countryside is now encrusted with innumerable shrines and temples whose construction these exiles have financed. Some schools and clinics are supported by the philanthropy of those exiled, particularly by the Jain and Patel communities, but these are not extensive. We once visited a post-*bhokam* village in the east, where Mr. Shah and myself were due to speak. Gunatitpur was architecturally not an interesting place, but as a thoroughly viable community it was almost perfect. All the houses—there were forty or so families dwelling there—were well built and clean and possessed toilets. There was no refuse lying about the place, and there were many flourishing trees. It was truly a model village. It had been built with Patel money sent from outside the country and with contributions from the government of Oman, where a Patel held a high position in the government.

A great number of young men who have neither the education nor funds to travel far manage to migrate towards the Gulf and the Emirates, where they work—sometimes for decades—sending money back to their wives and families and now and then returning for a connubial visit. Some will only work for a few years and come back with sufficient capital to buy a motor vehicle or to set up a shop. Those who start work on the dhows as deckhands and then proceed to other kinds of shipping often manage to earn large amounts of cash with which they establish their families in a more comfortable life, for labor on the dhows often supplies a man with seaman's papers and he is then able to go on to work in larger and more international fleets or sometimes on foreign oil rigs. Until recently, smuggling of consumer goods and gold "biscuits" was a lucrative source of black or "number two" income for Mandvi, but the gathering renovation of India with its escalating middle class and a subsequent production of luxury goods has led to a decrease in the return that contraband brings.

Topography, tree cover, human habitation, and social organization, the prevalence or incidence of diverse animal life: all these shift and change in time, even small amounts of time; nothing is firm. I have seen old watercolors and drawings of the Kacch from about two hundred years ago, and the views were very different then, being more desert-like, arid, and uncovered, for the advent of the non-indigenous acacia *prosopis juliflora* during the last century changed the organic system of vegetation by destroying native growth. Only camel can feed upon this plant, and its thorns embed themselves in the hooves of sheep and goats, causing whole flocks to limp. Yet now when monsoon came, if it did at all, the landscape would become transiently and finely green with a thin skein of grasses upon the mineral earth as the thornbushes sprang into sudden new foliage, often with tiny and delicate white blossom whose perfume was delicious, like a mimosa.

So the days proceeded, gentle cool wintry days with tall clear skies of dark sapphire and those icy-cold hours before dawn, when in the villages and along roadsides, men shawled in blankets and wearing woollen hats and scarves would crouch and huddle beside small fires of scrapwood; those dawns were often misty with dense white clouds of dew that lingered above the earth. Then in the mid-year, heavy pre-monsoon humidity and intense heat would give way to sodden and rotting downpours, that is, if the recalcitrant monsoon came at all. If it did not, there were the sad spirits of herdsmen and shepherds to be encountered as Leanna and I went out on our walks in the hills or to the fields. Cattle and flocks would be emaciated and tottering unsteadily and slowly in their gait, weighed down by the glaring rays of a ferocious yellow sun. In the cooler and easier, times there were lighthearted festivals like Diwali and the chaotic, slightly delinquent vernal days of Holi, a time of bonfires and topsy-turvy fun.

There were also occasional political times, as when Chief Minister

Modi came to visit Kacch to give a speech on the beach at Mandvi. On that occasion, thousands of vocal supporters were trucked into the port and the town itself was meticulously cleaned of its refuse and filth: all the littered plastic bags suddenly vanished one night. The Mandvi populace without exception turned out that day to promenade the shore and to listen to the speeches. Strangely enough, CM Modi—who was a short and stocky man—from the shoulders up possessed an uncanny likeness to the small limestone bust portrait of what is usually called the "priest king" of Mohenjo-Daro, the former Indus Valley city.

We had been returning from Jakhau that day, trying to avoid the hullabaloo, when suddenly a cavalcade of vehicles crossed our path at a junction. There were black commandos, the *black cats*, everywhere with their dark automatic weapons and threatening anxious faces—they were trained in Israel—as the white Ambassador automobile of the CM sped past. Never before in my life had I witnessed such a brash and outright demonstration of power with such potential for precise and systematic violence, and this was a terrifically unpleasant experience. I realized how privileged we were today in comparison to those times when the Stalins and the Maos held sway. The images of those rapid instants stayed with me for a long time afterwards, tainting and discoloring my naïve and idyllic view of Kacchi life. As Pragmulji once remarked, the barbarians are always there, somewhere, waiting on the other side of the frontier, ready to dismantle and steal our lives; discontent lingers quietly in the midst of civilization. A year or so earlier, when the European Community had refused Modi a visa because of his ostensible default backing of the riots in Ahmedabad, we had acquaintances—a German painter and his wife who were staying on the outskirts of Mandvi—who had been harassed one night by government officials in an overtly odious manner, although there had been no further consequences.

Perhaps one of the most aesthetically pleasing dimensions of modernism and its irresistible process lies in the realm of architecture, in that so much of rural vernacular design is in fact good. For some reason, unlike in other parts of the world, like Greece, where contemporary domestic and urban architecture is often dreadful and tasteless if not simply downright crude, in present-day India, popular architecture even at mundane levels is excellent. I am not sure why this is, if the phenomenon is due to the great depth and range of Indic civilization and culture, insofar as there are profoundly established traditions of architectural form that no profanity can delete, or whether architecture in India today has naturally received an inflexible stamp from such great men as Lutyens, Le Corbusier, Louis Kahn, and Charles Correa.

Whatever the genealogy or source of such imprint, modern vernacular architecture in India maintains a crisp and attractive sense of balance and volume. I am consistently amazed in both town and villages how modernism sustains beautiful ratios and formal shape. Even the garish buildings of the new rich, who would erect showy and ostentatious structures in their natal villages, demonstrate a sensibility for design and architectural inventiveness, even if the results are not always good. Not only that, but Indian architects and the local builders—in the tradition of Corbusier—are excellent colorists, to the extent that color itself often assumes or expresses architectural form.

It is a moot question as to why one culture—in how it developed and innovated—should succeed in a particular aspect of taste and another culture would fail: whether the influence was long term, and the traditions themselves were indelibly current, or whether the cause was human and individual, and the greatness of a few architects were deeply impressive? Certainly, the Moghuls directed much time, resources, and intellectual effort towards the creation of exquisite buildings, and this too has left its trace. It is remarkable, however, to pass through a small village and see something as simple as a concrete bus shelter or a column erected to hold bird food built with fine proportion and beautifully and brilliantly painted. It always puzzled me why the human sensibility for pragmatic and material beauty was such a complicated affair and was in no way natural but always varied from place to place; human civilization is perhaps more influential and indelible than we think.

Despite all these insidious and menacing intrusions of the present century, both pernicious and otherwise, in my mind's eye as I write these lines sitting at my desk at Jalaram Bag, listening to the taped music of Bismillah Khan, in this little circular room downstairs that is half sunken into the earth, I often find myself back in the Maharao's sanctuary at Pragsar, where we frequently used to go and walk during those early days and observe the birds—kingfishers and ibis and little bee-catchers—and the many silent floating crocodiles out on the lake. Once during those early years we noticed a spotted panther, a *chitro*, slinking away to the rocks; only a few now remain out of the thousands that once roamed all of Kacch. At the highest point in the landscape, the Maharao's lookout, we often used sit upon the stones for a while and drink some water and gaze out across that ancient panorama with its little crimson hills and former volcanoes. At the small nearby shrine sacred to Siva, we would sometimes pause and Leanna would make an offering in the shadows beneath the gulmohar trees. That old *pujari* is now gone, for Jehan sacked him for hacking off the paws of the dead panther with an axe, presumably in order to sell the claws; the new priest is somewhat shy and unspoken.

That is old Kacch, in contrast to this new society that is rapidly sweeping across the land. Some of the happiest and most lighthearted moments of my life have been spent at Pragsar, as we stared across miles of dry elemental terrain. Whatever anxiety or unease I had been feeling about how the environment throughout the world was deteriorating, that would be dispelled by the unusual air of supernal well-being that lingered throughout the place. Wandering on foot upon Pragsar's dusty earth, far away from human signs, I always felt at ease and untroubled, as if balance did exist within the cosmos and there was direction rather than merely incoherence and despoliation. I suppose there is a value in land conservation, but it does come with an exclusive and selective price.

It is autumn here and *Navratri* and the mornings are cool, the skies more declined and gentle, lacking that blazing summery quality; the light slants more obliquely and the shadows are darker and more precise. At this time of the year, the roads leading towards the town of Mata-No-Madh are crammed with pilgrims making their way on foot towards the temple of Devi Ashapura Ma. The lanes are crammed with folk and their banners and flags; they come from hundreds of miles away and sleep beside the roads at night and crowd the tea-stalls that have appeared along the side of the ways, just for a sight of the goddess in her shrine. This is one of the loveliest times of the year, for the land remains tinted green from the rains and has not yet been parched by the sun, and birds have begun to migrate back towards the shores and standing waters of the area, cranes and pelicans and gulls, and the fields are full and flourishing.

Sometimes I find myself recalling our past years in America, walking beside the broad sluggish river in Cambridge, watching the scullers. I puzzle over how tensioned and compacted my time was then, as university life circulated around the great library of that town. I had once been poet in residence at one of the undergraduate Houses and also president of an old arts and letters society, and I often recall those days spent with students and their boisterous and energetic habits: they were so full of excitement and ambition, those young ones. Sometimes I miss that academic and intellectual culture and its conversations, but until I wedded Leanna I had always been slightly lonely in Cambridge, never really part of that world no matter how I tried to understand it and study its history and manners, its arts and architecture and the establishment life of its museums and recital halls. I did manage to capture its aesthetic, but that was all, for emotionally Cambridge always evaded me. I never loved Cambridge no matter how I tried, like I love the Kacch, for there was never any unison. My time there had been like an arranged marriage that was not quite successful: it worked, but it lacked spontaneous joy or passionate desire.

At one point during that early time in the Kacch, when we were still attuning ourselves to the details and moods of daily life, almost every afternoon Leanna and I used to walk along the nearby coast, as the ocean boomed turbulent and brown, as the tides slowly moved with their frequent tempo up and down the sands, and the little spoonbills and terns roamed the water's edge. The Arabian Sea more than any other body of water has shown to me what emptiness means, glittering and saline and hot; it was not without life, but without visible life, for a strange unseen world teemed out there. Now and again on the shore near to the palace, young tawny-colored camels would be wandering, having come down to the sands to rest and ruminate. Our little daughter loved those animals more than anything.

Crossing that narrow bridge on foot towards Mandvi and seeing all those gigantic wooden ships in various states of construction and repair upon the mud, whilst boys scampered beneath the hulls and men with a few tools and nothing but their knowledge and words built those enormous and beautiful vessels, that view—even in my imagination—still fills me with a calm happiness. Even today, I often drive into Mandvi in order to go and sit alone at the *chai*-stall near the Customs House, just to watch the lives who are attached to those vessels. For the thoughts I have there are like instruments with which I can remove the compression of our contrived life in the West, with its artifice and cheap sensibilities, and live on earth more completely. Similarly, it is really people like the Phakirani Jaths, who so shun and scorn any possession of property, who are the only ones to actually remember and know—not only the old Kacchi life, but also what it truly means to be human and unencumbered by material. Those desert folk—the Rabari and Meghwal—have something in their eyes, an experience come of years of dignity and struggle and a profound symbiosis with the landscape, that troubles me and fills me with a strange desire to know what *genius* they possess in their hearts. Of course that is impossible and on my part mere romance, but that unique idea that they own, I still pursue.

What I have been describing concerns not only present-day Kacch but all of India and, of course, by extension, Asia. In other regions of sub-continent during the last hundred years, the destruction of tribal life—those forest communities like the Santhal, the Gonds, and Nagas—has been horrific. The modernization of traditional forms of social life, the increasing urbanization of human settlement, and the degradation of the natural world are conditions that are occurring more or less throughout all the East and most awfully in China. The Kacch just happens to be my own paradigm. Such transitions also happened in Europe and North America during the eighteenth and nineteenth centuries, but technology has developed to such an extent that homologies are not possible between the two times and two places, and what is present now can perhaps be construed as irreversibly damaging: no retrieval will be possible given the present degree of despoliation, and nothing can exonerate this.

Just as in Europe in the early modern period, the old religion of Marian and agricultural devotion was thrust aside by a burgeoning mercantile Protestantism, so in the Kacch today there exists a similar trend away from the worship of Devi and towards the more male-oriented and intrinsically urban Swaminarayan sect: an institution that is becoming increasingly powerful, both politically and economically, as it displaces the former *kshatriya* ascendancy. Deities as social metaphors are constantly shifting in themselves, migrating after their own fashion as they persist in professing universality. In this new century, Swaminarayan Hinduism becomes a vital component in the organization of identity among the Kacchi *émigrés*. The are the ones to finance the great *mandir*, a huge cathedral-like temple that is being constructed in Bhuj, just beside the lovely, ancient, and presently ruined Mahadeo shrines with their many hero stones. It will take years to complete, but its colossal marble ostentation says much about the new culture.

There exists no necessity to this paradigm, however, for Malayalam Kerala in the south has succeeded in making the transit, and modernity has brought with it a comfortable equilibrium, where the life expectancy and literacy of women—key markers in judging the quality of life—are the highest in all India and infant mortality rates are exceptionally low. There, an erstwhile social system of predominant matriliny has become—in time—a political system of Marxist communism with an admixture of ancient Christianity and a few grains of aged Judaism. Modernity is not inevitably offensive and opprobrious; it possesses no mandatory destiny, and a key signifier of success appears to lie in the privileging of femininity—in terms of education and property rights—that makes for less humiliating exclusiveness in society and for healthier innovation.

When the present Maharao expires—for he has no offspring—I wonder what will become of the Kacch and what will happen to his patrimony: what does the twenty-first century hold for this benign and harmonious place? Desiccation of the earth, contamination of the landscape, a flood of grimy cargo-vehicles on the narrow roads and tourists who drive out to photograph the Rabari villages and purchase from the women some item of authentic embroidery: is this the eco-touristic future? Can Kacch experience an *anabasis*, I wonder, without losing its inner tissue? The palace will become a hotel, and its pristine shores will become a place for bourgeois leisure, bikinis, and alcohol, and the new ports of Mundra and Gandhidham will become extensive conurbations, miscreant and savage in their struggle for survival. Present-day Kacch is without law, as the old equations falter and new trends of mistreatment and dominance appear, based upon novel formations of wealth—typically the urban—and where the old chicaneries of caste politics persist. Among the villages, former systems of caste supremacy still tend to operate, and Harijans and *adivasi* outcastes often remain thoroughly abused.

As the old systems of order and the monitoring of social life—paradigms of exchange and exclusion typically based on community and village—collapse and become redundant, there is suddenly a great lack of decent civic sensibility; by default, venality becomes an actual necessity if the new system is to function with a modicum of process and without formal infrastructure. Given the great rigidity of traditional society, a world of strict degree and highly tuned marital systems of exchange, I have often wondered if the dishonesty and bribery that now naturally flourish at almost every level as commonplace are not actually a cultural and received standard, having developed as a medium of vitality and energy in that previous restricted world, much as a *return of the repressed*. What we consider "corruption" was once in fact a normal reaction within the vascular system of hierarchic exchanges, which had ossified into a mere skeletal structure.

I recall being at a girls' school in Bhuj one evening with Mr. Shah. We had been asked to speak on some issue, and I remember talking about Nehru and his view of education. At the close of the program, as we were all shaking hands and bidding farewell, our host had introduced me to a blind man who had been playing the harmonium when a song recital had been given earlier in the proceedings. I watched him depart, being led by a purblind young boy; another blind youth had one hand upon the musician's shoulder, and similarly, another youth was so attached, and another, as they carefully and delicately made their egress. Human culture is like that, as is language: it is blind and might only continue, for change and innovation are rare if not irrelevant. No matter how conditions alter, culture will always go on regardless. It is simply a matter of metonymic association crossing time, unless the pressure upon the order of exchanges and limitations cracks, fissures, or erupts, and then the practice dissolves. For it is always terrain and its aspects, not society and ideas, that are fundamental and most profound in the motive effort that directs variance. Desertification, earthquake, climate change, and of course, migration influence human definition and substitution at a most initial level.

There remains this inalienable and potentially transcendental virtue of location, regardless of human precedent; it is the land itself that has created these small and vigorously private cultures. For me, being in the Kacch and wandering its plains and hills during various seasons allowed me to see what I had only previously envisioned in poetry and literary scholarship: an ideal landscape and rural populace that I had carefully imagined and slowly constructed only in words over several decades came into immediate existence. Suddenly it was as if time had been arrested in its process and what had only existed as an idea was briefly reified. Long ago when we came to the Kacch on a university fellowship to study the manifestations of the epic *Mahabharata* in the present day, I little realized that I would be spending my days pursuing those tropes and metaphors of literature in the extant and authentic world rather than in poetry, as I began to examine the lives of modern *kshatriyas* and all that surrounded them. So there, with my wife and children, I was able to ramble the terrain and be simply overwhelmed by its beauty and complexity and the amazing decency, kindness, and sweetness of the people, and to observe—for a while, because it too was vanishing—a world of extraordinary natural poise and equilibrium that appeared to hover in time rather than move with the days. Suddenly, it was as if human life itself was a remarkable and unique work of art, replete with perfect transparency, and for me, the aesthetic must perforce always behave morally in effect.

Once, when we happened to be visiting Lakhpat—I think that it was during a winter season, for I can recall the startling perspicacity and great altitude of the sky with an intensely blue coalescence and tracery of alto cirrus—my son and I passed through one of the broken old gateways with its massive doors and walked out into the Rann. People often used to call him Moksh, which in Sanskrit and in present parlance means release or deliverance, referring to when the soul or *atma* is at last freed from its material weight or conditions and earthly qualities fall away as the spirit is finally loosed from the necessity of rebirth and further compulsion. He was thus often curious about the soul and afterlife, and we would frequently speak of such matters when we walked alone together.

Leanna and little Manki had gone off to visit the Sikh *gurudvara* because they were thirsty, as we had drunk all of our water. Jagdish had wandered away in order to find something to eat and a place to take his siesta. So Max and I discovered the broken gateway alone and set off to walk for a while into the Rann, as the tide was then far out from the land. This was the region that Arrian had described as Kaumara. The sands were shining and firm and were littered with small convex calciform discs, and the sheen of wetness beneath our feet—a dun-colored slight brown— reflected the blue and white of the sky above; all was a delicate and milky color, gentle and airy, and it was as if were walking into great and fathomless space, without substance or level. I forget what we were talking about, but I seem to recall that in those years Maxim only talked about books and what he had read in books; his hero then was Wilfred Thesiger or anyone who wrote about camels and exploration.

There were some ruined and desolate fishing boats rotting on one of the banks, and we walked over to inspect their black shapes. Dead boats always inspired me with a wistfulness, for their bleakness and decomposition seemed to be so slow and relaxed, so easy, as the decaying form appeared to be perfectly natural and unobtrusive in the world, in distinct counterpoint to our fractious haste and desperation at the possibility of demise. We also walked out to what was a rocky islet where the stone wreckage of a former shrine or navigational mark had tumbled about upon the sandy ground. I could scarcely hear those old human voices from long ago speaking there as they conducted business; all was so vacant and abandoned, lost from time and human activity. It was as if having crossed through that deep gigantic threshold and the lopsided gates, we had suddenly entered upon another kind of universe, one where human activity and life was thoroughly absent and there was nothing but docile silence and a beneficent and absolutely open space where we had become merely two souls, attached but verbally apart. The magnitude and deliquescence of the volatile marine light was almost fluid and vivacious and itself supportive of life as we casually wandered hand in hand.

We strolled for an hour or so before setting off back towards the umber-colored walls of Lakhpat, which from the distance appeared dark and formidable. It was pleasant to saunter through so much empty volume, to be so patently horizontal and unencompassed and beneath such a colossal dome of open heaven. I recall at the time wondering if Maxim would ever remember that short walk, where he would be in life—both in time and place—when and if he did recall our brief ramble out across the Rann into nothing, and what the moment would signify for him. In fact, I often wondered how our days together in the Kacch would affect the metaphors and affinities that would run through his later life and what, if any, attachments would occur in consequence of those compelling necessities when boundaries are perceived and crossings are made.

For me, life has not only been composed of people but also of places; my intimate and emotional society has always been marked by the earth itself as well as by human population and amity. I wondered then if Max would grow up to know the world similarly, as possessing an equal and yet unspeakable valence with human life: what can be described as the decency of natural splendor and universal conscience. Yet a destiny runs within our arteries from conception, and, in a sense, all this has already been spoken.

VI. Mata-No-Madh:
The Unspeakable

Here on a shelf next to where my books are ranged lie various ceramic sherds that we gathered from Dholavira. There are some fired clay balls, shot for slings, and items of carved seashell that were used by women as jewelery, as well as some copper beads and some stone blades and a small archaic bull made of fired clay, decorated with indented circles. I also have some fragments of what is called painted grayware, pottery that Indian scholars typically associate with the period when *Mahabharata* flourished, although I do not really believe in that connection. There is the Kacch of terrain and an ancient and unspeaking dust, the plains and small peaked hills. There is also the Kacch of people, of communities and bucolic sandy villages and hamlets and of periodic transhumant migration. The traditions of these men and women and their patterns of dress and decorative apparel are so old-fashioned in the light of functional and global modernity, and that Kacch is far removed from the contemporary Western state. Then there is the new Kacch, which has come into existence since the earthquake, and new Bhuj, an emblem of this cultural movement towards the vastly permeable twenty-first century.

There are the languages of Kacch, the dialects and the different kinds of speech, and the metaphors that landscape has driven into common parlance: terms and phrases of life that derive from aspects of physical topography. It is not by chance that the central deity of all Kacch, Ashapura Ma, is *svayambhu*—that is, self-arisen or self-generated, meaning that she once appeared spontaneously and naturally from the earth itself, manifest at Mata-No-Madh. There is so much about Kacchi life that is *svayambhu*, and it is only modernity that has countered and restrained this phenomenon by thrusting its factories and warehouses and thousands of grimy oily trucks upon the old terrain.

On the one hand there is experience or personal narrative, and on the other hand there is research and scholarship: this book is an attempt to bind the two elements, these two wires of knowledge, and at some point to transcend that fusion. On the one hand there is sensation and emotion, and on the other hand there is a rational acquisition and organization of information; sometimes one form will predominate, and on other occasions the other is more adept and adroit. This is how human culture operates, fitting the received with events themselves, adjusting and sometimes conflicting, and this is how humanism makes its forays into accomplishing further equilibria. It is only at an observed boundary that an exchange of ideas occurs, and culture is patterned by these perceived limitations and substitutions, neither of which are natural.

It has always been a struggle for me, being aware of what I do not know and yet simultaneously needing to appear—being an academic—as an authority, one who possesses neither ambivalence nor equivocation. I have always been acutely conscious of how little Leanna and I comprehend about Kacchi life and time and how much our research and knowledge is profoundly superficial and actually trivial. This book is not a travelogue; there are too many of those on the market nowadays, nor is it a work of cautious scholarship, for I have done that elsewhere; nor is it poetry, which has been my life's central medium and art. I have studiously avoided that kind of literature within these pages. Here is an account of our *periplus* about the island of Kacch and its communities, that is all; it is an attempt to understand and to penetrate into ambiguity with language and sometimes knowledge. The Greek *théoros*—a term which gives us our word theory—was traditionally one who was sent like an ambassador to observe and report. This book is founded on a similar process. To travel is to *travail*, to create value; it is work, but mental and emotional work.

Other scholars have been drawn to Kacch in the last few decades. Judy first entered that world in order to research textiles and fell in love with the people. Edward Simpson, an English ethnographer from London, had in his youth wanted to become a boat builder and to apprentice himself to the trade and learn how to build wooden boats. Then as an undergraduate student he had bicycled the coastline of Gujarat, becoming captivated by the shipwrights of Mandvi, the group of men whom he later wrote about in his excellent study. Farhana Ibrahim is a radical feminist scholar of the effect of borders and boundaries. John McLeod is an American historian who is a friend of the Dhrangadhra Jhalas; he has recently written a lengthy and definitive article on the Kacchi *bhayad* in the nineteenth century. Rushbrook Williams was a historian of myth and legend who assembled a coherent—if not various and divergent—chronology of Pragmulji's lineage.

Of all the outsiders who have been drawn to Kacch and inspired by its landscape and society, Scottish MacMurdo was probably the most Romantic of them all, yet he passed away at the age of thirty-five. Unlike the sad little British cemetery outside of Mandvi, which dates back to the early nineteenth century and which has been systematically wrecked and vandalized—probably during Quit India times—MacMurdo's *chattri* continues to stand in picturesque isolation. In rereading his work and in coming across the sparse details of his life, I constantly had a sense of his great love of place and its various lives and of his enthusiasm and natural sensibility for Kacch. He was a true *théoros*.

This is a book about passions, the constant desires that flourish inside of our beings and drive us towards action. A passion for language, a passion for another human body, for the satisfaction and levelling that is uncovered by friendship; the passion to be walking upon a remote part of the planet's surface, the passion for the acquisition of knowledge itself and an extension of language and metaphor. There are many fugitive desires at work in this book, which I have attempted to weave and knit together into a single form. There is also the passion of the migrant to secure a place on earth that is both familiar and not unstable, for love to thrive therein and for death to be comfortable and not lonely.

Love, need, desire, temerity, all of these aspects of human emotion are threaded by constraint, for not one of these feelings exists in an unbounded manner. As sentient creatures, we reach out into a world and society and touch upon other beings, and thus emotional exchanges occur, those invisible transactions that actually constitute human awareness. Sometimes these take on a more permanent form when love is practiced and become a grounding for time: love that establishes the primary state of all human action and its codes.

This book concerns such human effort and the fervor, the ardor and the zeal that go into making a life more than itself, the fervor that takes us beyond a state of mere action upon an unknown stage. Sometimes people do become cognizant of their acting—that is arguably the postmodern condition—but rarely do they apprehend the situation and nature of their stage. For me, Kacch has been another metaphor where consciousness might find location: both Kacch and Leanna drew me out of myself and simultaneously limited me in my action and thought. Part of this trade, this economy of feelings, is given here in these pages in verbal form and expression. Some people would soundly aver that words are the only valid and true home of human life and that nothing further exists and there is no natural substrate, and hence we move only through language itself, in thought and in speech.

In my mind now I can locate many beautiful and amazing incidents during those Kacchi years of ours, wonderful moments that were marvelous and transporting, circumstances that changed the gravity of all of our life, which took us away and colored us indelibly with their sensations and perceptions and changed our value of being.

One such instant occurred—and I cannot recall exactly when this was in the cycle of the year's festivities; perhaps it was *Svatantradivas*—when there was a great fair in the town of Bidhada, and the untidy gentle village became a teeming body of music and crowds and smoky pungent dust. I never liked masses of people, and Leanna and the children had gone alone during the early afternoon, leaving me at the house reading and typing up my notes. They returned two hours later, excited, perspiring, and grimy, insisting that I return with them, as the event was much fun. So we set off again down the sandy track towards the village, Manki in the rucksack upon my shoulders and Maxim's shirt stained with melon juice and the various kinds of sweet festival drinks that he had consumed. An air of amusement and holiday was about the place, and everyone was dressed up and sauntering; no one was working, and all draught animals were hobbled. Camels and ponies and bullocks all stood and stared in wonder at the rowdy swarming hubbub.

Bhavesh, a young man who worked as Mr. Shah's personal servant and who also tended to the cultivation of flowers at Jalaram Bag—he did not work among the fruit trees—was singing that day. He was the favorite of Leanna among the staff, youthful, unmarried, and infinitely kind, and she used to rely on him for help about the household and for questions about manners and convention; he was her *confidant*. The rest of the staff resented him for being closer than they were to Mr. Shah and also for the fact that his work was different and less laborious; he was also more intelligent and dynamic and was profoundly devoted to his *guru* and deities. His *kuldevi*, the guardians of his community, were the Jakhs, the equestrian figures who reputedly once came from Byzantium to the Kacch. His marriage had already been arranged and he had given us a photograph of his prospective *fiancée*, whom he had met once or twice and bashfully adored. During his afternoon siesta when everyone else slept, Bhavesh would study the *Gita* or the words of his *guru*, or he would lie on the terrace and listen to recordings of devotional songs that he had downloaded onto his cell phone.

On that day he was himself singing—for that was his private and most ambitious life—and when we arrived at the *maidan,* the central open space of the village, there he was in his best tight jeans and tight patterned shirt upon a dais with drummers and a harmonium player, singing into the microphone surrounded by many hundreds of attentive and circulating festive villagers. Upon the broken walls about the area, almost like puppet figures, dozens of boys were sitting or crouching and overlooking the party. The atmosphere was hot, and a cloudy dust had been raised by the many feet; the amplified noise of drums and of Bhavesh's voice dominated the scene; it was too loud for anyone to talk. Max—who appeared to be known by everyone in the village and was constantly greeted and hailed—kept on disappearing, wandering about and then returning with news of what he had found. Leanna was charmed by Bhavesh's vocal and stylish expertise, and little Manki was childishly astonished at the dense quantity of laughing and gay humanity. After Bhavesh had finished, he joined us for a while and we strolled together, and he insisted on paying for the children to have drinks and fruit and to take rides on the several welded iron swings and roundabouts that had been set up in the village.

There were also *funambules,* two children who worked a tight-rope that was stretched about twelve feet above the thronging multitude whilst their father went around touting them and holding out a tin for donations. For me, the desperate little faces of those two hungry and overworked children were the one dissonant point in the afternoon. Such acrobatic folk were perhaps the only true nomads that existed any more in India, as they went about the country from fair to fair, year after year pursuing a hard, grueling existence. Bhavesh was proud and happy that day and looked smart in his number-one clothes, although he was thoroughly drenched with sweat and darkened with grime. Eventually he went off with some friends, exhausted because he had been up all night singing at his village temple before returning to Bidhada. He made a good amount of money that day, which he was saving to make a compact-disc recording of his songs at a studio in Bhuj, the prospect of which was most satisfying for him.

Soon the music was playing again and all the teenagers of the village began to dance, boys with boys and girls with girls, each one with a pair of sticks or wands that they rhythmically struck against those of a moving partner in time with the music as they circled and stepped about the earth floor. It was a scene of great enjoyment and mirth, and many of the young men danced exultantly whilst the girls were far more reserved. The parents stood about or sat on benches or stones at *chai*-stands watching the unmarried, the future grooms and brides of the village, who were celebrating their youth and good looks. It was a scene that made me content also, for its promise and its beauty and its easiness, its glad hilarity. There are few moments in life that are absolutely delightful, like marriages, for instance, that are cheerful and good in an irrefutable fashion—in the same way that odd numbers and even numbers are absolutely distinct—and communal joy is filled to a maximum. I had once witnessed such unmixed instants in Greece at Easter, village celebrations that were pure and unaffected and full of rare, unalloyed pleasure. To see the parents and grandparents and uncles and aunts of Bidhada standing apart from the dancing and watching the juvenile and unwed young perform the *danda-rasa*, the stick dance, was something appealing and remarkable and wonderfully stately, and I too felt unusually glad.

After that event there occurred a contest among the male youth to break a clay pot with a bamboo cane. The large pot was placed on a stool and had been filled with water, and this was set in the middle of an area cleared amongst the crowd. Successive youths and boys were blindfolded by a master of ceremonies and given a cane, and having been spun about a couple of times by his assistants in order to disorient them, they were vocally encouraged by the crowd to locate the pot and with one firm downward blow to free the waters. This, with much cheering and hooraying as contender after contender made their assays, was only completed after more than an hour, and the victor awarded his triumph.

We walked home that evening in the slow dusk, thirsty and oily with perspiration, exhilarated and exhausted by so much busy and noisy display and the agitation of the many people. As the air grew dark and shadowy and the shapes of cattle stared at our passing, we spoke about the afternoon and its wonderful humor and community. It had been an outstanding few hours of shared contentment, hours that had been lightly and pleasurably separated from the usual days of work, sustenance, sleep, and the repetitions of dawn and night. There was nothing exceptional about that day, but its emotions had been profoundly rewarding for reasons of glad association.

In our travels over the years about Kacch, we had come across several beautiful villages; some old Jain villages in the south about the region of Jakhau had been especially lovely, with finely made patrician houses and exquisite temples. Bidhada still had some handsome buildings, embellished with sculpture and wonderfully proportioned, although most of them had been knocked down by now and replaced with bigger and more recent concrete structures; it was not an appealing model village by any means, and I never felt passionately about it as I did, say, for Mandvi. Yet as we wandered home that evening I felt a warmth and affection that I had not experienced before, a recognition and an acceptance of our slight peripheral and yet strangely integral role there: integral because of our children, who were known and welcomed by everyone. I felt simply human that evening, pleased with the smallness and imperfection of life, with its modest capacity for ordinary happiness.

One day in the late spring when the season was already hot—the neem trees were blooming and the gehena were putting out their light feathery flowers—Bhavesh had come to the house after work had finished and asked that we join him for horse racing out to the west of the village; that was the area that Leanna and I often walked of an evening, where we would stroll and review the day. It was the festival of Hajjipir, the Moslem saint whose *dargha* was up to the north on the edge of Banni; Leanna had already heard about the races—both pony races and ox-chariot races, and there were also supposed to be wrestling matches—and she was keen to be present. Maxim was of an age where he did not really want to have to do anything with his parents, yet he joined us. Little Manki was still portable in the rucksack, yet she was becoming heavy. As usual Bhavesh was perfectly gentlemanly and behaved as our host, which Leanna enjoyed; at one point he introduced us to his brother and brother-in-law, both of whom had sugar-cane juice stalls.

I was adamant to attend this occasion, as the year before I had missed a celebration for Bhima—one of the heroes of the *Mahabharata*—that was supposed to venerate the termination of a fast which he had endured. Of all the Pandava heroes, Bhima was the glutton, so a fast was unusual. There was the town of Habaya to the northeast of Bhuj, where this day was dedicated to remembering Bhima as a divine herald of the monsoon, and I had kept on missing the event. I wanted to see how the modern world dedicated a day in honor of an epic hero; it would be akin to Cambridge commemorating an event in the life of Achilles.

We went out of the Jalaram Bag gates and left towards the open fields and commons; it was an area that I was always fond of, and I sometimes went walking there alone in the late-night darkness. Soon we were among many hundreds of people—all men—who had lined themselves up along a track of about two kilometers in the sand. It was a serious gathering and slightly tense, and here and there nervous ponies were being groomed or stood on tether. We walked down towards the right, where sounds of applause and shouting emanated: that was the *kushti*, the wrestling, and we arrived just as it was ending.

I kept my distance, but Leanna, Max, and Bhavesh elbowed and shoved their way towards the center of the ring, where two men in cotton shorts and zonal belts were in the grips of a bout, grunting and growling. Now and then as the circle of several hundred men swerved sideways, like an animal, I caught a glimpse of the match. The cheering was intensely loud, and bets were obviously being laid. I always felt apprehensive among passionate crowds, and I felt particularly uneasy that day because I had a small child upon my back, so I left and wandered back towards the race-track. The others soon joined me, as they too had been overly confined by the swaying *melée*. Leanna was the only woman present out there and I felt just a little less than indifferent: the thoroughly masculine audience was not a joyous body, but was serious and intent and very male.

Soon the first young ponies, ridden by youths on bareback, went cantering past looking beautiful and graceful. Then a while after that came the low wooden-wheeled chariots, each drawn by a yoke of oxen, the drivers twisting the tails of the beasts in order to gain more speed. The crowd was live with shouting and encouragement as the various competitors sped by us. Bhavesh kept on quietly directing that we stay clear of certain groups of men, as they had been drinking country liquor and would be unpredictable; I wanted to leave as soon as the races were concluded, but Leanna insisted on roaming around and looking at people. She greeted many of the men—shopkeepers who sold her sweets, the potter and his brothers whose household she sometimes visited; we met several farmers whom we knew. Now and then we glimpsed a few women hidden in the rear of *tum-tums*, *saris* concealing their faces, but that was a strangely if not eerily male assembly, and I had not experienced such before in the Kacch.

What did interest me was that the festivities were in praise or memory of the Moslem *pir*; his day was being remembered with athletic contest and performance. In Cambridge I had on certain occasions lectured on the genealogy of athletics, for this was something that had hypothetically originated with the death of a hero, when the companions would conduct funeral games in his honor. Thereafter, the events were held annually or seasonally in recollection of those heroic deaths and became, in time, what we know today as the Games or *agonés*, a word cognate with our term agony or antagonism.

For me, *Iliad* was the most perfect poetry that I was aware of, and my research with *Mahabharata* had always been secondary to my Homeric studies. I loved the Kacch because very often it allowed me to sight an old heroic world that had everywhere else vanished, and once again, on that day—and this was not a *kshatriya* festival—I was suddenly able to perceive how it had once probably been: to slip through an interstice and to join with another kind of time and be witness. I loved those moments of temporal freedom, as I well imagined MacMurdo—also trained in classical scholarship—must have loved his views of another world: not a feudal and romantic world, which had been so captivating to the British imperial imagination, but a world that was still unconsciously enacting or repeating a former poetic age when heroes had existed and walked the ground.

Only once, and that was brusque and instantly transient, did I really experience any contact with that primordial and thoroughly terrestrial genius of the *Kshatriyas*, something elemental that I knew from literature and epic, but that I had not until that moment actually understood in its core as a mindful emotion. We had been visiting Bhuj in order to see what was new on Kamlesh's book-shelves and had then gone to call upon the Bhujwalas at Camp. There we chatted and had tea in English teacups whilst the children played in the courtyard and Katie showed us some recent pictures from their life at Kanha. Then, as *muezzin* began at the mosque next door, we decided to go for a drive and set off with Jagdish towards the small hill-temple of Tapkeshvar.

It is odd how in life some of the most revealing instants come quickly and unexpectedly and then directly vanish, and one's comprehension, suddenly confounding all time and depth, exists more as an amazing and vital retrospect than as any kind of mediate reality.

The temple was in the hills above Bhuj in an area where the military trained and practiced; firing ranges were there and obstacle courses, and cliff faces were marked with large painted directions so that the young soldiers could follow particular ascents. Mottos like *Shoot to Kill* were stenciled on the rocks in tall twelve-foot letters. The temple to the goddess Devi was tiny and recent—its earlier form must have been destroyed by earthquake—and the situation was similar to that of the great Buddhist site at Ellora in Maharashtra, being of a horseshoe-like form, with dozens of little monastic cubicles, arcades, and rooms being carved into the stone face on either side of the *mandir*. As we drove up the narrow winding road at dusk, higher and higher into the range, we passed many young men dressed in shorts and running shoes who were also going in that direction. They were young officers from the army base below on their way to make an evening *puja* to the goddess. Some of them were quietly running uphill, others were arm in arm or hand in hand, some were solitary and serious of mien.

We halted and parked and left Jagdish to enjoy himself alone. Leanna and Katie went with the girls and sat upon a high terrace, and Jehan took the boys uphill towards some caves. I wandered about, not so much concerned with the place, but with the men who were arriving and washing their feet and often exclaiming *Jai Mataji*, or *Jai Hind*. They completely ignored us and almost seemed to resent our foreign presence, which was unusual, for people were always welcoming in the Kacch; here, the cadets did not even look in our direction, so intent were they on their business. Quietly and casually they made their way and halted at a spring to remove shoes and bathe their feet before entering into the shrine, where a *pujari* greeted them as they sat down upon the ground. I rested on a high parapet and pretended not to watch. Then the drums and bells began to sound and an unhurried monotonous chanting began.

That sound was the deep inner current of *kshatriya* India. These young and devout if not fanatical warriors were singing of their joy and adoration to the goddess, she who was their soul and spirit of their earthly world, an image that they were trained and prepared to kill and die for, and in whose name, and in friendship with their companion soldiers, they were presenting a unified voice.

The singing went on and on, changing in tempo and sometimes in diction as the mantra shifted pace, and I almost felt the wetness of tissue or soul, the awful indescribable moist nature of that invisible nucleus of India to which these young officers were prepared to sacrifice their lives: and it was a sacrifice, quite certainly, for the blood involved represented the indestructible verve of that terrific deity whom they were presently invoking as their spiritual envelope. Those rhythms and sounds, the slightly soft syllables and nasalized vowels droning on and on repetitively, accompanied by clapping and drumming and the clanging of triangles, told me more about India than I had ever before received. That was also the *Hind* that Pragmulji—in the various complex rites that he led—sought to maintain as an evoked and elicited ideal, an idea that had been long transported by song through time.

Jehan returned; Leanna and Katie were anxious to take the children homeward, and Jagdish was ready to proceed. He too had loved the spot and he had been impressed by the vigor and virility of the *javans*, the youthful warriors. Often have I tried to recollect the details of that brief visit, trying to reformulate its meaning and its signs, but it happened so quickly and then we departed. I wanted to remain there in the agate twilight among the rocks, drawing in that tremendous old spirit that was so available to those men and so familiar to me but never experienced except in poetry. Momentarily I had the nerves and veins in my hands and could sense the vibration and pulse of that material body: an invisible and unimaginable flesh that so composed the ancient landscape and human souls who dwelled and walked upon its terrain and whose blood was the spirit and reflex of that earth. I say this not in praise of the inane cruelty and folly of war and violent death, but simply as an observation upon the intrinsic and genuine nature of human society in that place at its most irresistibly tragic. For an instant there had occurred a partition of things, and I had suddenly witnessed an interior lust and true figure of pitiless, cold moral wisdom. Unfortunately where death is made beautiful, there is no hope.

Another time, Maxim and I were returning from somewhere along the coast road to the east of Bidhada. We were passing an area that once had been rich and fertile with date plantation, but now all the mature trees were dry stumps. For some reason the water in that area had disappeared and the irrigation necessary for date cultivation had become inadequate, and on that day as we drove past fields of dead trees, it was as if the place had been scorched. One of the loveliest sights on earth, to my mind, is an orchard of date palms in fruit with orange branches heavy and ripe; now, this ghastly view of deadened and pale tree trunks was not prepossessing.

Not long before we were due to turn northward and away from the coast, we passed a small temple within a walled precinct. I had often noticed this spot before but had never paid much attention, as it was always deserted and a mood of abandon hung upon the air. On this day, however, there were many small automobiles and motorcycles parked on the sand beside the gate, and we could hear a sound of chanting being amplified from loudspeakers. I stopped our little car and we parked and walked back towards the site. Inside the walls the compound was crowded with people, mostly men, and a large canvas tent without walls had been erected in front of the small temple and decorated with green palm fronds and necklaces of marigolds. Groups of men were sitting upon chairs in the shade talking and drinking tea and being served sweets by completely veiled daughters-in-law; some women were grinding meal at querns. Max and I made our greetings and went directly to the temple, going inside to pay our respects: the shrine was dedicated to a cobra deity, *kshetrapal*, who was protector of fields. I spoke with a young fellow outside who came to chat with us and who told us that the temple was new and had been erected upon the ruins of a much older structure, which the earthquake had demolished.

Below us, upon the ground beneath the *shamiana*, the tent-roof, were four fire altars where brahmins were performing a quadripartite sacrifice, reciting Vedic hymns and pouring oblations of clarified butter into the flames as assistants tended the fires with chips of wood. Each one of the priests had a wife attached to him by means of a knotted scarf. The men were all bare-chested and wore orange *dhotis* and their foreheads were liberally marked with sandal paste; they all wore thick caste threads across one shoulder.

In my youth I had studied and worked on translations of the Rig Veda but had never actually attended a reenactment of those rites, and this was a wonderful moment for me. Maxim was fascinated and full of questions; it was exactly the kind of scene that would spark his phantasy. We went and sat upon some chairs and were given tea as we watched the ritual being performed; it was going to continue for several days and nights, and we were asked to return for the final elements of the *yajna*.

We were hot even in the shade and thirsty, and the priests were perspiring as they labored and chanted mantras. I tried to assimilate the recreation of what they were attempting but could not: that old Aryan world of hymns and sky-deities and lengthy complex ritual was not quite right. It did not seem to work any more, and this was a mere palimpsest, a showy synthesis of something long vanished. The words and gestures were orthoprax, but the spirit no longer existed and it was middle-class artifice. It was beautiful to see, for the light from the dazzling sun illuminated the sacrificial ground and the smell of the consecrated fires and burning oblations was heady as the verses droned on with strong nasal diction and tempo. I admired the fact that this was still being attempted, even if the interior of the ritual was now hollow and there was no spirit to the system; it was a bit like the date palms across the fields, desiccated and moribund for lack of refreshment. I felt that the officiants were dressed up and play-acting and would soon return to their world of trousers and cell phones, to their motorcycles and automobiles; this was just a show.

We soon departed and drove homeward, and yet the images of those moments remained with me for a long time afterwards; even now in my mind I can recall them distinctly. The unreality had not been so slack and casual after all, and my scholarly *hauteur* was unjustified. I often pondered the event—the reenactment of something several millennia in age—and felt privileged to have glimpsed it. I suppose it does not really matter if the vision no longer exists, so long as liturgical precision is maintained and transmitted onward through time: for something persists in the code and human experience, and artistry is not lost. It is akin to trying to replay Greek tragedy in modern theaters when the social, political, and mythical context is no more, for the alternative is only further dross. One must not become too arrogant about building small walls and preserves against death, for at least some genetic replication occurs, and who knows what the future already holds in store? It is a situation akin to the fact that there are more tigers now in North America—particularly in Texas—than there are in India, or reputedly more Buddhists in Colorado than there are in Ladakh. Max certainly was never to forget that afternoon with its concentration of ancient prosody and syllables and its startling visual definition.

Apart from the solitude above Pundi, which always easily returns to my inward vision, there are other moments and places that continue to inhabit me in a similarly indelible fashion, not being subject to *amnesis*. I have pictures in my heart that come from one terrific monsoon time when, one day, as much as two feet of rain came down upon us at Bidhada. The gigantic mass of cumulus nimbus that hung above the Mandvi coast was then otherworldly in its giant dimension, sparking with delicate silvery thunderbolts. A few days later, when we were on our way up towards the Rann with Jagdish, the Black Hills about Bhuj were covered with clouds of mist, like a Himalayan *terai*, and there were many small, rapid streams of clay-colored water beside the roads; the desert to the north was verdant and full of pools where flamingo and spoonbills waded. Even Nanamo that day was hidden by fog and mist and was almost Alpine in appearance.

As much as I loved the strong ascetic beauty of the desert, I always enjoyed those green times: the silence and exclusiveness that we would find at Rohar then, for instance, where so many birds filled the high air with their voices and the ruins were sheathed in grasses. At Syot, where the Buddhist caves were—a small enclave that overlooked the Rann—and where the walls were marked with so much strange and ancient *graffiti*, I discovered a silence that was completely atemporal if not mysteriously substantial, as if human life had never occurred, where small owls and a strange envelope drawn from the Rann's spacious distance adhered about the site. Perhaps more than any other spot in the Kacch, there I was admitted into an unearthly and inhuman fellowship of quiet and gentle sovereigns.

There was one small village, not far from Syot, where we often visited, particularly because Leanna enjoyed the company of the wife of the leading man of that hamlet; this was the village of Dhordo, which was on the margin of the Rann. Abdul, the son of a famed head-man, lived in that wonderful solitude near to the Sindhi border. He had family on the other side and often sent his racing horses to compete in events there. His ponies were his passion, and he bred them to trot and to race and also to dance, a particular Sindhi occurrence; he was also a judge of camel fighting, another competitive event. I spent many an hour with him in the men's quarters watching videos of such contests; he even had small films of his horses on his cell phone.

He had married his paternal cousin, Popli, a woman well known for her art of embroidering, a skill that derived from old Indus traditions. They had nine children together, each one now grown and married and with their own *bhungas*, each *bhunga* with its own crib. Love for this happy and distinguished couple had been a matter of destiny, as it was with most of their children. Marriage had been a structural affair; there was no question of emotion being at stake: Popli had been married to her paternal cousin, and that was simply how it was. In Dhordo affective life was very different from how it occurred in the West, was far more organic and always immediate. Leanna always enjoyed visiting there and bringing presents.

Perhaps the finest of those special occasions which continue to linger among my memories—and there are not too many of them now, minutes when we seemed to actually participate and become momentarily incorporated into the Kacchi world—occurred one night as we were returning from one of our long trips, another of our topographical surveys. I think that we had been out up in the region about the Chari Dhand visiting a *kshatriya* village where the women were still in a state of strict seclusion. It must have been winter, for the evening was dark and cold. Jagdish had been driving for at least twelve hours and was obviously hungry and exhausted. He suggested that we pause at Mata-No-Madh and take a meal at the temple, which had large communal kitchens where pilgrims and visitors were fed each night after the *arati*, the evening *puja*. We agreed, as all of us were tired and the children were becoming fractious and disagreeable.

Jagdish dropped us off at the gates to the precinct, where all the stalls and gift shops were brightly illuminated. We left our shoes on the racks and entered, Maxim and Leanna instantly vanishing somewhere, leaving Manki and me to wander about the smoothly polished courtyards. The air was chilly and dark, and shadowy figures in shawls were gliding about in anticipation of the *arati*, cramming the entrances to the main shrine. I squeezed and forced a way into the temple, through all the herdsmen and widows and young men, and Manki and I stood for what seemed a long time among the crowd, who were becoming increasingly but gently agitated, awaiting the imminent emergence of the goddess. The atmosphere beneath the stone roof was gray and sweet with incense, and only one or two exposed light bulbs hung from wires, emitting a faintly jaundiced glow. It was damp and cold, but the smell and proximity of sweat and clothing and human breath charged the air with a state of animal heat.

Suddenly a youthful *pujari*, wearing only an orange *dhoti*, appeared before the shrine and the rites began; simultaneously, the temple bells, enormous brass pieces that were hanging near to us, were repeatedly and monotonously struck. Two drummers were at the side and began to keep up a fast *allegro*, and the crowd began to surge and sway, everyone stretching their bodies upward and forward in order to catch a glimpse of the goddess. Within the sanctum, the youth was moving about the ochre-painted stone figure of the deity, and in the dim light, her gaudy bright tone caught the flames from the dish that he was offering her as obeisance, where heaped carbon and raw incense were burning, reflecting an almost savage and flickering radiance. It was a scene of great candescence and concentration: the fast loud clanging of many large bells, the rapid and unending rhythm of beaten hand drums, the urgency and passion of the crowd, where children were being held up in order to view the Devi, as combustion and smoke fused in the enclosed sanctum and glared with uncanny vigor about her orange form, her four large black eyes staring mesmerically as the figure of the priest moved swiftly about, swaying the *arati* dish before the features of the goddess as he revered her.

I cannot recall how long this lasted, perhaps half an hour, perhaps more. Both I and little Manki, who was in my arms, were completely possessed by the sight: what in fact was a vision of the divine herself, carefully staged and thoroughly fortified with the extreme sensations of fire and smoke and a strident metallic and rhythmic noise. The lurid, vivid air and the ecstasy of the worshipers were confounded within that small dark space, with its delicately carved and shadowy sandstone statuary. Then it all suddenly ceased and people lined up to receive the *prasad*, edible tokens from the deity, which she had graced.

We stayed there for a brief while, somewhat dazed and yet intoxicated by the sensuality and intensity of the apparition. Leanna and Maxim came and found us and asked why we had been so long, for they had been waiting for us in one of the halls where food was about to be served. Jagdish was nowhere to be seen, for he had gone ahead and already stood at the front of the queue with a steel plate, ready to take the evening meal. We too joined the refectory line and took our places at the tables and ate in silence. There were educated *bourgeois* wives present, mothers and daughters, as well as many brahmins and also young unmarried men; there was even a Rabari herdsman, who stood out from the gathering because of his dress. We spotted him later as we were departing, sitting on a wall talking on a cell phone. Then we were on the road again, driving through the night and darkness away from lights and life, encircled by the bare and limitless Kacch. It was not long before Jagdish halted the vehicle because we had a puncture, and he and I struggled in the complete dark to change a front tire.

I shall always recall that night, for its humanity and its epiphany of the Deity and the strong clamoring sensations that surrounded her revelation. It is not so much the emotions that I remember, nor the experience itself, but the feeling that I had of being momentarily part of that land and its origins, of being briefly incorporated—in the literal sense of the word—with something apart from myself. Some element in my soul went out as I stood there holding up my little daughter to the light, and something of that was received in exchange for a glimpse, a small shot of perception, of that which did not really exist.

VII. Kacch: Art of Walking

One morning I set out from the house at Jalaram Bag, having said goodbye to Leanna and the children. Walking through the grounds and going beyond the gates and down the dry sandy track towards Bidhada, I felt slightly uneasy about my departure. On the edge of the settlement, I took a rickshaw and went all the way to Mandvi, hopping out as we crossed the bridge and skirting the rear of the town, taking the road that ran westward and roughly parallel to the coast. Once away from the crowds and the noisy hurly-burly of traffic, I began to feel better, lighter and slower and more inured to anxiety. I was setting out on a long walk, this time without my wife, and with no particular destination. I had said that I would be gone between two and three weeks.

I was wearing local wear, *choyani*, baggy cotton trousers that farmers used, and a loose shirt. I had a piece of printed cotton wrapped about my head, as men always wore some kind of headdress in the country, and I had a swordstick hidden inside of a thin linen blanket that I had rolled up and tied with line and slung across my back. In my bag I had a new notebook and pen and ink, a large bottle of water, a small torch and steel cup and some dates. That morning as I embarked, slowly settling to a swinging pace, my heavily nailed Rabari shoes clicking on the stones as I went, I felt a great relief to be at last footloose and without imperative. I missed Leanna and the two children and felt guilty at leaving them, but knowing how well they would be at Jalaram Bag and knowing that they would probably not even notice my absence, I soon begin to think about the surrounding landscape. My only disquiet concerned dogs, the wild dogs that were everywhere in Kacch; hence the swordstick, rather than simply a heavy or reinforced cane.

Even though I had often walked through that topography and crossed its terrain, I was often actually oblivious of my environs and unaware of India. The flatness of the land, its dustiness and slowness and its hazy visual quality, were now suddenly acutely present; it was as if the natural world itself was observing me and wanting to be asked a question. There is about the Indian landscape an elusive but overt sensibility of the antique, of great and careless age, of the deeply worn edges of time, conscious and unspeakable.

Place is frequently difficult to identify and to experience; it is not easy to receive a place into one's psyche, and with India I always felt that it was there, watching with complete disregard. Figures would come and go without any presence, as if they were ghosts upon a scene that was inherently untimed; the sun did not rise and fall, but it appeared and vanished, approaching and receding as if its being was more a matter of attention than of actual physical occurrence. India was unique in that way, in how it hovered weightlessly about one like a network or reticulation of things and shapes and sometimes sounds. It was as if the supra-awareness that constituted the Indian terrain was quietly lamenting the human condition and its excessive years and efforts and signs of life. This became more and more apparent as I walked out that morning, slowly moving across the plain.

This was a world of powdery heat and cawing crows, of lost human ages and lineages and also of the imagined specificity of deities—Surya, Siva, Devi—those constant forces that inhabited the temporal, the potential, and the merely inferential. Visceral and simultaneously conceptual, India gathered about me as I progressed westward that day, generous and yet piteous for all of human suffering and endeavor and for the centuries of small human effort, emitting a heat that gave time its impulsion and the blood that made love wet. India was always awaiting human accomplishment and the extent of human love, desperate for innovation and freedom from human vicissitude.

There is earthly India, the audible India—drums, bells, the sound of shells being blown, the never-ceasing voice of birds, the old *recitative* of poetry—and there is spatial India of void and silence, that hollow immaterial emptiness that is so ghastly and yet so profoundly attractive and compelling. Then there is something else that can only be inferred or imagined, but which is perhaps the most exacting and the most constant of all of these, and this is the presence that has most to give to a pedestrian, someone who is going only on foot.

I had always admired the Rabari whenever we passed them on the road, as they proceeded with their migrations in search of pasture or as they returned from grazing far afield, moving in a long-strided ambling and loping gait that swayed slightly. In fact I was in complete awe of those people whenever Leanna and I used to encounter them on the highway, and we used to slow down our vehicle in order to stare and observe their ponderous and loaded camels. There was such a mysterious air about their physical unhurriedness and their impassive faces, and I would feel envious of their contact with a world that we were simply speeding through without pause. They knew and experienced something that we did not. I always wanted to go and speak with them whenever we spotted one of their temporary camps but felt abashed at our western and inquisitive manner, at our distance from their pedestrian reality.

When busy human efficacy is discarded or superseded, there exists a fragrance come of that bare vacancy, a duration that is live and vivacious, fluent and yet thoroughly attendant. That is this hovering India of the Rabari, streaming with disquiet as time possesses no recess: ultimately fugitive and yet simultaneously liberal, wholly beneficent, slow and profoundly unconfined. For it is only gentleness that can break suffering, an immutable light that as one walks reveals its compassion, gradually becoming apparent. It is as if there is always a duality about India, as if a woman had two brothers and her thought was so patterned and impressed as her brittle soul divided among the cadence and spray of years. We are worn away by those years, and youthfulness is exchanged for night, but a fertile and flourishing night of great but arid sweetness whose moist surface, the color of coral and diamond, is stained by an oily smoke that adheres to us, who are its bitter or tasteless instruments. This is the India that envelops the pedestrian, and the accompanying emotion is one of amity and of love.

As I continued, the days wheeled past with a gentle and almost circular motion. I was always thoroughly tired by evening, but my physiology soon adjusted to being afoot all the hours. Sometimes I would take a siesta if I came across a quiet and secluded spot that would be snakeless and dogless, and then I used to walk at night. Having set off when the moon was touching its third quarter, I had sufficient light to guide me through the dark; otherwise the hours would be absolutely black. Water was not the problem that I had imagined, and I always found someone to offer me a drink and to refill my bottle. It was not always good water—sometimes stale or brackish—but it was never bad water. Sleep was not a problem either: I would stay in village *ashrams* or sleep on the terraces of farmhouses, and sometimes I would spend the night on a *charpoy* at tea-stalls where truck drivers would also halt to refresh themselves. Now and again I slept out, but only if I was sure that there would be no dogs to trouble me; as it was autumn, the nights were not cold and the days were not burning hot, although the pre-dawn dews were always lavish.

Perhaps for the first time in my life, I felt a great unearthly tranquility descend about me and envelop the hours. This was something that I had never experienced before, although I confess, I do not actually remember much about my years. Certainly, marriage with Leanna and domestic and household ways had introduced a wonderful happiness into my life, a feeling that I had never experienced before, but this was not simply happiness but calm, a profound sense of stability and equivalence, as if one had a place on earth at last. I realized—despite all the years that I had spent in the West—that I was strangely Asian, and that here in the Kacch I had found a home and could substantiate that emotion. Certainly, we had lived a privileged life in Cambridge, intellectually and socially privileged, but it had never been true home. There was something about Kacch, the strangely insular and remote island of Kacch, that had given us a ground to walk on that we could love. I loved the terrain, its flat, stony, and gritty quality, with its hot waterless mineral earth and small conical and volcanic hills: that was my body in a way, where my substance felt its most worldly and attached.

However, on that morning I was aware that my detachment and liberty were artificial, that the lack of property and the lack of residence and emotional connection were mimic if not staged, just like the clothes I was wearing. I was pretending to be something, and then I would go home to Leanna and our nice house. Nevertheless, for a short while the experience of being so without social and material relations apart from the immediate was a sublime feeling. Without doubt the act of walking—the migrant way—is one of the most fundamental exercises of the human mind, insofar as human beings passed their early centuries and millennia as wanderers upon the earth, as *homo habilis* moved out of Africa and began its slow population of the planet. Walking and carrying little and sleeping in different places each night—as an activity—are thus deeply impressed upon the human soul. Walking was also like poetry, insofar as it explored a world whose signs were not always overt and whose traditions were not material and its form of being was not always immediately accessible: just like poetry.

On that walk, the first of many—when I would set out at different times of the year, but never in the hot months, as walking during those times was unendurable—I made my way slowly up towards Jhara, just east of Lakhpat and bordering on the Great Rann. I had a map and compass and kept to all the small ways and tracks. Jhara had been the site of an important battle in the eighteenth century, when marauding Sindhis had invaded Kacch and defeated the assembled *kshatriyas*. I loved the deep and gentle hills of that region; the lanes there were without trucks and there were no Turfans, those maniacal communal jeeps. There were yokes of oxen and herds of cattle and many flocks of sheep and goats; otherwise the unmetalled, dusty lanes were empty.

Lakhpat *taluka*, once a great producer of rice grain, is now a poor district with scarcely any water, and what few Moslem communities lived in those hills were without wealth whatsoever. A lot of the water was actually tanked in by the army, which maintained a presence in the area due to the border being only a few miles away across the Rann. The people of Jhara were always kind and generous to me, and so dignified that I loved being among them and often would actually pray in their small and minimal mosques, or at the open *musalla* that I sometimes came across in my wandering. Never before had I experienced such surrender nor such joy in surrender, this was a complete submission to aniconic nature that I had never before even admitted.

On another occasion, I walked about and across the Banni during the cool time of January, when the sands were not hot but were sheathed in delicious blonde-dry grasses and when the sky was endlessly tall and a startling pure cyanine blue. I often walked at night then, for the moonlight was strong and potent and the skies were clear and the silence was weighty and material, like a thick dense atmosphere about one, and that was heady and exhilarating. Sometimes I would sleep on the sands beneath my blanket, and one pre-dawn when I was in an area south of Khauda— an area where many buffalo were herded—I woke in the thin watery twilight aware that I was being watched. Slowly I opened my eyes and looked about, wary and mildly fearful, only to realise that upon a long stone wall that was about fifty meters away, a dozen motionless vultures were perched and imperturbably staring at me. On other nights I would find a village where someone would allow me the use of a *charpoy* on his terrace, and I would be given tea and *chapattis* in the morning. Wherever I went, no one would ever accept any rupees in return for the gifts, so I used to give the children my coins and small notes as they invariably followed me through and out of the hamlets at dawn, curious and confused by my strange and itinerant presence.

Leanna would always be worried that I would come down with typhoid or dysentery, but it never happened. Occasionally I would be trembling and dizzy with hunger, but that rarely occurred, and never did I run out of water for too long a time. Only once did I use my swordstick, one night when I was being trailed by some dogs; I think that they were probably more terrified than I was, and when one of them ran past me, I automatically drew the blade from its thin brass scabbard and slashed at the shadowy air. The sound of the steel being swiftly removed and the thin flash of reflected moonlight upon the polished blade—it was a razor-sharp saber—was something that I will never forget. I had never drawn a sword in self-defense before, and it was a curious sensation, as I prepared myself for the attack. Of course nothing happened, for the frightened dog was merely trying to flee, but all my youthful fencing lessons were suddenly and completely with me again. The horripilation that accompanied that half-minute stayed with me for days afterwards, for it was as if I had crossed some conceptual frontier in my manner, and I did not really worry too much about dogs after that night.

I loved the quietness of darkness when I was on foot, when all the insects were resting and there was only space and sleeping earth and a delicate fluttering of the air. It is only in full solitude that the human soul completely exposes itself, and briefly we experience the true nature of our beings. There was the enormous whispering volume of the heaven above, so fertile as to seem to be a most exquisite water, with its millions of small seminal stars and a few gleaming planets. From their view we are merely creatures crawling towards death. Now and then a spurting meteor would enter the atmosphere and almost seemed to hiss as it was instantly extinguished, shooting quickly across the cosmos. Those kinetic meteors were probably the fastest thing that I ever saw in life, as they thinly burst across tens of thousands of miles in less than a second's fracture.

The air was warm and redolent and empty, and the shadows of rocks and an occasional small tree were soft and indefinite. All was unlit except for the moon and for the afterglow of a rare lamp when I was passing human habitation. The ground and stones would still be tepid from daylight, and the somber ancient dust felt as if it were sentient and living. If I ever slept on a *charpoy* at a *chai*-stand or outside someone's house, I would always sleep deeply and absolutely and would waken thoroughly relaxed and refreshed. I relished those string beds with their uneven balance and simple comfort, and to settle down upon their rough webbing and allow the intoxication of sleep to rush through one's sore limbs was a sensation close to ecstasy. My solitude come from those walks actually had no place and no light, for the days were without person and without name or body, were fully undiscerning, and the perspicuous genius of India with its desolation and its soundless music always caressed me.

I used to return to Bidhada somewhat dirty and soiled by the landscape, my body rather oily and grimy and my beard usually uncut, although now and then I would pause at a village barber's stall for a shave. Generally I would take a bus or Turfan for those last miles, for the mystique of walking would always vanish as I neared home and I would only want to hasten my arrival. Sleeping in a room and on a bed again was always disconcerting for the first night, but then, there was Leanna beside me. Her person and being were my only real home, and the shape of her body next to me during those initial evenings back at the house was always a wonderful and profoundly familiar and archetypal joy.

Now, as I close this book, I feel at rest again, for now all has been said, and the transformation that writing implies and necessitates is complete. There remains no more compulsion nor premonition, and days are perfectly balanced by only days and the present is simply organized by sunlight and sometimes by the presence of rainfall. The old fluency of life and time and person possesses an almost spiritual quality, or at least a feeling of the durable. Sometimes I waken in the cold pre-dawn hours and listen to the jackals whooping and screaming outside the walls of Jalaram Bag, and all the emptiness and solitude of Banni and old Kacch returns to me, filling me with an ancient and abstract longing.

Of all the happiness that I have known in life, I think that walking in the early evening towards the fields on the western side of Bidhada, as herds and flocks would be returning homeward, walking out along the deep tracks through those fields and hedges, as ibis, lapwings, and kestrels rose into the twilight, hand in hand with Leanna as we spoke about the day's events and the morrow: those moments were the best of all occasions, the most memorable and human, when my being joined with another without the intervention of time. Yet that unity was inseparable from the landscape; the topography was intrinsic to our personal amity. For the witnessing of love is an unbearable perfection; fugitive and nameless, it pauses in no one place, is always to be seen through and cannot be exchanged. Such love cannot be withheld and never keeps to just one way, and its beauty does not change; ingenuous and motive, it keeps us in one state.

This book has been an attempt to snare, entice, or grasp some of that human experience with words, images, and the emotions that at times inhabit such a weaving. There does exist a moral force in the world, a moral beauty mediated by human affection, by love of place and love of person and ideally without partition between the two. I have been told that a Moghul emperor in the late sixteenth century declared Gujarat to be "the beauty and ornament of India." In my experience of the Kacch, I have found this to be true.

Bibliography

Agrawal, Arun. *Greener Pastures*. Durham, NC: Duke University Press, 1999.

Ali, Salim. *Birds of Kutch*. Published for the Government of Kutch by Humphrey Milford, Oxford University Press, 1945.

_____. *The Fall of the Sparrow*. New Delhi: Oxford University Press, 1985.

Arrian. *Anabasis of Alexander and Indica*. Loeb Classical Library. London: Heinemann, 1933.

Arunachalam, B. *Tradition and Archaeology*. New Delhi: Manohar, 1996.

_____. *Traditional Sea and Sky Wisdom of Indian Seamen*. New Delhi: Manhohar, 1996.

Askari, Nasreen, and Rosemary Crill. *Colors of the Indus*. London: Victoria & Albert Museum, 1997.

Aziz, Ahmed. "Epic and Counter-Epic in Medieval India." *Journal of the American Oriental Society*, 83 (1963), pp. 470–76.

Baines, Sir Athelstane. *Ethnography (Castes and Tribes)*. Strassburg: Verlag von Karl J. Trübner, 1912.

Baland, J.M., and J.P. Platteau. *Halting Degradation of Natural Resources*. Oxford: Oxford University Press, 1995.

Banerji, R.D. "The Andhau Inscriptions of the Time of Rudradaman." *Epigraphia Indica*, Vol. 16, No. 5 (1922), pp.19–25.

Briggs, G.W. *Gorakhnath and the Kanphata Yogis*. Calcutta, 1938.

Bright, Richard K. 1975. *The Coinage of Kutch*. Dallas: Numismatics International, 1975.

Bunting, Ethel-Jane W. *Sindhi Tombs and Textiles*. Albuquerque, NM: Maxwell Museum of Anthropology, 1980.

Burnes, James. *A Narrative of a Visit to the Court of Sinde; A Sketch of the History of Cutch and Some Remarks on the Medical Topography of Bhooj*. Edinburgh, 1831.

Carnegy, Patrick. *Kachahri Technicalities*. Allahabad: Mission Press, 1877.

Chaudhuri, A. *Trade and Civilization in the Indian Ocean*. Cambridge: Cambridge University Press, 1985.

Choksi, Archana. *Pastoral Adaptation in the Late Harappan Tradition of Gujarat*. Unpublished MA thesis, University of Baroda, 1991.

_____, and Caroline Dyer. *Pastoralism in a Changing World*. International Institute for Environment and Development, Issue Paper No. 69, 1996.

Clark, William L. *The Modern Coinage of Kutch*. New York: Wayte Raymond, 1952.

Crooke, William. 1879. *Materials for a Rural and Agricultural Glossary*. Delhi: Oxford University Press, 1989 (originally published 1879).

Dange, G., ed. *Mud, Mirror, and Thread*. Ahmedabad: Mapin Publishing, 1995.

Daruwalla, Keki N. *Sword & Abyss*. New Delhi: Vikas, 1997.

Dayton-Johnson, J., and P. Bardhan. *Inequality and Conservation on the Local Commons*. Berkeley: University of California, Department of Economics, Working Paper, 1996.

Dhamija, Jasleen, ed. *Crafts of Gujarat.* Ahmedabad: Mapin Publishing, 1985.

Dilipsinhji, K.S. *Kutch in Festival and Custom.* New Delhi: Har-Anand, 2004.

d'Orazi Flavoni, Francesco. *Rabari.* Delhi: Indira Gandhi National Centre for the Arts, 1990.

Drèze, Jean, and Amartya Sen. *An Uncertain Glory.* Princeton: Princeton University Press, 2013.

Eck, Diana L. *India, A Sacred Geography.* New York: Harmony Books, 2012.

Elson, V. *Dowries from Kutch.* Los Angeles: UCLA Museum of Cultural History, 1979.

Elwin, V. *The Baiga.* London: John Murray, 1939.

Farroukhi, Lyes. "An Ecologically-Sound Water Harvesting Under Threat. A Case Study of the Banni Pastoralists' Knowledge in the Grasslands of Kachcch District." Swedish University of Agricultural Sciences, Working Paper 226, 1994.

Fisher, R.J. "Nomadic Groups in the Caste System." *Man in India,* 61(1) (1981), pp. 55–66.

Forbes, A.K. *The Ras Mala.* London, 1856. Repr. in Two Vols., Delhi: Low Price Publications, 1997.

Frater, Judy. "Rabaris of Kutch." *The Illustrated Weekly Magazine,* May 9, 1976.

_____. "Rabaris of the Barda Hills." *India Magazine,* June 1984.

_____. "This Is Ours: Rabari Tradition and Identity in a Changing World." *Nomadic Peoples,* Vol. 6, 2002.

_____. *Threads of Identity.* Ahmedabad: Mapin, 1995.

Fuller, C.J., ed. *Caste Today.* Delhi: Oxford University Press, 1996.

Geevan, C.P., A.M. Dixit and C.S. Silori. *Ecological-Economic Analysis of Grassland Systems: Kachchh District (Gujarat).* Bhuj: Gujarat Institute of Desert Ecology, 2003.

Ghosh, Suresh C. "Fresh Light on the Peninsula of Gujarat in the Early Nineteenth Century." *Journal of the American Oriental Society,* 96,4 (1976), pp. 570–575.

_____. *The Peninsula of Gujarat in the Early Nineteenth Century.* New Delhi: Sterling Publishers, 1977.

Goswami, Chhaya. *The Call of the Sea.* New Delhi: Orient BlackSwan, 2011.

Goswamy, B.N., and A.L. Dallapiccola. *A Place Apart.* Delhi: Oxford University Press, 1983.

Grant, C.W. "Memoir to Illustrate a Geological Map of Cutch." *Geological Society,* Series II, 5(25) (1837), pp.289–389.

Gujarat Ecology Commission. *Current Ecological Status Of Kachchh.* GEC, Baroda, 1994.

Gupta, D. 1969. *The Kutch Affair.* Delhi: U.C. Kapur & Sons, 1969.

Habib, Irfan. 1976. "Jatts of Punjab and Sind." N.G. Barrier, ed., *Punjab Past and Present,* pp.92–103. Patiala: Panjabi University, 1976.

Harshraji, D. *Kacch Kaladhar.* 2 Vols. Bombay: Suman Prakashan, 1988.

_____. *Kacchna Santo Ane Kavio.* 2 Vols. Bombay: Suman Prakashan, 1988.

_____. *Kacchni Rasadhar.* 4 Vols. Ahmedabad: Gujarat Grantharatna Karyalaya, 1972.

Hirway, Indira, and Darshini Mahadevia. *Gujarat Human Development Report.* Ahmedabad: Mahatma Gandhi Labour Institute, 2004.

Ibrahim, Farhana. "Defining a Border." *Economic and Political Weekly,* April 16, 2005, pp. 1623–1630.

_____. "No Place Like Home." *Nomadic Peoples,* Vol. 8(2) (2004), pp. 168–190.

_____. *Settlers, Saints and Sovereigns.* New Delhi: Routledge, 2008.

Jain, Kulbhushan and Minakshi. *Archi-*

tecture of the Indian Desert. Ahmedabad: Aadi Centre, 2000.

Jeffrey, Patricia. *Frogs in a Well.* New Delhi: Manohar Publishers, 1979.

Jeffrey, Robin. *Politics, Women and Well-Being.* London: Macmillan, 1992.

Jethi, Pramod. *Kutch: People and Their Handicrafts.* Bhuj, nd.

Jhala, Angma Dey. *Courtly Indian Women in Late Imperial India.* London: Pickering and Chatto, 2008.

_____. *Royal Patronage, Power and Aesthetics in Princely India.* London: Pickering and Chatto, 2011.

Joshi, Jagat Pati. "Excavation at Surkotada 1971–72 and Exploration in Kutch." *Memoirs of the Archaeological Survey of India,* No. 87, 1990. Delhi: The Director General, Janpath.

Joshi, P.N., V. Kumar, M. Koladiya, Y.S. Patel, and T. Karthik. "Local Perceptions of Grassland Change and Priorities for Conservation of Natural Resources of Banni, Gujarat, India." *Frontiers of Biology in China,* Vol. 4, No. 4/December 2009, pp. 549 556.

Kalhoro, Zulfiqar Ali. *Vanishing Visual Heritage: Sati and Hero Stones in Nagarparkar, Sindh.* Unpublished paper, 2009.

Karve, Irawati. *Kinship Organization in India.* Bombay: Asia Publishing House, 1965.

Khara, P.D. "Ethnography of an Earthquake." *Economic and Political Weekly,* Vol. 37, No. 11, March 16, 2002.

Laidlaw, James. *Riches and Renunciation.* Oxford: Oxford University Press, 1995.

London, Christopher W., ed. *The Arts af Kutch.* Mumbai: Marg Publications, 2000.

Lyon, Peter. *Conflict Between India and Pakistan.* Santa Barbara, CA: ABC-CLIO, 2008.

MacMurdo, James. "An Account of the Province of Cutch." *Transactions of the Literary Society of Bombay,* Vol. 2 (1820), pp. 205–241.

_____. "Papers Relating to the Earthquake which Occurred in India in 1819." *Transactions of the Bombay Literary Society,* Vol. 3 (1820), pp. 90–116.

Mallinson, Françoise. "Saints and Sacred Places in Saurashtra and Kutch." Phyllis Granoff and Koichi Shinohara, *Pilgrims, Patrons, and Place.* Toronto: University of British Columbia Press, 2003.

Mankekar, D.R. *Twenty-Two Fateful Days.* Bombay: Manaktalas, 1966.

Mayne, C. *History of the Dhrangadhra State.* Calcutta and Simla: Thacker, Spink and Co., 1921.

McGrath, Kevin. "Acts and Conditions of the Gita." *Studies in the Bhagavad Gita,* Vol. 1: "Ontology." Steven Tsoukalas and Gerald Surya, eds., Lewiston, NY: Edwin Mellen Press, 2014.

_____. *Comedia.* Philadelphia, 2008.

_____. *Eroica.* New York: The New Book Press, 2013.

_____. *Heroic Krsna.* Cambridge, MA: Ilex Foundation, Harvard University Press, 2013.

_____. *Jaya.* Cambridge, MA: Ilex Foundation, Harvard University Press, 2011.

_____. "Landscape, Poetry, and the Hero." In *Paintings of the Floating Desert.* Jayasinhji Jhala, ed. De Gruyter Open: Warsaw. (Forthcoming 2015.)

_____. *Raja Yudhisthira: Kingship in Epic Mahabharata.* (Forthcoming 2015.)

_____. *The Sanskrit Hero.* Leiden: Brill, 2004.

_____. "A Short Note on Arjuna as a Semi-Divine Being." *Journal of Vaisnava Studies,* Vol. 21, no.1 (fall issue 2012), pp. 199–210.

_____. *Stri.* Cambridge, MA: Ilex Foundation, Harvard University Press, 2009.

_____. *Supernature*. New York: The New Book Press, 2012.

_____. "The Swim as a Work of Art." *Keats-Shelley Review*, Vol. 17, 2003.

_____. "To Windward." *The Harvard Review*, 44 (2013).

_____. "Walking in the Morea." *Temenos Academy Review*, 6 (2006).

McLeod, John. "A Numerous, Illiterate, and Irresponsible Bhayati: The Maharaos of Kutch." *Journal of Imperial and Commonwealth History*, Vol. 35, No. 3 (2007), pp. 2371–391 (1999).

_____. *Sovereignty, Power, Control: Politics in the State of Western India*. Leiden: Brill, 1999.

Mehta, Lyla. 1997. "Contexts and Constructions of Water Scarcity." *Economic and Political Weekly*, Vol. 38, No. 48, November 29, 2003.

_____. *Water, Difference and Power*. University of Sussex, Institute of Development Studies, 54 (1997).

Miller, Barbara Stoler. "Contending Narratives: The Political Life of the Indian Epics." *Journal of Asian Studies*, 50:4 (1991), pp. 783–792.

Millot, J. "Le Paye De Kutch Et Ses Paradoxes." *Objects et Mondes* 9(4) (1969), pp. 341–82. Paris.

Ministry of Information & Broadcasting. 1965. *Pakistan's Aggression in Kutch*. Delhi–6: Publications Division, 1965.

Nakane, Chie. *Garos and Khasis*. Paris: Mouton, 1967.

Nilsson, Sten A. *Jaipur*. Lund: Magasin Tessin, 1987.

Pandya, Vishvajit. "Hot Scorpions, Sweet Peacocks." *Journal of Material Culture*. Vol. 3(1) (1998), pp. 51–75.

_____. "Nose and Eyes for Identity." *Journal of Material Culture*. 7(3) (1999), pp. 296ff.

Parkin, David, and Ruth Barnes, eds. 2002. *Ships and the Development of Maritime Technology in the Indian Ocean*. London: Routledge Curzon, 2002.

Patel, G.D., ed. *Gujarat State Gazetteers: Kutch District*. Admedabad, 1971.

Pearson, Michael. *The Indian Ocean*. London: Routledge, 2003.

Postans, Marianna. *Cutch or Random Sketches*. London: Smith, Elder and Co., 1839.

Postans, W. "Account of the Ruins and State of Old Mandavi in Raepur." *Journal of the Asiatic Society of Bengal*. Calcutta, 1837.

Prasad, R.R. *Pastoral Nomadism in Arid Zones of India*. New Delhi: Discovery, 1994.

Raikes, Stanley Napier, and Charles Walter, et al. *Memoir and Brief Notes Relative to the Kutch State*. Bombay: Bombay Education Society's Press, 1855.

Randhawa, T.S. *Kachchh: The Last Frontier*. New Delhi: Prakash Books, 1998.

_____. *The Last Wanderers*. Ahmedabad: Mapin Publishing, 1996.

Rao, Aparna, Michael J. Casimir, and T.N. Madan. *Nomadism in South Asia*. Oxford in India, 2003.

Rathod, P. *Kutchanu Sanskriti Darshan*. Ahmedabad: N.S. Mandir, 1990.

Rice, William. *Tiger Shooting in India*. London: Smith, Elder, and Co., 1857.

Ronald, Emma. *Ajrakh*. Jaipur: Anokhi Museum, 2004.

Rothermund, Dietmar. *India: The Rise of an Asian Giant*. New Haven, CT: Yale University Press, 2008.

Roy, Arundhati. *The Cost of Living*. New York: Modern Library, 1999.

Rushbrook Williams, L.F. *The Black Hills*. London: Weidenfeld and Nicolson, 1958.

Salzman, P.C. "From Nomads to Dairymen: Two Gujarati Cases." *Economic and Political Weekly*, July 30, 1988, pp. 1582 1586.

Sampat, D.D. *Kacchni Lokvarta*. Ahmedabad: T.K. Thakkar, 1943.

_____. *Kacchnu Vepari Tantra*. NP, 1935.

_____. *Sagar Kathao*. R.R. Bombay: Sethni, 1940.

_____. *Shahshik Sodagaro*. Bombay: Bharati Shahitya, 1950.

Sen, Amartya. *Violence and Identity*. New Delhi: Penguin Books, 2006.

Shah, A.M. *The Family in India*. Delhi: Orient Longman, 1998.

_____, and I.P. Desai. *Division and Hierarchy: An Overview of Caste in Gujarat*. Delhi: Hindustan Publishing Corporation, 1988.

Sharan, Girja. *Dew Harvest*. Ahmedabad: Centre for Environmental Education, 2006.

Shastri, Durgashankar K. "Bhagwanlal Indraji Commemoration Volume," *Journal of the Gujarat Research Society*, October 1939.

Simpson, Edward. 2004. "Hindutva as a Rural Planning Paradigm in Post-Earthquake Gujarat." Zavos, J., Andrew Wyatt, and Vernon Hewitt, *The Politics of Cultural Mobilization In India*. New Delhi: Oxford University Press, 2004.

_____. *Muslim Society and the Western Indian Ocean*. London: Routledge, 2006.

_____. "State of Play Six Years After Gujarat Earthquake." *Economic and Political Weekly*, Vol. 42, No. 11, March 17, 2007.

Simpson, Edward, and Kai Kresse. *Struggling with History*. New York: Columbia University Press, 2007.

Singh, Jaswant. *A Call to Honour*. Delhi: Rupa and Company, 2006.

Singh, Y.D. *et al. Ecorestoration of Banni Grassland*. Vadodara: Gujarat Ecology Commission, 1998.

Smith, J.D. *The Epic of Pabuji*. Cambridge: Cambridge University Press, 1991.

Snodgrass, Jeffrey G. *Casting Kings*. New York: Oxford University Press, 2006.

Sontheimer, G.D., and L.S. Leshnik, eds. *Pastoralists and Nomads in South Asia*. Wiesbaden: Harrassowitz, 1975.

Srivastava, Vinay Kumar. *Religious Renunciation of a Pastoral People*. Delhi: Oxford University Press, 1997.

_____. "Who Are the Raikas/Rabaris?" *Man in India*, 71(1) (1991), pp. 279–304.

Tambs-Lyche, Harald. *Power, Profit and Poetry*. Delhi: Manohar Publishers, 1997.

Tarlo, E. 1996. "The Genesis and Growth of a Business Community." P. Cadène and D. Vidal, eds. *WebsoOf Trade*, pp. 53–84, Delhi: Manohar Publishers, 1996.

Tiwari, Jugal Kishor. "Gray Hypocolius, *Hypocolius ampelinus* in Kachchh, Gujarat, India." *Indian Birds*, Vol. 4, No. 1 (2008), pp. 12–13.

_____. "Jurassic Park." *Hornbill*, 2 (1995), pp. 25–27.

Tiwari, Jugal, and Asad R. Rahmani. "The Common Crane, *Grus Grus*, and its Habitat in Kutch, Gujarat, India." *Proceedings of the Salim Ali Centenary Seminar*, pp. 26–34, 1996.

_____, and Uffe Gjol Sorensen. "Two New Birds for Gujarat." *Indian Birds*, Vol. 5, No. 1 (2009), pp. 14–16.

Tyabji, Azhar. *Bhuj*. Ahmedabad: Mapin, 2006.

Udamale, Sanjay. *Architecture for Kutch*. Mumbai, 2003.

Vaishnav, M.N. "Social Forestry in the Rann of Kutchh." R.K. Kohli, ed. *Social Forestry for Rural Development*, pp. 40–46. Solan: Indian Society of Tree Scientists, 1987.

Varadarajan, Lotika. *Traditions of Textile Painting in Kutch*. Ahmedabad: New Order Book Co., 1983.

Varadpande, M.L. 1991. *Mahabharata in Performance*. Delhi: Clarion Books, 1991.

Vasa, Dr. Pulin. *Nani Rayan*. Kalikalsarvajna Shri Hemchandracharyas, Ahmedabad, 2007.

_____. *Oceans of the Heart*. Mandvi, Kutch, 2009.

Westphal-Hellbusch, S. "Changes in Meaning of Ethnic Names." Sontheimer and Leshnik, 1975, pp. 116–138.

_____. *Hinduische Viehzuchter im Nord-Westlichen Indien 1: Die Rabari*. Berlin: Duncker and Humblot, 1974.

Williams, Raymond Brady. *An Introduction to Swaminarayan Hinduism*. Cambridge: Cambridge University Press, 2001.

Wiser, William Henricks. *The Hindu Jajmani System*. Lucknow Publishing House, 1936.

_____, and Charlotte Viall. *Behind Mud Walls*. Berkeley: University of California Press, 1971.

Wyllie, J.W.S. "The Rao of Kutch and His Bhayad." *Essays on the External Policy of India*, W.W. Hunter, ed. London: Smith Elder, 1875.

Yagnik, Achyut, and Suchitra Sheth. *The Shaping of Modern Gujarat*. New Delhi: Penguin Books, 2005.

Index